Black Queer Flesh

Black Queer Flesh

REJECTING SUBJECTIVITY IN THE AFRICAN AMERICAN NOVEL

Alvin J. Henry

MINNESOTA

University of Minnesota Press
Minneapolis
London

The University of Minnesota Press gratefully acknowledges the financial support provided for the publication of this book by a Faculty Research Fellowship Award from St. Lawrence University.

Unpublished materials from the Ralph Ellison Papers at the Library of Congress are published with permission.

Published by the University of Minnesota Press
111 Third Avenue South, Suite 290
Minneapolis, MN 55401-2520
http://www.upress.umn.edu

ISBN 978-1-5179-1005-1 (hc)
ISBN 978-1-5179-1006-8 (pb)

A Cataloging-in-Publication record for this book is available from the Library of Congress.

Printed in the United States of America on acid-free paper

UMP BmB 2020

Contents

Introduction: Rejecting Subjectivity *1*

1 Passing into Racial Anxiety *21*

2 Nella Larsen and the Emergence of Black Queer Flesh *59*

3 Queer Underworlds in Ralph Ellison *105*

4 Social Protest and the Aesthetics of Flesh in Richard Wright *159*

5 Toward a Black Queer Utopia *197*

Acknowledgments *223*

Notes *227*

Index *241*

Introduction

Rejecting Subjectivity

> It was the time for sitting on porches. . . . It was time to hear things and talk. These sitters had been tongueless, earless, eyeless conveniences all day long. Mules and other brutes had occupied their skins. But now, the sun and the bossman were gone, so the skins felt powerful and human. They became lords of sounds and lesser things. They passed entire nations through their mouths.
>
> —Zora Neale Hurston, *Their Eyes Were Watching God*

Zora Neale Hurston wrote tirelessly against the dehumanization of African Americans as "tongueless, earless, eyeless . . . brutes." She sought to reveal her subjects as oppressed, but dignified and "human," who "hear things and talk." When "the sun and the bossman were gone," "they became lords" over themselves. Not surprisingly, this agency over the self represented—and continues to represent—the triumph of liberal human subjectivity in the West. In lockstep with conservative Black thinkers and artists of her generation, Hurston unwittingly produced an ableist Black subjectivity that celebrated speaking, listening, and seeing as part of self-ownership. This deep preoccupation with self-possession, self-determination, and self-reflection defined the parameters of Black subjectivity for much of the twentieth century and catapulted an ableist discourse of subjectivity onto the scene of culture and politics that has held sway in the critical literature ever since.

Black Queer Flesh intervenes in this discourse, interrogating the age-old problem of "making the self" whose antecedents date to the rise of power/knowledge we inherited from liberal humanism, which emerged in the sixteenth century and subsequently produced the idea of the self as subjectivity well into the nineteenth century. This idea of the self made into a subject with subjectivities adopted the key tenets of liberal humanism, giving primacy to the notion of sovereignty over the self and of self-possession, since ownership over the body founds the first act of sovereignty. It gave rise, also, to the notion of bodies bounded by skin (no more escaping essence or spirit), coherence between body and mind (later supplanted by simplified models of the Freudian ego), and agency or self-determination. Hurston's "sitters," according to this resounding liberal humanism, exemplify the human subject who is responsible for managing subjectivity, one in which power imbues the self with sovereignty and self-governance that, as Michel Foucault points out, serves "to efface the domination intrinsic to power."[1] This new form of knowledge about the self—a species of biopower—seeks to conflate the idea of the self, the subject, and the human by collapsing difference into something that renders self-formation the dominant mode of being. In this regard, Black queer self-making, too, becomes, in the words of Roderick Ferguson, a project of "one-dimensional queer" subjectivity.[2] Given this logic of domination, to reject, challenge, or modify subjectivity is necessarily to damage the self, to dehumanize African Americans—and similar logics apply to altering the other two ontologies. A consequence of this conflation, Walter Johnson cautions, is that when enslaved or marginalized people are assumed to lack heroic agency or full self-determination, they become dehumanized. He warns that it is "harmful" to suggest "that enslavement [inevitably implies] 'dehumanized' enslaved people."[3] They were indeed humans, but not by the light of liberal humanism's view of the subject. Suppressed agency in fact leads to charges of dehumanization precisely when the terms collapse into each other. Yet, power obscures how the self, the human, and the subject—like self-determination—can be predicated on multiple ontologies; self-making need not inescapably proceed from liberal human subjectivity and its insistence on agency and liberal human morality.[4]

We humans, I argue, can assemble the self-without-subjectivity: Black queers, in fact, have been dynamically engaging in acts of self-making that have not subscribed to subjectivity for a long time. These Black queer people were indeed "selves," yet unrecognizable when viewed through the obfuscating optics of subjectivity. Understandably, for readers seduced by one-dimensional queerness, any challenge to Black subjectivity will ostensibly entail a challenge to Black humanity, but this project seeks to topple this investment in subjectivity and liberal humanism as sites of knowledge production about Black queer lives to indicate just how Black queers can—and have been—both human beings and selves, beyond the ideology of subjectivity. I am interested to uncover to what extent dispossessed knowledges might emerge when self-making proceeds without the hermeneutics supplied by liberal humanism. To this end, this undertaking and book join scholars who have questioned the role of liberal humanism in Black life. *Black Queer Flesh* seeks not only to challenge but also to redress the Eurocentric ideal of "Man" in modern discourse to propose another way of experiencing the self.[5] Delving back in time, in studies of post-Emancipation America, Saidiya Hartman finds that liberal humanism attempted to standardize African American identity by endowing it with "individuation constitutive of the liberal individual and the rights-bearing subject."[6] This transformation from dispossessed slave to "sovereign, indivisible, and self-possessed and as fungible and individuated subjects" enabled power to police these newly formed subjects (117). No longer property without agency or self-possession, the remaking of slaves as selves understood as subjects also opened them to power. Hartman herself casts doubt on the "prized designations like 'independence,' 'autonomy,' and 'free will' . . . conscience, self-knowledge, responsibility, and duty" (122). At the same time, she reveals that African Americans can become liberal human subjects "as long as they are seen as lesser, derivative, or subordinate embodiments of the norm" (123). Questioning this fallout of subscribing to self-making through liberal humanism raises the idea of the Black self, one not beholden to liberal humanism but one whose Black queer flesh can recover feelings and narratives of slavery.[7]

Black queer flesh thereby emerges as a complementary system of knowledge to the idea of Black flesh—not a queering of Black flesh but rather a mode that centers queerness as an intersectional identity whereby Black queer flesh distinguishes itself as both a mode of being that fosters another practice of self-making and one that functions as a living archive of Black queer life. Yet, before attending to the specifics of Black queer flesh, a history of Black flesh is required, given that I engage with, and extend, the concept of Black flesh postulated by Hortense Spillers in a now famous essay, "Mama's Baby, Papa's Maybe." There she indicates how anti-Black racism cleaved the enslaved Black body into two parts: skin and flesh. The skin, in a poststructuralist sense, for her constitutes the site for discursive formations of African Americans and the space of the performance of the self. Spillers provides a few examples to illustrate this point: "Peaches" and "Brown Sugar," "Sapphire" and "Earth Mother," "Aunty," "Granny," "God's 'Holy Fool,'" a "Miss Ebony First," and "Black Woman at the Podium."[8] These signifiers limit the subjectivities that African American women can create for themselves at the level of skin. Instead of women enacting full self-determination, their beingness is represented and determined, in large part, for them. What is more, this discursive skin, which can often be the metonymic site of the social construction of race, suffers another transformation, so Spillers therefore proposes that the captive Black body can be further dispossessed of agency beyond the linguistic and social in what she terms "the pornotrope." She describes this process in four steps. First, the captive body becomes an object by severing "the captive body from its motive will, its active desire" (67). Second, the captor continues partitioning the body into skin and flesh as they create an "absence from subject position[s]" for the captive body. Third, without access to subject positions of gender, ability, or class, the now object serves as the locus of cultural "otherness." Finally, this "other" object comes to register "powerlessness" in a culture in which the object can be written upon and forced to represent or produce anything desired by the captor—from a source of sexual pleasure and deviance to powerlessness. Sapphire can become a legitimate identity, or subject position, because it has been authorized by anti-Black racism. This reading of flesh supports claims by Afro-pessimism that "characterizes blackness as a site of accumulation and fungibility," or steps 4 and 3, respectively.[9] However, while the captive body, from the perspective of the captor, loses its subjectivity, the self that remains, Spillers theorizes, exists as captive flesh. The pain and suffering associated with each cleavage of self-determination can only be registered in captive flesh. In this sense, Black flesh accumulates histories of the body "seared, divided, ripped-apartness, riveted to the ship's hole, fallen, or 'escaped' overboard" and the body's abuses: "lacerations, woundings, fissures, tears, scars, openings, ruptures, lesions, rendings, punctures."[10]

Black skin should be the site for the expression of subjectivity and social identities—that is, what is normally the substrate for race, gender, and racialization. Black skin, after slavery, constitutes the site where discursive constructions register, to reiterate Hartman's claims. For Spillers, the enslaved possess limited control over skin and the representations and the reading practices associated with the performance of Blackness. Captive flesh, on the other hand, occurs where "liberated subject-positions" must go once skin is co-opted. This means that flesh lacks access to subject positions (and their performance), which Spillers regards as a negative attribute, joined by scholars in the field who believe that subjectivity must be recovered. Furthermore, "before the 'body' [skin] there is the 'flesh,' that zero degree of social conceptualization that does not escape concealment under the brush of discourse" (67). Flesh, therefore, comprises the pain, suffering, and death associated with slavery, including additions from the skin (the series of cleavages of agency and identity from above) that have been forced out of hegemonic representation.[11] Because all of these are not part of hegemonic discourse, they become unrecognized parts of discourse, as it were; flesh does not necessarily constitute fragments of discourse but rather is unmarked and unmarkable by discourse and representation. The markable parts of the body are skin. Thus flesh is conceptualized as the repository for negative affective histories that are not "recorded" in the dominant narrative or that cannot sufficiently be recorded. Flesh, to be clear, is not physical skin—it is not literal flesh. In more ideal conditions, we can extrapolate that skin, or racialization, emerges out of flesh ("before skin there is flesh").[12] As a historical set of experiences, Black flesh is not simply part of the Real—that which resists and cannot be symbolized—but rather a materiality and history that has not (yet) been interpreted and absorbed into the hegemonic Symbolic and Imaginary. Flesh cannot enter normative representation because it entails the negative dimensions of Black life—and hegemonic power relations refuse to let Black suffering be fully expressed. These experiences and histories must be denied and silenced. For Spillers, they become flesh, and the body then performs and embodies them. (Work songs and spirituals are keen examples of Black suffering gaining representation.) Flesh should be understood as a reservoir of knowledges and histories that cannot be easily translated into networks of power or representation.

The making of Black queer flesh encompasses not just Spillers's pornotrope model but also another avenue of creation and curation. Amber Musser has argued that "since becoming flesh depersonalizes and removes subjectivity, we can understand the production of flesh as one of white supremacy's tactics of domination."[13] Instead of whites enacting the removal of subjectivity, Black queer flesh entails the self-abnegation of subjectivities by Black queers themselves. By taking the reins of ablation to subjectivity, Black queers commandeer the process of Black queer flesh making. Abnegation destroys the liberal human self and subjectivity, but the person remains human. After all subjectivities have been destroyed, the human reaches a condition of Black queer flesh, and rather than functioning as a site of pain, horror, and death, Black queer flesh includes the rich histories and experiences of living gay, lesbian, bi, trans, bulldagger, punk, and other queer identities from the past.[14] The characters from literature in this study destroy their subjectivities, but at the same time, they do not forget their lived experiences: they add these memories to the fabric of Black queer flesh. The use of the term *queer* here encompasses the histories of those socialized and policed into specific, historically contingent categories of nonnormative sexual and gender practices, especially acknowledging the time when gender and sex were considered one and the same. This exploration recognizes the vast histories of bodies, practices, and experiences that now live under the aegis of *queer*. In recognizing that the modern categories of sexuality and gender orient and produce bodies in specific formations—just as liberal humanism produces selves in specific formations—the making of gay or lesbian identities emerges from a power/knowledge system that cannot be taken as given but rather as belonging to a specific genealogy. As such, this book honors historical formations of gay, punk, or lesbian that might be in flux in this period. Consequently, this inquiry discusses characters not only through a contemporary understanding of queer but also through historically relevant identities. It is the experiences of being made a punk and performing punk identities or being rendered disabled and performing Black disability, for example, that are brought to Black queer flesh. While the subjectivities that constitute a punk or the historically reprehensible category of handicap might be abnegated, the lived experiences while a punk or disabled remain.

Black queer flesh should be defined according to context: with or without subjectivity. The book largely explores the question of Black queer flesh at odds with subjectivity. When the main character still has a subjectivity, either normative or deviant, Black queer flesh exists as a simmering, cloaked reservoir of queer histories and as a vibrant life-force, a psychic drive rooted in the histories of Black queer cultures: drag, cross-dressing, coded and fanciful language, covert and not-so-covert queer sociality, queer domesticity, queer labor, queer stubbornness, passing for straight, and queer cultural production, as well as the full constellation of "Blackness" in all of its ambiguity and complexity. Black queer flesh as a life-force, however, is not easily recognizable to a self crafted as a subject: the former reveals subjectivity as an oppressive social and psychic structure. Instead of recognition, the subject feels Black queer flesh unable to gain representation except as the effect of racial anxiety. Frantz Fanon, the Martinican philosopher, captures this eruption of racial anxiety as the "muscular spasms" of the colonized.[15] Within these muscle spasms, Darieck Scott finds a "reservoir of resistance to the colonizer's acts of subjugation and enslavement."[16] Although Scott views corporeal spasms through the prism of abjection, I want to stress the psychic dimension of the spasms: for me, they constitute manifestations of racial anxiety. Black queer flesh literally erupts into subjectivity, causing the self and subjectivity to literally tear open through feelings. Because Black queer flesh functions as a psychic drive, it cannot enter language proper. Harnessing racial anxiety goes against normative logic but aligns with queer-of-color critique.

As *Black Queer Flesh* aims to show, racial anxiety propels desubjectification. After successive self-abnegations of gender, sexual desire, family, and race associated with subjectivity, for example, the character joins others existing as Black queer flesh. By centering Black queer flesh as a new ontology for being, remaking the human can proceed from queer knowledges; in this case, Black queer flesh transcends liberal humanism.

Embracing the process of self-abnegation, however, does not come easy: subjectivity does not willingly depart; the body and psyche do not magically transform from liberal subject to nonliberal subject. The journey of self-abnegation requires dedication and risks actual death. The self defends itself from attacks. By evoking what Jacques Lacan defines as surplus *jouissance,* or extra pleasure that is false pleasure, the self quells and mitigates fits of racial anxiety. This means that the body must forcibly elicit regular bodily enjoyment rather than its organic emergence. Such surplus pleasure distracts from how the body experiences anxiety or that Black queer flesh might exist. Additionally, the pleasure contains a critical moment that reveals the "extra" pleasure as false. By simply providing not only pleasure but also more-than-needed pleasure, surplus jouissance both calms racial anxiety and obscures it, producing a forgetting that racial anxiety even happened: the subject merely remembers the surplus jouissance. For this study, the false dimensions of pleasure ensure that Black queer flesh does not rear its head or that the subject does not remember an encounter with it. This investigation focuses on a particularly useful false pleasure: the pleasure of being a unified, agential self, as a subject. The ideology of liberal humanism grants the subject the feeling of self-possession, self-determination, and self-formation. In evoking these attributes, the abject Black queer subject can feel a part of society, can feel normative. And feeling normal at a time when queerness was criminalized alongside escaping misogyny and racism is a powerful curative to psychic and social stress. In these ways, surplus jouissance disciplines with a proverbial carrot rather than a stick.

Aligned with surplus jouissance is the *Bildungsroman.* Emerging as liberal humanism cannibalizes Western thought and culture in the late eighteenth century, the novel of self-formation promotes subjectivity in the realm of aesthetics and culture. These novels follow a protagonist from childhood or young adulthood as she crafts her subjectivities to merge with society's norms. This genre appealed to African American authors who wanted to vehemently challenge the status quo and racism so that Black people could find their way into society and subjectivity. It is no surprise that the Bildungsroman is the most prominent genre of Black fiction; its idea of racial uplift and its many afterlives, too, parallel the idea of Black self-formation, but in the social rather than aesthetic and cultural sphere. African American authors strove to articulate self-formation, self-possession, and self-determination via the Bildungsroman. Indeed, it is the perfect vehicle for narrating and policing rebellious or queer liberal human subjects. Whether telling the story of feminist rebellion like Harriet Jacobs or the story of surviving meth-addicted parents in the work of Jesmyn Ward, the Bildungsroman was and remains the choice genre to construct Black subjectivity. Although the Bildungsroman, and its story, is a cultural form of surplus jouissance for many, it also hides the fact that African Americans were coerced into shaping themselves along the axis of liberal human subjectivity. The genre presents this journey as normal, as pleasurable, as right; it is surplus jouissance for the masses.

Black Queer Flesh treats texts commonly classified as part of this genre—the Bildungsroman—as case studies to explore the power of surplus jouissance to keep liberal humanism intact and Black queer flesh suppressed. After examining this process, the study examines another group of Bildungsroman for how they overcome surplus jouissance, allowing racial anxiety and self-abnegation to proceed. By examining the question of self-making first under the aegis of liberal humanism, the book can then unpack how Black queer authors advocated self-abnegation through different intersectional identities. Gay, punk, bi, trans, and lesbian characters self-abnegate differently. They also relate to Black queer flesh differently once subjectivity has been purged from the self. As such, my central fascination and focus here concern how a human person proceeds as a self in the world, but without subjectivity, without a coveted "I" and ego. Throughout, I wonder about this steering question: how might self-making unfold with Black queer flesh as the source of knowledge?

The self merges with and becomes part of the soul of Black queer folk after the end of subjectivity. Recalling the multiplicity inherent in Blackness, the self blurs into Black queer flesh, and vice versa. Without an ego and subjectivity, the self manages to feel itself as part of a larger history and collective self. Black queer flesh becomes the basis for knowledge and self-making. When viewed through the prism of subjectivity, Black queer flesh might appear as chaos, uncivil behavior, or a unified actor. After the demise of subjectivity, it becomes and functions quite differently: chaos gives way to improvisation; racial anxiety gives way to queer sociality (including loving arguments and fights); a unified actor gives way to existence and expression as plurality and multiplicity. Black queer flesh without subjectivity is by this means conceived of as a collective constellation of Black queer histories, experiences, and cultural practices. This includes the remnants—residuals—of uplift, accommodationist practices, and other neoliberal ideologies. It even includes the good and not so helpful histories too. At the same time, Black queer flesh aligns with Judith Butler's formulation of queer as a "point of departure for a set of historical reflections and futural imaginings" that "in the present, [is] never fully owned, but always and only redeployed, twisted, queered from a prior usage."[17] Black queer flesh simultaneously encompasses past "prior usage[s]" and visions of the future: it is the elsewhere that queers, frustrated with subjectivity, seek. Moving beyond subjectivity also requires relinquishing the hold over Black queer flesh, or, as Jennifer Nash advises, a "letting go" by Black feminists of "making property of knowledge."[18] Black queer flesh is therefore more of a reservoir and an unheld, unowned holding place of history, the future, the present, the body, Blackness, and queerness; it is for all intents and purposes the soul of Black queer folk. Characters inhabit or are Black queer flesh rather than owning it. Black queer flesh adapts, expands, and contracts as more experiences add to its richness.

Constructing a self from Black queer flesh knowledge leads to the creation of a plural self. Tavia Nyong'o terms this "life lived in the singular plural" in adaptation of Deleuze's formulation, while Amber Musser develops a model of "plural selfhood" that emerges from brown jouissance.[19] Josh Chamber elaborates further on these ideas of existing as a plural entity: "we're not quite one thing but instead a singular being made up of the many."[20] In each instance, scholars of queer-of-color critique understand the self as multiplying subjectivities or, in the case of Musser, as reshaping the self from sensual pleasures. Black queer flesh adds another facet of making the self plural. In doing so, the self is not constituted by self-possession, self-determination, or agency. Rather, these "self"-centered qualities give way to a they—a plurality. And this does not remain stagnant, does not solidify into a permanent or semistable they. As Snorton might describe the process of Black queer self-making, these new forms embody trans practices of having the "capacity to change form."[21] This capacity is put into full play as the self remakes itself as Black queer flesh. The self shifts, drawing on its capacity to change—as an endless journey of discovery. Through Black queer sociality and exploration, improvised or not, the self makes itself/themselves into Black queer flesh, which itself never stops growing.

As socially located humans, selves of Black queer flesh will need to engage subjects. How can human subjects interact with humans without subjectivity? These fleshy bodies are, to cite Paul Gilroy, a "living, disorganic formation" that operates through improvisation instead of through subjectivity. Black queer flesh is an unordered, living amalgamation of experiences and histories from which queers can cite in performance of provisional, fluctuating selves. When the self needs to interact with bodies authored by subjectivity, Black queer flesh calls forth from itself. First, a call goes out to Black queer flesh for the need to craft a legible self-without-subjectivity. Fred Moten would describe this as "a nondetermining invitation to the new and continually unprecedented performative."[22] In response to this call, random dimensions of flesh arrive, and that group improvises an ensemble of "the many," to borrow José Muñoz's phrase, which helps describe wild queer sociality, which will performatively construct a self-without-subjectivity that is able to relate to that specific subject (or group of subjects). And this temporary entity draws upon their capacity to change form to respond to dynamic situations. In this way, the self-without-subjectivity evokes Tavia Nyong'o's concept of fabulation, where those bodies and identities present "all wind-up implicated in the continual transformation, breakdown, and remaking" of the queer sociality.[23] Black queer flesh in this context of interacting with subjects, especially those subjects in self-abnegation, follows Nyong'o's understanding of Black queer performance as an "improvisational and relational process" that is open to accommodation and permeation.[24] This radical freedom of unpredictable improvisation is key to Black queer flesh. After the self-without-subjectivity is no longer required, this entity can self-abnegate back into Black queer flesh, and its history further augments the collective. In these ways, Black queer flesh and performances of it embody trans practices as articulated by Riley Snorton: "a movement with no clear origin and no point of arrival."[25] The ensemble of flesh resists order and logic, while the temporary performance of a self-without-subjectivity and its abnegation ensure no arrival point but rather an always-changing form.

My arguments about Black queer flesh ask us to recalibrate our approach to questions of race and recognition and to come to a greater understanding of how it continually redynamizes itself and defies interpretation as determined or fixed. In other words, in adapting E. Patrick Johnson's description of Black queer culture, Black queer flesh entails a "mutual constructing/deconstructing, avowing/disavowing, and expanding/delimiting dynamic that occurs in the production of" Black *queer flesh performances.* This unpredictable dynamic "is the very thing that constitutes 'black' culture" as such.[26]

Living as Black queer flesh necessarily involves an arduous journey, one in which Black queer-of-color subjects must endure racial anxiety if they respond to its call for self-abnegation. And desubjectification, too, entails tremendous effort, resiliency, and dedication to a path that lacks a telos, even when one arrives at that otherworld. If complete self-abnegation is achieved, the next task is to explore and elaborate a self that has transcended subjectivity. This demands narrating and approximating the first stages of a queer utopia. African American authors must imagine and represent a character who is not a subject, who does not have an ego or who does not think through a unified and bounded psyche—one who is not usually legible to the normative world and who performs nebulous Black queer flesh. Saidiya Hartman takes up this challenge in her *Wayward Lives, Beautiful Experiments: Intimate Histories of Social Upheaval.*[27]

This project theorizes Black queer flesh as an alternative phenomenology, as an experience of the Black queer body that thrives on queer sociality, acting to decenter subjectivity and identity. It exemplifies queerness as creatively regenerative and thus inherently open to dynamic fluctuations and collaborative revision. This approach contrasts with that of many scholars who characterize Black flesh as determined wholly through passive and personal experiences. The contrast inherent to my theorization introduces a significant difference to the state of current scholarship insofar as it helps us understand how queerness sustains flesh, how it reinterpellates it and enables it to become no vestige of defeat but a power that is fully capable of fighting against subjectivity's reign over the Black queer body and mind.

Black queer flesh has been articulated as a method, life-force, critique, awareness—issuing a call from utopia, submission, waiting, knowledge, and pleasure. This amalgamation of definitions is messy and a set of inequalities because Black queer flesh manifests differently when subjectivity holds the body and once it has been abnegated. As characters attempt to liquidate the structures of subjectivity—and moreover disentangle power's grasp on Black queer bodies and psyches—Black queer flesh can be transformed into the aforementioned resources as needed in the fight against subjectivity. There is no pristine or fully mapped out Black queer flesh: the myth of organization, harmony, and structure belongs to subjectivity and not Black queer flesh. This study approximates Black queer flesh, and the descriptions will always be insufficient in capturing the entirety of Black queer flesh. Black queer characters, in aiming to rupture and terminate subjectivity, tap into the plasticity, the disorganic character of Black queer flesh, to advance their projects. In these ways, the description of Black queer flesh not only seems to vacillate in terms of definition—a characteristic of radical queerness is to be constantly shifting and to avoid being one, definable, and normative thing—extending beyond our understanding. Readers with subjectivity will demand distinct categories and boundaries to aid in classification, to aid in controlling the information about Black queer bodies. While Black queer flesh within subjectivity has more concrete yet varied examples, Black queer flesh after subjectivity proves more difficult insofar as it runs the gamut of the souls of Black queer folk.

Black Queer Flesh embraces queer-of-color critique by disidentifying with the ideology of subjectivity (and its cultural partner, the Bildungsroman) and its ability to reproduce and structure Black and queer lives within a network of oppressive power at the level of social critique, personal action, and aesthetic practices. The project contributes new scholarship given the need to disidentify from normative aesthetics and canonical literature. It disidentifies with the ideology of subjectivity due to its strong hold on the reproduction and structuring of Black and queer lives within oppressive networks of power/knowledge. In this regard, it decenters liberal humanism as the de facto sense of self, illuminating suppressed ways of Black queer existence and the performance of nonsubjectivity, including disavowed knowledges, ceding to the self rather than privileging subjectivity as the sole mode of self-fashioning. The project rejects hegemonic identity making, at the level of the individual, in favor of emptying out subjectivity and giving way to the self as Black queer flesh—contributing to a new sphere of queer-of-color critique that problematizes aesthetics. The project contributes a new sphere of queer-of-color critique by problematizing aesthetic practices. By revealing the futility of racial and sexuality minorities in their adaptations of a white literary form such as the Bildungsroman, this book proposes ways by which we may reject hegemonic aesthetics to discover what might emerge in their place. The domain of aesthetics has often been a refuge for queers of color to reinvent and express themselves, but the beauty and the pleasure of normative art forms must be equally challenged. A triple vacillation between the social, individual, and aesthetic domains highlights the need to reject both systems of knowledge and material conditions that reproduce anti-Black thought, homophobia, homonormativity, sexism, and *normative pleasure.*

Black Queer Flesh draws crucially from the methodologies of Black and queer Black performance studies. Its interventions are grounded in psychoanalysis and are simultaneously indebted to performance studies because of its insight that queer African American experiences represent material conditions and not mere discursive conundrums. Just as a performatively constituted psyche with double consciousness cannot be resolved by linguistic undoings alone, so, too, real bodies and minds have been organized by the ideologies of subjectivity. Bodies and histories have material effects while at the same time showing that these material conditions are not necessarily linear with neat genealogies. In pursuing this line of thinking, Jafari Allen's rhizomatic metaphor of Black queer experiences is quite relevant: a deterritorializing and reterritorializing as it were, depending on the conjuncture.[28] Specifically, Black queer flesh as performance represents a work in progress, never quite settled and never quite knowable beyond the ephemeral. Riley Snorton's conceptions of trans capture this spirit, while José Muñoz captures this queerness as "fleeting moments and performances."[29] His strand of Black queer performance studies emphasizes in its supple and flexible methodologies a polyglot communication, a wide and open outlook, and a nuanced analysis.[30] In treading the intellectual terrain of Jennifer Brody, Roderick Ferguson, E. Patrick Johnson, Fred Moten, José Muñoz, Tavia Nyong'o, and Michelle A. Stephens, I locate and understand Blackness as a concept and lived experience that is both performative and embodied. In her analysis of E. Patrick Johnson's performance art *Strange Fruit,* Brody underscores how Johnson "does" Black gay art while being aware of racial stereotypes and essentialized histories. Her methodologies remind scholars to analyze how art performatively constructs a dimension of Black queer life while also locating Johnson's critiques within specific yet shifting intellectual conversations on gay Black representation.[31] My work grounds itself in these questions of Black performance, specifically Johnson's question of "what happens when 'blackness' is embodied" and "what happens in those moments when blackness takes on corporeality."[32] From these historical traditions, I am less interested in what the novels say about subjectivity and more interested in what these authors and their novels "do" to transcend subjectivity by honing in on the Black queer body and its embrace of deviance.

Chapter Summaries

Black Queer Flesh traverses three intellectual clusters. The first discusses the clash between racial anxiety and surplus jouissance, the lure of the Bildungsroman, and the cultural mandate for subjectivity. Chapter 1, "Passing into Racial Anxiety," presents novels that tarry with self-abnegation only to be won back over by the surplus jouissance associated with a journey of normative and deviant self-formation. This chapter explores how African American authors adapted the Bildungsroman genre as a vehicle for perpetuating the ideology of subjectivity. In particular, this genre provides the secrets of achieving successful self-formation, self-determination, and self-possession. At the same time, the characters find it nearly impossible to extricate themselves from the grasps of subjectivity even when they encounter racial anxiety over and over again. James

Weldon Johnson's *Autobiography of an Ex-Colored Man* (1912), Nella Larsen's *Quicksand* (1928), and Jessie Redmon Fauset's *Plum Bun* (1928) all register these frustrations about subjectivity and its imperative as told by the Bildungsroman. As each author seeks to dismantle subjectivity, they also manage its defense mechanism: surplus jouissance. While attempting to showcase the emergence and preliminary acceptance of Black queer flesh, they begin to practice self-abnegation, ultimately reverting to the comforts of subjectivity and self-formation. They cannot overcome the surplus jouissance supplied by a journey of normative development and its promised outcomes of a sovereign subjectivity.

The second section presents a variety of authors who defy surplus jouissance and the Bildungsroman and who have their protagonists abnegate until they transcend subjectivity. Each author outlines a different mode of self-abnegation, which reveals that there is no formula for how or when desubjectification occurs. Moreover, this section is not meant to represent all novels within this genre but to exemplify the tradition with clear examples of a journey of abnegation. Chapter 2, "Nella Larsen and the Emergence of Black Queer Flesh," argues that Nella Larsen, in her novel *Passing* (1929), inaugurates a new genre: the novel of self-abnegation and Black queer flesh. Larsen imagines her characters' frustrations with subjectivity and how they escape the lure of surplus jouissance. They reject the pleasures of normativity and deviance and instead forge a mimetic, queer relationship that allows each to assist the other in her self-abnegation. This chapter untangles how Clare and Irene cast aside their identities as mother, wife, socialite, and even dominated Black woman in a journey of self-abnegation. Instead of holding tightly or curating these subjectivities, Larsen plots out how they respond to the call of Black queer flesh to liquidate. For Larsen, queer love sparks self-abnegation. Moreover, the two women nearly simultaneously complete their journeys of self-abnegation and start new lives within Black queer flesh. However, Larsen can only gesture at the transcendence of subjectivity insofar as she abruptly concludes the novel once Clare and Irene reach Black queer flesh. This dramatic narrative closure ensures that whoever Clare and Irene become after subjectivity, they are not narrated and described through hegemonic discourse. In this way, Larsen refuses to redominate the characters back into subjectivity; she does not want only to create a new and better subjectivity but rather to destroy subjectivity so that Black queer flesh can emerge. Ultimately, Larsen ushers in a new literary genre—with a unique Black queer aesthetic. Her novel sparks a quiet revolution in African American queer culture.

Chapter 3, "Queer Underworlds in Ralph Ellison," offers the proposal that scholars have long misread Invisible Man as cisgendered, heterosexual, and able-bodied. By placing the novel and materials from the Ralph Ellison Archive at the Library of Congress in conversation with disability studies, this chapter illustrates how Ellison crafts a theory of Black punk disability. As an early thinker of Black disabled experiences, Ellison imagines a character who has an "invisible" disability: queer punk sexuality. This disability renders the protagonist abject, yet Ellison reclaims this dismissal from subjectivity: his protagonist finds pride within his disability and in turn embraces society's exclusion of him from qualifying as a subject. This act of embracing disability, at a historical moment when disability was widely seen as a shameful bodily experience, helps Invisible Man launch a journey of self-abnegation. Ralph Ellison previews life after as Black queer flesh. In the prologue and epilogue, the unnamed narrator is not a subject. A case in point: when the narrator speaks to the reader, they (I presume neither cisgendered pronouns nor the moniker Invisible "Man" apply to the narrator once he transcends subjectivity and lives within Black queer flesh) performatively constitute a temporary self-without-subjectivity such that they have access to (hegemonic) language. To be heard by those dominated by subjectivity, the narrator, too, must perform an ephemeral self-without-subjectivity. In other words, Black queer flesh improvises a disposal identity so they can be heard and seen by those who haven't made the journey of self-abnegation. Ellison's interventions thus help scholars theorize mid-century questions of disability, race, and sexuality.

Many readers might be surprised to see the inclusion of Richard Wright in a book on Black queerness. His *Native Son* (1940) tends to invite a critique of his portrayal of brutal, heterosexual masculinity, and his writings are not always the most hospitable to representations of women or sexual minorities. Wright, a good friend and intellectual sparring partner of Ralph Ellison, began contemplating the question of Black queer life in his later works. Chapter 4, "Social Protest and the Aesthetics of Flesh in Richard Wright," examines Wright's neglected and final novel published in his lifetime, *The Long Dream* (1958). Wright engages with the intellectual conversations between Larsen and Ellison and adds his own perspective on Black queer flesh. As with *Invisible Man,* the novel appears to be a Bildungsroman and to narrate the protagonist's journey of self-formation. Instead, *The Long Dream* plots an arduous journey of self-abnegation: the protagonist destroys parts of his subjectivity and ego until nothing remains. Unlike the beautiful and often sensual language that Larsen and Ellison employ to represent self-abnegation, Wright returns to the gruffness characteristic of the protest tradition found in his *Native Son* and *Black Boy* to illustrate Black queer flesh as racial anxiety. Wright captures the brutality inherent within stripping the self of subjectivity and the brutality of subjectivity's hold on the Black queer body. At the same time, he also hints at the pleasure the protagonist enjoys, thereby thwarting the control mechanisms imposed upon Fishbelly's body by hegemonic culture.

The final chapter of the book explores Black queer flesh after subjectivity. How might lived experience proceed for a self-without-subjectivity? How does the self relate to, become, and perform Black queer flesh? Chapter 5, "Toward a Black Queer Utopia," analyzes the self practicing living without subjectivity and as Black queer flesh. This chapter takes up the improvisational and relational qualities of Black queer flesh as characters, narrators, and what Saidiya Hartman terms "the chorus," who endure numerous trials and tribulations of performing Black queer flesh; they do so while negotiating an existence that is multiple, indeterminate, and unpredictable instead of singular, unified, and bounded by subjectivity. The chapter begins with an examination of Ralph Ellison's character Jim Trueblood, who constitutes an unexpected example of the self-abnegation of subjectivity and the reignition of the self as Black queer flesh. The chapter then turns to Hartman's *Wayward Lives, Beautiful Experiments* and her invention of the concept of "close narration,"[33] whose style dissolves the boundary between narrator and character. The fusion of experiences and histories here exemplifies plural selfhood that is not bound to a unified, liberal human ego or liberal humanist sense of self. Hartman's style offers a mode of narrating Black queer flesh, particularly its vast experiences, given that she and her characters craft temporary selves-without-subjectivity. Within this configuration, close narration also includes a third voice: that of a chorus. Written as a call and response, the chorus, Hartman, and the characters speak among themselves; at times they might interrupt one voice, follow up a comment with an outburst of agreement or dissent, or provide their own perspective on the topic at hand. Unlike Hartman and the characters who perform selves-without-subjectivity, the chorus embodies the ensemble of Black queer flesh that remains a fleshy amalgam and does not form a singular, speaking self-without-subjectivity. The chorus thereby comprises the parts of Black queer flesh that comingle, listening to the story told by Hartman as well as the other characters in text. They shout, sing, and stomp their opinions, insights, and emotions—interruptions that the text designates with italics. *Wayward Lives* effectively creates an aesthetic that allows Black queer flesh to interact in the world without being dominated, without regressing back into subjectivity. Rather, the text promotes a plethora of characters who have rejected subjectivity and embraced Black queer flesh as a new sense of self.

1 Passing into Racial Anxiety

> "When you gone to get married? You need to have some babies. It'll settle you."
>
> "I don't want to make somebody else. I want to make myself."
>
> —Toni Morrison, *Sula*

Surplus Jouissance and Racial Anxiety

Inspired by Marx's ideas of surplus and exchange value, Jacques Lacan devised surplus jouissance as the object-choice of anxiety. He reasoned, quite understandably, that anxiety is placated in a number of ways, particularly through the idea of acting out, which includes throwing a tantrum or perhaps committing suicide. The most common way of mollifying anxiety, however, occurs through the pursuit of surplus jouissance or through overwhelming pleasure. This inordinate component of pleasure exposes the inequalities papered over by exchange value. The pursuit of pleasure, for the French psychoanalyst, in the context of anxiety, is therefore similar to repression; the surplus pleasure distracts by forcibly eliciting "regular" bodily enjoyment. Additionally, the surplus contains a critical moment that reveals the "extra" pleasure as false. By providing not simply pleasure but also more than needed pleasure, surplus jouissance both calms anxiety and obscures it, producing forgetting that anxiety even happened: the subject merely remembers the surplus jouissance. For this study, the false dimensions of pleasure ensure that Black queer flesh does not rear its head or that the subject remembers an encounter with anxiety and Black queer flesh. Put differently, surplus jouissance acts as a form of both repression and distraction that explains pleasure rather than coercion at the level of the subject, including violence from state actors. Surplus jouissance disciplines with a proverbial carrot rather than a stick.

While Sigmund Freud initially envisioned anxiety as fear of a specific object—say, a bear attack while out camping—and ultimately expanded this to fear of an imaginary object, Lacan understood anxiety as an encounter with the objet cause of desire. Frantz Fanon, by contrast, modifies this account for the Black experience and claims that it is not the object cause of desire doing this work. Rather, anxiety is Black queer flesh registering being trapped and dispersed by subjectivity. Fanon signals toward this idea when describing the Black body as phobogenic—a stimulus for anxiety—for both the colonizer and Blacks. In *Wretched of the Earth,* Fanon captures my understanding of racial anxiety:

> In the colonized world, the colonized's affectivity is kept on edge like a running sore flinching from a caustic agent. And the psyche retracts, is obliterated, and finds an outlet through muscular spasms that have caused many an expert to classify the colonized as hysterical. This overexcited affectivity, spied on by invisible guardians who constantly communicate with the core of the personality, takes an erotic delight in the muscular deflation of the crisis.[1]

Within these muscle spasms, Darieck Scott finds a "reservoir of resistance to the colonizer's acts of subjugation and enslavement."[2] Although Scott views corporeal spasms through the prism of abjection, I want to stress the psychic retraction and obliteration as manifestations of racial anxiety. In this scenario, I see Black queer flesh erupting into the Symbolic as a spasm, as a disruption of the skin's false account of Black subjectivity. I propose we think of Scott's interpretation of muscle spasms as Black queer flesh making an appearance in the Symbolic world. The body jolts when the boundary between the Real and Reality, Black queer flesh and Black skin, becomes ruptured. Even as there is no object to cause anxiety, the drive of Black queer flesh keeps forcing the body to experience racial anxiety as a way to remanifest itself and liquidate subjectivity. Thus anxiety is really Black queer flesh being called forth from the body as a life-force, and, at the same time, its appearance tears apart subjectivity. Flesh at this juncture exists as an unacknowledged life-force: it lacks a shape or form.

As Fanon illustrates and Scott indicates, the Lacanian Real body (not to be confused with the Symbolic-Imaginary body constituted by language) reveals Black queer flesh attempting to manifest itself in the Symbolic and Imaginary. I want to underscore that Black queer flesh is not part of the Real but rather the drive system that transverses the Real and Symbolic-Imaginary. The muscular twitches of anxiety show the body attempting to re-create Black queer flesh. These moments are indicative of unconscious racial anxiety. During moments of anxiety, Black skin and subjectivity are ruptured. With continued rupturing, subjectivity eventually falls apart or is destroyed. I conceive of this process as self-abnegation, as one that occurs after repeated bouts of anxiety and that is its by-product: the ablation of subjectivity.

On the other hand, surplus jouissance works to disavow the existence of Black queer flesh and, more important, Black queer flesh as a viable ontology and mode of being queer and African American. Attempts to quell and forget anxiety—rather than sustaining the encounter as in self-abnegation—manifest surplus jouissance through the ideology of a unified self. This ideology counters the possibility that subjectivity can be dissolved, that anxiety breaks apart a unified ego. Moreover, the ideology of subjectivity appears as many ideologies: self-possession, self-determination, and self-formation, with the fetish of subjectivity consolidating and collapsing them. In this way, the Bildungsroman—the cultural product that narrates and perpetuates these myths of self making—is the vehicle par excellence that delivers surplus jouissance. In this chapter, I examine three novels that flirt with anxiety, only to fall back on the side of surplus jouissance rather than self-abnegation. Each of these texts represents a character tortured with anxiety who ultimately selects the pleasures of a hegemonic ideology instead of anxiety's negations. Each accepts the pleasures of self-formation as a way to forget about anxiety and Black queer flesh. Not until Nella Larsen's radical queer intervention in *Passing* does the project of surplus jouissance come to an end: in this narrative, she rejects it and its main vehicle, the Bildungsroman, and the notion of self-formation. Larsen renders the Bildungsroman a failure and, in doing so, opens a way of thinking about Black identity outside of subjectivity.

The Bildungsroman as Surplus Jouissance

The theories of racial uplift espoused by Booker T. Washington, W. E. B. Du Bois, and Marcus Garvey stressed the importance of the development of a new African American race—giving pride of place to how individuals forge this new reality while directing their own lives. For these leading men, racial uplift marks the transformation where self-possession shifts from a dream or ideology to a cultural practice. Historically, uplift prescribes the ideals of new African Americans who leave behind rural life and poverty for middle-class comfort and privilege. Under this widespread propaganda, uplift promised to improve the race via higher education and the pursuit of professional and vocational careers, amounting to nothing more than distant ideals and unattainable commodities. Middle-class incomes and the purchasing power for homes were distant luxuries to dream of for most African Americans—not for all, but for a vast majority in that period. In the rural South, pristine Sunday outfits, education, and other luxuries that made for a minimally decent standard of living were unavailable because of meager wages that sharecropping, like other forms of indentured servitude, afforded in the aftermath of slavery. The project of racial uplift promised to remake the race by ensuring that each individual endlessly and dutifully toiled, including the inspiration, indoctrination, and support of family members along the way, especially during the Great Migration. The collective feeling of a positive future in the North appealed to so many African Americans that it is not surprising that most subscribed to some version of racial uplift, irrespective of their social location. The pleasure of success—of improving one's life and future generations—tapped into the mythology of American Exceptionalism and the American Dream, the strict purview of white Americans at the time. It would seem that African Americans could now share in Alexis de Tocqueville's grand vision of American optimism and its trappings: "the charm of anticipated success." Enacting racial uplift in the everyday life choices for African Americans, the ideology promises, would undoubtedly secure their economic, political, and social uplift.

Indeed, the quest to remake the self relies upon a larger social phenomenon concerning the role of the individual in society or, put another way, regarding the parameters of being an individual subject. The idea of self-formation, almost by definition, requires an agent capable of making the self, including the freedom to identify one's pursuits. Liberal humanism asserts self-possession as the first act of agency in its ideology of subjectivity. Since the advent of that philosophy, self-determination has gone hand in hand with self-formation. A unified subject, "my" subjectivity, negotiates with society the construction of a specific form of person, and in thrall to this mythology, subjectivity must be constantly reworked. And this reconstruction constitutes, in turn, agency, self-possession, and self-determination. It is futile to say that self-determination causes self-formation since the ideologies all reinforce and remake one other by excluding the possibility of alternative modes of existence. One can only be a subject by this logic since subjectivity ostensibly endows one with self-possession, self-determination, agency, and self-formation (or vice versa).

The development of the liberal human subject stressed the idea of a unified subject that possessed autonomy over herself. To disseminate this emerging idea of the subject, Europeans invented the genre of the Bildungsroman to help illuminate the relationship among autonomy, self-determination, and a unified subjectivity. Historian Reinhart Koselleck underscores this fact in his tracing of the genealogy of the concept of *Bildung* across cultures, noting also key differences among various incorrect English translations of the genre, which take the forms of formal education, imagination, self-education, or self-cultivation; yet, in his estimation, Koselleck finds that "self-formation" *(Selbstbildung)* best captures the meaning of the German phenomenon. He demonstrates that Bildung does not imply a pregiven social identity but involves an evolution that is predicated upon self-reflection and self-determination.[3] Thus subjectivity must be developed and forged, and this is why African Americans after slavery were eager to adopt the ideology of subjectivity. They, too, could partake in the ventures of self-formation, practicing bold self-determination.

Only after the 1848 revolution does the concept of Bildung attain its hegemonic position as the ideology that accounts for self-formation. Franco Moretti concurs with Koselleck's social and political conclusions in a digital humanities study where he notices a surge in the authorship of novels written in the style of the Bildungsroman post-1848.[4] Furthermore, sociologist Viviana Zelizer, by contrast, contends that a dramatic decline in infant mortality rates, along with a concomitant rise in the bourgeoisie's fetishization of the child, enabled the cult of self-formation to gain traction, allowing it to proliferate in the middle of the nineteenth century.[5]

With the rise of the African American novel in the same period, the choice genre was none other than the Bildungsroman, which included early notables such as *Our Nig* (1859) by Harriet Wilson, *Iola Leroy* (1892) by Frances Ellen Watkins Harper, and *The Marrow of Tradition* (1901) by Charles Chesnutt. After the end of human bondage, the narrative of slavery—exemplified by the writings of Booker T. Washington—also followed the trajectory of the Bildungsroman. It often compressed the period of childhood, privileging the idea of racial uplift as well as the successes brought in its wake. By interlacing racial uplift into the fabric of the Bildungsroman, African American writers of the period worked through the logic of uplift—testing it out as a model of African American identity, anointing the genre as the vehicle for telling two simultaneous stories: Black self-determination as the ur-text of self-formation and self-possession, including the narrative of uplift's successes.

These novels reflected the choices and journeys that ultimately depicted the making of a subject by capitalizing on self-determination and self-possession as the fiercest of choices. Likewise, the genre promulgated by these texts required self-formation as the necessary precondition for becoming a unified, autonomous subject. From either perspective, the result and methods were the same. As a political project, the African American Bildungsroman vehemently challenged the status quo and racism so that African Americans could find their way into society—documenting while also performatively constituting the reality of uplift's promises. Success and respectability could be achieved by African Americans provided they practiced and championed uplift as self-formation. Washington's Bildungsroman narrative of slavery, *Up from Slavery* (1901), exemplifies this pathway into subjectivity in its resounding commercial success.[6] Du Bois propagated his own take on uplift through his literary output—novels, autobiographies, and sociological studies as well as the NAACP's *The Crisis* and its short-lived children's magazine *The Brownies' Book.* Each of these influential texts laid a blueprint for African American self-determination. And the beauty of Du Bois's approaches was his suggestion that multiple pathways account for the intersections of identity, including but not limited to age, gender, class, location, family history, marital status, parent and grandparent status, relationship to slavery, and skin color. Besides ignoring queer sexuality and assuming a cis-able body, Du Bois's work displayed how self-formation in each of these domains was required to become a Black subject.

Uplift stories and practices packaged the supposed creation of subjectivity into "unique" identities, not as cogs within a stream of Black commodification but instead as the fantasy of self-directed, autonomous self-fashioning. This entire venture of subjectivity hides the fact that African Americans were coerced into shaping themselves along the axis of liberal humanism's subjectivity. One way out of subjectivity is to destroy the apparatus through anxiety. In her epic novel *Beloved,* Toni Morrison demonstrates how the residents of 124 Bluestone Road experience anxiety and their reactions. Howard and Buglar run away to avoid anxiety; Denver adopts it for a while but quickly turns to normative subjectivity by flirting with a peer, working, and immersing herself in the Black community. Sethe, on the other hand, embraces anxiety.

African American authors ultimately strove to articulate self-formation, self-possession, and self-determination via the Bildungsroman. Each struggles with anxiety and self-abnegation only to return to the havens of subjectivity and self-formation. In what follows, I analyze Nella Larsen's *Quicksand* (1928), James Weldon Johnson's *Autobiography of an Ex-Colored Man* (1912), and Jessie Redmon Fauset's *Plum Bun* (1929), focusing on the ubiquity of surplus jouissance and the missed opportunities beneath moments of false pleasure. Two novels explore the theme of racial passing, and Fauset's in particular reveals the limits of uplift that I seek to trace. In the tragic mulatto novel, a light-skinned, mixed-raced protagonist racially passes for white, only to experience the futility and angst of such endeavors in the long run. At the end of the story, the protagonist somehow returns to the race—although in Johnson's case, the reverse happens, as the text ends with the decision to racially pass after a frustrating Black existence. My goal here, then, is to show not only how African American authors modified the Bildungsroman to advocate self-determination but also how they embedded surplus jouissance into their plotlines as a way of bolstering liberal humanism's unified subject and keeping alternative modes of being at bay. In performing these analyses, I hope to stress not only that the Bildungsroman is the quintessential genre in African American literature—rivaled only by protest prose and poetry—but also how subjectivity, as an ideology and practice, continues to plague and stifle Black culture even as it purports to offer freedom.

Plum Bun: A Novel with Surplus Jouissance

In Fauset's *Plum Bun,* the protagonist Angela Murray decides to pass for white and move to New York after the death of her Black parents. She mistakes, in her experiences, her light-skinned mother's passing as moments of enormous joy. As a child, she goes on weekend adventures with her mother while co-passing in the white world and reveres them as the pinnacle of success, as the rewards of life: "the great rewards of life—riches, glamour, pleasure,—are for white skinned people only."[7] Moving her body into the realm of whiteness would often bring her "joy and freedom which seemed to her inherent in mere whiteness" (14). She mistakes that race inhibits her from achieving success, namely, self-determination. Ultimately, she realizes that following the subjecthood offered by racial uplift cannot bring her the "joy and freedom" it promises: instead, white subjectivity allows for self-possession and self-determination. Angela spends the remainder of her time courting wealthy white men as suitors while also pursuing drawing. As a single "white" woman without family support (aside from a meager inheritance she receives after her parents' early deaths), Angela seeks a white husband for a variety of reasons. At first, she believes that "she would need even protection; perhaps it would be better to marry . . . a white man" (88). Protection soon morphs into another set of beliefs about marriage: "I might marry—a white man. Marriage is the easiest way for a woman to get those things [position, power, wealth], and white men have them" (112). Later, marriage for Angela provides "the assurance of relationship," and finally, at the novel's end, it includes all of these comforts: "protection, position, untold wealth, unlimited opportunities for doing good" (275, 320). And yet, as her life situations shift, so does her perspective on marriage to white men. Love, we notice, rarely enters the equation of marriage, at least to white men. Fauset satirizes the idea that marriage is the antidote to female troubles, while additionally mocking the Bildungsroman's prospect of Angela marrying to afford her social and personal status and fulfillment. At the same time, though, Fauset invests in the idea of self-determination as a curative by showing Angela constantly preening her subjectivity.

The attainment of a white husband—or simply a husband—authors Angela's, or Black women's, quest within the narrative of Bildung. She can only forge her own "real" identity once she has married. This idea aligns with critic Rita Felski's view that early twentieth-century women can only go on a journey of self-formation after marriage.[8] Fauset powerfully tethers Angela's potential identities to her husband's social status and wealth. Deborah McDowell, in the introduction to the novel, argues that "both marriage and passing are means by which these two disenfranchised groups [women and African Americans] hope to gain access to power."[9] On one hand, the novel explores the limited ways in which African American women can conceptualize their participation in the social sphere by subverting social norms, especially in marriage and romance. With alacrity, Angela relinquishes her racial identity to pursue the chance of gaining power—albeit through the privileges of a white husband—as she also dismisses or ensures the rejection of marriage proposals from wealthy white men. By ensuring that racial passing and white marriage are bound to fail, Fauset successfully eradicates the surplus jouissance associated with the female quest for marriage as the sure path toward uplift and selfhood. While the pursuit of marriage causes Angela grave anxiety, it simultaneously ensures her journey of self-formation. In trying to make herself as attractive to male suitors as possible, her journey brings her enormous amounts of surplus jouissance in the process. Rather than feeling the pain of racial passing or the turmoil of double consciousness, Angela obtains pleasure from dedicating her life to securing a husband. To the extent that Fauset prescribes a Bildungsroman plot for women like Angela, her protagonist hardly feels the domination she has consented to—surplus jouissance eradicates the feeling of domination.

Along the way, Fauset interrupts this journey of self-formation and thwarts the marriage plot, throwing Angela into a spiral of anxiety. Black women, under the aegis of the ideology of subjectivity, had to marry upstanding men. This preoccupation with marriage and its subsequent failure seems to dovetail nicely with McDowell's assessment that "Fauset focuses on the powerful role fairy tales play in conditioning women to idealize marriage and romantic love" (xvii). These fairy-tale marriages produce surplus jouissance in abundance. When Angela ends her courtship with a white man, for instance, the surplus jouissance also flees, leaving her in anxiety. Without surplus jouissance to distract her from feeling racial anxiety, Angela becomes wretched in the process, given that "she began to husband her clothes . . . her face lost its roundness, the white warmness of her skin remained but there were violet shadows under her eyes; her forehead showed faint lines; she was slightly shabby. Gradually the triumphant vividness . . . left her" (234). With the resounding failure of self-formation, therefore, comes the failure of youth, of beauty itself.

When marriage is denied to Black women, Fauset ingeniously turns to another available resource: self-formation through a profession. Angela becomes a designer for a fashion magazine, and this new program of development promises to empower her. The text seems to supply a surfeit of surplus jouissance to Angela through the trappings of economic power and the seeming ability to make herself now that she has gained purchasing ability and social status as a designer for a top fashion magazine. McDowell echoes this excitement, claiming quite assuredly that "her work becomes empowering." More specifically, McDowell reads the return of self-formation as a "good" thing: "Angela's self-development begins in earnest when she becomes gainfully employed as a designer for a fashion journal while continuing to refine her portrait painting."[10] When Angela returns to the path of self-determination by securing professional work, McDowell wants to affirm the reappearance as "self-development."

Indeed, Angela's glowing face returns, along with the concomitant quest to assimilate into society. Surplus jouissance resurfaces for Angela and readers alike.

After Angela is fired for racially passing, or for being dishonest about her race as the white liberals castigate her, work offers no more surplus jouissance, and she subsequently spirals back into anxiety. She begins to experience tremors and utter despair and loneliness. Barred from white husbands, having spent all of her inheritance, and rejected from a profession, a journey of self-formation has nowhere else to turn: these are the three plotlines that form the genre and supply surplus jouissance. She nevertheless manages to alleviate her racial anxiety by seeking stability in the form of an old acquaintance from childhood. In fact, when she visits her old home during a bout of depression, Angela comes across a former potential lover, reigniting the marriage plot and summoning up surplus jouissance. Whereas in their initial encounter, she partially rejected him because of his predictability and unquestioning conformity to racial uplift, she now finds solace and some kind of stability. Her crying and anxiety seize just at the moment when she takes comfort in his stability, in his pursuit of uplift. The tears cease when she calls him out for "read[ing] [his] paper and be[ing] all homey and comfortable" (365). The memories of her old home life temporarily quench her loneliness, and in particular, Matthew's former courting of Angela and the trope of marriage once again become a "tiny island of protection reared out of and against an encroaching sea of troubles." Angela returns to the surplus jouissance that marriage can bring by telling Matthew that "[she] was thinking what a little haven a house like this could be; what it must have meant to my mother" (366). By this point, with only a few pages remaining in the novel, Bildung characteristically returns in the guise of marriage, and not simply through memories from childhood. Fauset refuses to let anxiety take hold, refusing also the Black queer flesh driving anxiety.

True to form, Angela's sister marries. Angela herself weds as well, and both experience incessant joy. In a wild turn of events—just a few pages shy of the novel's closing—Matthew ends up marrying Angela's sister, and Angela's sister's former fiancé ends up marrying Angela. The latter was also the man who found the design position for Angela and who had outed himself as an African American male passing for a white man within her circle of friends. At the end of the text, which seemed to reject marriage as a fantasy that operates to oppress African American women, the novel concludes with two marriages, one in which Angela finds her "happiness" through a husband as well as his status—all of the things Fauset seemed to critique in the novel. In *Plum Bun,* Fauset began to reject marriage and the "meaning" making it forced African American women to accept, and perhaps even obtain, only to then subvert it. By the end of the plot, Angela marries, and Fauset seems to legitimate marriage as the curative for African American women. As Fauset undoes the plot she spun of self-formation, she equally reinforces this plot by incorporating fantasies of love that further oppress African American women. At the same time, she unwittingly naturalizes marriage as a legitimate core focus, one whose quest serves as a legitimate source of surplus jouissance for African American women. Rather than embrace anxiety as manifested in loneliness, the loss of work, the loss of marriage, and the loss of family, Fauset embraces the normative. The quest for female subjectivity—and thus comfort and surplus jouissance—wins out over any radical transformation, any rejection of hegemonic ideologies.

Forgetting *The Autobiography of an Ex-Colored Man*

The intersection of gender, class, skin color, and race constricts and aids Angela's journeys as well as her ability to find her way in the world. While she racially passes to escape the miseries and disadvantages that she interprets as integral and constitutive to the experience of being a Black woman, James Weldon Johnson's unnamed narrator in *The Autobiography of an Ex-Colored Man* lives most of his youth as an African American male. Like Angela, the ex-colored man does not need to try to pass, as he is, according to his presumptuous benefactor, "by blood, by appearance, by education and by tastes, a white man."[11] The world reads and constructs him as white—something he relies on when he decides to pass for a different race. In passing, he refuses to claim agency for assuming whiteness, thereby taking the passive position, knowing full well the outcome of his lack of choice: "I finally made up my mind that I would neither disclaim the black race nor claim the white race . . . and let the world take me for what it would" (90). After traveling across Europe and America, he is always read as white; in fact, he is never even mistaken for being of mixed heritage. In certain situations, he must nevertheless convince others of his Blackness. Not being phenotypically "black," the ex-colored man goes on a journey of self-formation that is in large part dictated by others. Those who socially read him as white invite him on journeys in which young white men would partake as they curate their own subjectivities. His light phenotype combined with misreadings allows him access to a normative, white journey of self-formation—with all of its surplus jouissance.

The gender privilege of the narrator equally contributes to the extent to which surplus jouissance affords him access to self-determination. Angela could not embark on a journey of self-formation that included making herself a gambler, drunk, or valet to a white man. The ex-colored man's male privilege opens up various forms of surplus jouissance that appear to be more hedonistically pleasurable. The narrator can "command" a room with his male presence and handsome face and thus dictate, in part, how he is read and how he navigates social spaces. Angela cannot "command" a room; she must leverage her beauty and her fragility to seduce and manipulate the actions, perceptions, and thoughts of others. I caution at this point that we resist the temptation to read narratives of racial passing, as we do gender, among other intersectional identities, in terms of how they shape the journeys of our protagonists. For Johnson's male narrator, enjoying being read as white is in large part possible because of the social status of educated white men; Angela, by contrast, must constantly fret about being outed. She cannot take much pleasure as a white woman without means or family. For Angela, moreover, Black women must carry the memory of being Black as well as the kinship ties they are sacrificing. This normative stereotype that women are more nurturing and emotionally caring prevents her from forgetting the past. The unnamed narrator, however, can forget; his male privilege (along with being essentially an orphan, although he does have a living white father and half sister) is surplus jouissance from the act of forgetting his horrific encounters with racism and anxiety. Unlike Angela, who "forgot" anxiety by pursuing the next form of self-formation, the ex-colored man forgets anxiety by pursing another "male" adventure.

The Autobiography of an Ex-Colored Man is the quintessential Bildungsroman. The protagonist loses his mother when he is finishing high school, becoming an orphan at a pivotal moment during his childhood, compelled to decide whether to leave for college or stay in his town with his mother and develop a relationship with his white father. He leaves for college in Atlanta, but dire circumstances direct him elsewhere: a cigar factory in Florida, which he cheerfully embraces. He then enters a variety of successive experiences as an ingenuous young man, if only to fail and struggle at first and then triumph. At the end of the novel, he integrates into society by marrying, having children, and gaining moderate wealth. Structurally, the novel could not be more of a Bildungsroman. It concludes with a round character, and we, as readers, gain access to his interiority; we can empathize with his decisions and celebrate the life he has made for himself. Even though the narrator decides to racially pass, his ego and identity remain solid and complex. The novel, though, evinces the obstacles the narrator must endure to "become" who he is, to "become" himself. To develop in each of his journeys, the narrator must not only face trying situations but also ostensibly learn from them. Yet, Johnson reveals that this learning is not possible: Black men cannot go on journeys of self-formation as do their white counterparts. To the extent that racism guides and to a large extent overdetermines the narrator, the ex-colored man does not necessarily drive his own journey, nor is he in control of it. This is due in part to the artifact of literary Naturalism and the representation of the uncontrollability of "life"; but Johnson emphasizes the forceful and undeniable entry of racism into questions of Bildung. To advance to the next journey, the narrator must "forget" why he must advance; he is not always becoming less naive or mature. The difficulties of racism and its effects propel the journey, and forgetting their weight and costs constitutes a powerful form of surplus jouissance that essentially keeps racial anxiety—the acknowledgment of it, the feeling of racism acting on his mind and body—at bay. To reiterate, a white male character could advance to the next step in his journey by writing off mistakes or misfortunes—think Huckleberry Finn or Augie March—but African American males must "forget" those experiences with surplus jouissance to advance. Their subjectivities must be temporarily shattered and reconstituted for the next journey to begin. Only by drawing upon surplus jouissance can Bildung and self-determination continue.

When the ex-colored man makes the trek to Atlanta for college, an African American Pullman porter who befriends him along the ride steals his tuition money. Unable to afford college, the ex-colored man finds a job making cigars. The abject poverty of African Americans in the period and the criminal act of the porter cannot be contextualized by the effect of racism in the country; for his part, the narrator forgets the event and moves on. He does not mature as most other protagonists do in a Bildungsroman, forgetting as a way of terminating anxiety. Moving on from his attempt at college, he travels south in search of work and ends up making cigars. With his new Cuban colleagues at the cigar factory, he "learned not only to make cigars, but also to smoke, to swear, and to speak Spanish" (32). His self-formation also takes a turn for the worse at this point, becoming not mature but unwise: "from their [Cuban colleagues] example I learned to be careless about money; and for that reason I constantly postponed and finally abandoned returning to Atlanta University" (39). Notwithstanding, he relinquishes his hopes of an education by embarking on his next journey: New York City. Forgetting is integral to his transition north: the narrator quickly tells the reader that the factory had shut down and he had decided to go with a few friends to New York. Beyond the plant's closing and the tremendous fear that most workers experience in these situations, the narrator cannot recall what happened because he forgot: "for some reason, which I do not now remember, the factory at which I worked was indefinitely shut down" (41). The narrator, who proclaimed in the same sentence to be ready to settle down in Florida, and who had the opportunity to create a family and work in another plant in the area, conveniently "forgets" why he had left. He decides to turn his back on his supposed dream, so his act of forgetting prepares him for the next phase of his journey without remembering the accompanying anxiety.

This pattern of forgetting figures centrally in the novel. In New York, the ex-colored man becomes a gambler and a great ragtime musician: "I had the name at that time of being the best ragtime player in New York" (53). His tragic life as a gambler is abruptly cut short as he becomes a musician for hire. The text is silent on the circuits of poverty, illegal gambling, and violence that play such a key role in forging the identities of so many young African American males in the period; the ex-colored man simply forgets these life "choices" and proceeds to become a musician. The narrator further employs forgetting on the sexual plane: rather than experience the racism involved in an older women trying to seduce a so-called young primitive—and highly sexualized Black man—or discuss how his music playing at the nightclubs is policed by race, the narrator simply forgets such a life and tells the story of his time with his white benefactor. The surplus jouissance of forgetting wipes away the anxiety of being a criminal or of being made to perform the dominant view of an aggressive Black sexuality and gender. The text placates—covers up and links—these feelings of anxiety with the pleasures of forgetting by crafting an immediate transition to the narrator traveling in Europe with his benefactor. Anxiety cannot remain active in the text except as ephemeral moments, even though traces of anxiety—via surplus jouissance—riddle the novel.

As he travels about Europe with his benefactor, playing music for the latter nearly each evening, much to the narrator's exhaustion, the ex-colored man learns French and German, wears new clothes, and accidently encounters his half-sister and father at an opera house. As one would expect of a Bildungsroman, the ex-colored man expands his horizons abroad and seems to acquire new knowledge and experience; but he does not mature or grow until he encounters a musician who shows him how to infuse ragtime with classical musical structures. With this new inspiration—and after not having matured in Europe or faced much difficulty (or at least he might have, but forgot them)—he decides to return to America on a whim, to "go back into the very heart of the South, to live among the people, to drink in my inspiration first-hand" (66). Back home, he journeys through the South, having forgotten that his benefactor has in fact transformed him into a commodity by appropriating his Black music. The white benefactor literally buys the narrator after a party and takes him to Europe in tow as his valet and as a ragtime-on-demand musician. The exploitation of the narrator's Black culture and the Black male body is forgotten in the morass of travel and foreign encounters, including money and languages. Not surprisingly, these items powerfully contribute to the surplus jouissance needed to erase the narrator's conversion into an object of pleasure for the benefactor. The narrator forgets these experiences upon his arrival in the South as he takes on a new adventure.

The narrator's attempts to recode the Black aesthetic through classical music's structures and rules comes to a crashing halt as he witnesses the lynching of an African American man in an unnamed southern town. This final journey of Black self-formation concludes by the narrator's becoming a white man, husband, and father. He forgets his journey to create Black music, to create Blackness for a life without shame: "I knew that it was shame, unbearable shame . . . that was driving me out of the Negro race." "Shame," he continues, "at being identified with a people that could with impunity be treated worse than animals." His naming of racial anxiety as shame is quickly placated by surplus jouissance of the highest form: giving up his Black identity. Since his passing will be his final Bildung journey as a Black identified man, he conjures the quest as one not of his own making so that he does not need to forget it: "I would change my name, raise a mustache, and let the world take me for what it would; that it was not necessary for me to go about with a label of inferiority pasted across my forehead." The narrator does not choose to pass, but he does choose to avoid racial anxiety and racial "inferiority." He must escape anxiety by passing, and he erases that escape by framing the decision to pass as "let[ting] the world take me for what it would" (90).

Recall that Angela from *Plum Bun* experiences a similar moment when she attempts to relinquish her agency as a form of surplus jouissance that enables the world to dictate her process of development. After having lost her job and suitors, she desperately proclaims, "Whatever move I make is always wrong. Let life take care of itself" (314). For the narrator's part, his circumvention of the racial anxieties associated with being an African American male is one that turns on defending his psyche with surplus jouissance. When he informs the reader that as a white man, he earned a college degree, made a modest amount of money, and raised two children (and had a white widow), he has by all accounts achieved success and managed to stave off the anxieties of race. He concludes his journey in the novel not only by integrating into society as typical of the Bildungsroman but also by disavowing ever being psychically or culturally Black, and in doing so, he makes us forget that he has practiced the art of forgetting to mitigate racial anxiety, as when he admits that "sometimes it seems to me that I have never really been a Negro, that I have been only a privileged spectator of their inner life; at other times I feel that I have been a coward, a deserter, and I am possessed by a strange longing for my mother's people" (99). The threat of racial passing infuriated whites and fascinated many Blacks with the question of "when they'd be found out." In the ex-colored man's case, he successfully escapes his racial destiny, and his story—which most readers believed to be an actual autobiography—scandalized the reading public.

By the time Johnson reissued his classic text of African American literature in 1927 during the height of the Harlem Renaissance, racial passing had already taken hold of the American imagination. The novel had already stunned the reading public when it first made its debut in 1912. Posing the most hotly debated moral question of the period, it raised key questions pertaining to the morality of passing, even when African Americans sought to assuage and safeguard their offspring from the horrors of racism, particularly from the violence of race riots and lynching as well as the social-psychic costs of economic and perceived inferiority. The fantasy of passing could serve as a form of surplus jouissance for some African Americans, but Johnson's text served a more important role: not simply to revitalize the Bildungsroman during the literary flowering that was the Harlem Renaissance but to stoke the fantasy that African Americans could have a hand in crafting their own journeys of self-formation, reinforcing the hegemony of subjectivity. In each of the ex-colored man's journeys before passing, Johnson curiously depicts each adventure, each moment of development, as if racism had no say in the life of the narrator, as if it did not enter the picture; it appears as if the narrator was in full control of the journey—as if his life merely happened to him and he had full agency, full cognition to make choices without a psyche terrorized by double consciousness. Johnson's great feat overpowers the novel with surplus jouissance both in terms of the plot and in terms of the overall treatment of the genre. The racial anxiety in each journey is therefore forgotten so that each successive journey ostensibly starts afresh, unhindered from and untethered to the previous one. Forgetting serves as the "passing" device that makes this possible in terms of genre and in terms of plot advancement. More important still is the very framing of self-formation itself and its resolution in marriage, profession, and wealth, which all seem to justify the narrative that also helps to pass over the reality of the narrator's inability to craft his own Bildungsroman, in which we are left to forget that racial anxiety powerfully inflects and also structures the plot, character, and conclusion of the novel. Thus Johnson valorizes subjectivity at the cost of embracing racial anxiety.

No More Surplus Jouissance and the Failure of the Bildungsroman in Nella Larsen's *Quicksand*

African American authors such as James Weldon Johnson and Jessie Fauset began to derail surplus jouissance and to decouple it from the idea of racial anxiety—no longer needing to elicit pleasure as a mechanism to combat anxiety but instead to embrace it. They assumed that subjectivity must be maintained and preened to achieve self-determination at all costs. To go about this preening, they believed that Bildung was possible for African Americans and that the Bildungsroman could be retooled for the Black experience: they assumed first that subjectivity was available for the Black experience and second that subjectivity benefited rather than hurt African Americans. This is strikingly dramatized by Johnson's narrator in his attempt to infuse ragtime and southern Black music with (white) classical music elements. In their works, these authors sought to combat the racial anxiety springing from what they believed was the inability of African Americans to assert and define themselves in the public sphere. And the Bildungsroman offered the surplus jouissance necessary to placate that reality. While Johnson, Fauset, and their Harlem Renaissance counterparts embraced the surplus jouissance of the Bildungsroman and its power to disavow the Jim Crow racism and anxiety moderating Black lives and psyches, Nella Larsen rejected surplus jouissance and brought racial anxiety to the forefront in her novels. She is frustrated with subjectivity and trying to make it work. The effort is all consuming, and it does not always deliver on its promises. She takes the first step toward self-abnegation and rejecting subjectivity as something that is not really possible to preen, to manage, and to adopt. Larsen attempts to call into question that her character, Helga Crane, can exercise self-determination such that she molds her own subjectivity. Agency becomes quite limited under the performance of subjectivities since power dictates the breadth of what Helga, as a middle-class, single, essentially orphaned, heterosexual woman, can draw upon. Power relations grant a certain range of subjectivities to express. Larsen communicates this process by exposing how development is not possible under the regime of Bildung—rather, selecting prefabricated subjectivities is confused as making and performing subjectivities—and in the process, critiques African American authors for perpetuating such an oppressive fantasy, to say the least of the surplus jouissance embedded in the concept of Black self-making. Larsen deftly portrays the consequences inherent in viewing African American self-formation and subjectivity making as central to the mission and direction of Black youths: for her, Blackness itself becomes a commodity and Black Bildung by contrast a near futility, a distraction of sorts that keeps up the face of uplift, specifically when it is overinvested in a genre. In *Quicksand,* Larsen reconfigures surplus jouissance in the form of forgetting, racial uplift, and the Bildungsroman; it no longer contains the ability to quell racial anxiety, but instead surplus jouissance lets it rupture the neat plot of the text. She gives up on adapting a white genre to represent a Black aesthetic and a Black experience—what she accomplishes in fact is no less than the beginning of the project of dismantling this genre to create something new that captures Black "development." In *Quicksand,* Larsen critiques the Bildungsroman. It is not until her next novel, *Passing,* that she develops an alternative model for subjectivity and ultimately invents a new queer literary genre.

Most critics agree in the assessment of *Quicksand* as her literary masterpiece. Larsen's aesthetic acrobatics move us through exotic landscapes while simultaneously keeping us treading on the shores of Helga's ever-changing emotional current. The novel captures each of Helga's journeys of self-discovery. It follows her from a young college teacher in the South to her splendid adventures in Europe and America. Each episode builds upon the other, appearing to transform Helga into a more complex character and culminating as a Bildungsroman typically does for a female protagonist—with marriage. In this case, marriage tragically destroys Helga through the tribulations of childbirth and a life of struggle in the rural South. Despite Helga's apparently radical journeys and transformations, Larsen represents a fate bestowed upon Black women: the reproduction of oppression via motherhood. Literary critic Abdul JanMohamed calls such a state of affairs "death-bound-subjectivity."[12] He defines this position as one that is constituted by the fact of Black subjectivity being constructed by and for death and labor. In the case of African American women, he argues that they are "bound" to their children and that if they question the kinship, they in effect risk their very lives by doing so. Thus a radical change in the life of an African American woman most certainly implies death as a possible outcome. In the novel's end, Helga retains only her life, and even that, Larsen hints, she would be glad to relinquish were it not for the question of her children's care. The conclusion of the Bildungsroman for African American women, according to Larsen, turns on their occupation as wives and as producers of African American children—a future Fauset seemingly buys into. By writing this ending, Larsen shows that marriage and motherhood are not only forms of surplus jouissance but also ways to cover up racial anxiety. In the course of the novel, Helga struggles to avoid both of these death-bound-subject positions; she twice questions the imperative for reproduction, asking "why add any more unwanted, tortured Negroes to America," since "giving birth to little, helpless, unprotesting Negro children [was] a sin, an unforgivable outrage . . . more dark bodies for mobs to lynch."[13] Helga's statement asserts the claim that African American lives are destined for oppression from the moment of birth. To her mind, all African American children will grow up to be oppressed and socially abject: she voices a concern from early in the novel that African Americans do not develop on their own accord but rather are filtered into specific subjectivities. Helga rejects that subjectivity is possible within the Bildungsroman and attempts to argue that these African American students are simply occupying socially mediated and enforced subject positions: self making is not an option. The stringency of her perspective nevertheless poses the question of whether this philosophy encompasses Helga herself.

Critics tend to converge in their sense that the ending of *Quicksand* constitutes an aesthetic failure on Larsen's part in that it expresses or imagines an ending that is outside of the conventions expected of a middle-class reader and character. In many regards, Helga's ultimate self-destruction by way of marriage comes off as an unoriginal and flat conclusion. I suggest, however, that the real failure of *Quicksand* lies neither in the language of the novel, which is consistently graceful, nor in the spectacular unfolding of Helga's tragedy. While the text involves experiences that superficially satisfy the requirements that meet the usual classifications of the novel as a Bildungsroman, and while, thus, it should culminate with Helga's transformation into a "mature" and thriving subject, Larsen questions the productive dimensions of any such journey. The author subscribes to the narrative conventions of the white Bildungsroman. However, she mistakenly assumes that she can modify the Bildungsroman to accommodate a narrative of Black self-formation. What Larsen does in effect is to ask if Helga *can* develop an identity within a hostile genre. Over the course of the novel, Helga learns that self-formation for African American women is nothing short of a fantasy. No matter the level of negotiation or subversion of the social order she attains, Helga does not have access to Bildung because African Americans are given a range of prefabricated identities from which to select. Helga, at most, can slightly modify this "inherited" racial identity, but she cannot *develop into* a more complex character, given that her subject position is already fully formed. She is the tragic mulatta, for instance, and nothing can stop this destiny from unfolding. Thus writing the novel of education reveals to Larsen the impossibility of an African American Bildung within the context of a white genre.

While the Bildungsroman encompasses an attempt to narrate a life contradictory to this fate, Larsen acquiesces to the limitations of the Bildungsroman as a mode to express an alternative form of African American development. She discovers that the genre only permits her to write a history that ostensibly documents how Helga comes to perform the subject position granted to her. In *Quicksand,* Larsen accepts that not even a modified white literary form can express Black self-formation. No matter how much Helga struggles to develop her subjectivity, and no matter how much Larsen infuses the white Bildungsroman with a Black aesthetic, the genre and the social world delimit and contain the latter's ability to narrate a journey of development. The novel does not trace a journey of development, therefore, but it does culminate in an ending that seems entirely out of place. Helga's life contracts into the oppressive role of motherhood in which she is cast and is consequently hindered by continuous pregnancies. The domestic sphere radically destroys and ends Helga's journey of self-formation; yet, it endows her with the permanent subject position of mother. Larsen concludes the novel with Helga's deformation, but the novel does not logically lead into such a state.

With *Quicksand,* Larsen borrowed a previous century's aesthetic form and altered it somewhat while representing Black female development. Although she changed the racial designation of the characters, she remained fiercely wedded to the idea of self-formation as a struggle that ultimately ends in heterosexual marriage. This repopulation of an autonomous work of art flattens the genre and diminishes its critical reach. To paraphrase Theodor Adorno, Larsen cheats readers out of the Bildungsroman's promises. For one, the promissory note of Bildung issued by plot and packaging and genre is indefinitely prolonged; the reader must be satisfied with reading the nineteenth-century Bildungsroman rather than the twentieth-century African American Bildungsroman.[14]

By recovering Helga's Bildung, I aim to demonstrate how Larsen's mirroring of white Bildung moments turns out to be incidents that discipline the Black body into a normalized and bounded African American subject position with a limited but still enshrined subjectivity. Each of Helga's episodes functions not as *self*-formation but more powerfully to performatively reconstitute a subjectivity belonging to a middle-class African American woman. At the same time, each episode of *Quicksand* quietly registers the absurdity and terror of articulating Black development through an inherently anti-Black aesthetic. These episodes, in an almost picaresque fashion, offer insights into the failed project of a Black Bildung. Helga's journey of development turns out to be a series of scenes of subjection that do not develop her as an independent Black woman but reinforce—or discipline—her into a socially predetermined identity: self-determination is exposed as an ideological trap.

As scholars have pointed out, Larsen struggles to articulate a response to the story of the tragic mulatto that is psychically torn between her white and Black heritages. Larsen introduces a complex yet binary configuration of Black and white culture to address Helga's biracial troubles. As might be expected, in doing so, she draws upon historical and contemporary myths related to Black and white identity. The world of whiteness and its supposed refinement, and particularly its reserved "calmness" and self-reflection, are represented in Helga's relationship with her mother, stepfamily, and experiences in Copenhagen. On the other side, Blackness manifests in the novel as something "savage"—as a terrifyingly unknown quality that is closely tied to the erotic—and also Black "radiance" as the allure of Black sociality and folk culture. Larsen complicates these historical fables, however. First, since Helga cannot pass for white, she adopts a "proper" middle-class Black position that reflects the calmness and self-reflection that she attributes to white culture; racial uplift as surplus jouissance helps distance Helga from the "Black" experience when it is labeled as savage, too emotive, and too expressive—only when she embraces the savagery and radiance of Blackness will Helga find solace in the African American community at large. These tamed "white" qualities can be seen in the characters of Anne Gray and later in Irene from *Passing.* The focus of my reading does not pivot around Larsen's critique of the Black bourgeois interpretation of whiteness. Helga grapples with her own Black bourgeoisie sensibility and its negotiation and appropriation of white culture. I want to interrogate Larsen's reinterpretation of the stereotype of African Americans as primitives within this context of the Black bourgeoisie. She has Helga, for instance, pursue and slowly become the Black savage over the course of the novel as her mode of Bildung; Larsen attempts to replace the surplus jouissance of uplift (as an approximation of whiteness) with something more visceral and another form of Bildung in circulation at the time. Appropriating the primitive is Larsen's flirting with the methods of queer disidentification and exposing Black queer flesh, even if in controlled glimpses. First, though, Helga must endure a traditional process of (white/Black middle-class) self-formation: she must undergo a proper education. After failing at uplift, Larsen tries to salvage Bildung by turning toward her belief in an essential Black journey of development: the primitive, or what she terms "radiance" in the novel. This section first covers the normative white model of Bildung and then returns to the "primitive" model of Bildung.

Trained to become a teacher at the all-Black boarding school Naxos, Helga finds herself immersed in the ideology of racial uplift. Upon graduation, she takes on the task of indoctrinating Black students to become proper gentlemen and ladies of the Black middle class. After eight years of uplift, her enthusiasm begins to wane. Helga thinks of the school as one that emits "a depressing silence . . . [as] the automatons moved" (46–47). Instead of learning about Black history and culture, Helga witnesses the transformation of young minds into a burgeoning Black middle class. On one hand, these students will become the Black elite—Du Bois's "Talented Tenth"—a group capable of leading the fight for civil rights; on the other, the methods of formation enforced by Naxos's pedagogical machinery prove abhorrent to Helga and to anyone truly talented or enlightened. The school does not teach African Americans to be critical or creative but rather to adopt and perform the oppressed subjectivities planned out for them by none other than Black educators at a Black university. For Larsen, any induction into the world of middle-class values and cultures serves to inhibit African Americans from pursuing their own self-formation: she exposes the project of self-determination as a myth given that uplift determines so-called self-determination. Helga describes the young students, who are not much younger than herself, as "human beings who were prisoners . . . in the midst of all this *radiant life*. They weren't, she knew, even conscious of its presence" (49, emphasis added). What Larsen does in effect is to refer to the Black rural South and to the collective existence of the African Americans at Naxos as exhibiting a "radiant life" that is nevertheless ignored by students and faculty. The students take more of an interest in the industrial and technical education that will bring about the trappings of financial reward rather than enjoying and learning from Black "radiance." At this point in the novel, Black radiance—coded language for the "folk" and seemingly more authentic Black experience—evokes anxiety, one that must be assuaged by the veneer of financial success, another manifestation of surplus jouissance.

Helga locates the "authentic" dimension of race within the folklore and history of rural Black people and *within* those who come to the school with expansive family histories; not surprisingly, Black radiance comes to figure as an innate quality of African Americans. By comparison, an education of uplift is by all accounts bleak, silent, colorless—and white—and unnatural. It serves as a color metaphor, a mode of critiquing the values of the Black middle class as "whitewashed." Twenty years later, Ralph Ellison extends Larsen's critique of Black higher education as ignoring and suppressing the Black culture from which they emerge and by which they are literally surrounded in *Invisible Man*. Ellison, like Larsen, praises the radiant "Black" knowledge of characters like Jim Trueblood over that of the educated and uplift proponent Bledsoe. Larsen, as does Ellison, describes the school as "no longer a school. It had grown into a machine. . . . Life had died out of it" (39). Instead of a vital Black institution, the school produces Black subjects who lack life, who lack Black "radiance," and whose education will not allow them to critically reflect upon their own formations. The school manufactures the lives out of Black subjects.

When Helga realizes that her own identity has compromised her autonomy, she decides to leave the college. During her resignation meeting, Dr. Anderson speaks of the project of uplift, managing to temporarily convince her to stay so she can help him transform hardworking youths into Black leaders. Driven in part by a newfound sexual desire for Anderson, Helga has a change of heart and stays. Anderson's rhetoric of uplift pulls her desire back toward the improvement of the race. Indoctrinated by her education and middle-class milieu to desire and adopt the form of uplift propagated by Naxos, she is easily drawn back in by the institution. The power of Anderson's words—along with his sexual attractiveness—produces in Helga an "actual desire to stay, and to come back next year," because "he had won her." This feeling—this obvious surplus jouissance of lust—dissipates, while her disgust grows, as Anderson assures her that she is valued as a teacher because, as he puts it directly to her, "'You're a lady. You have dignity and breeding.' At these words turmoil rises again in

Helga Crane" (54). The abrupt change in attitude surfaces most assuredly upon the hearing of the word "lady." Helga refuses to perform a socially determined position imposed upon her, which turns out to be in actuality one that represents a nonnormative "breeding": "she could neither conform [to social norms] nor be happy in her unconformity [anxiety]" (42). According to Anderson, however, her tendency to act out by wearing provocative clothing or by being a hermit does not obscure her "good stock" (55). In terms of her actual effect on peers at Naxos, Anderson claims that Helga occupies and performs her socially constructed position as a professional Black woman of the middle class. To ensure his power of persuasion, Anderson insists that Helga *is* a "lady" to her students, peers, and fiancé. The insistence upon this reality—that even in her unconformity, she is a lady—encourages Helga's flight from the college. The horror that her own self-education has transformed her into a middle-class race woman is too terrible for Helga to bear. When she tells Anderson of her scandalous origins, she attempts to disrupt her performance of "lady," but to no avail. By this moment, in the development of Helga, uplift as surplus jouissance passes into racial anxiety. Larsen cleverly extracts the surplus of pleasure, revealing its more illicit oppressive machinations. Her immanent critique directs surplus jouissance into anxiety itself as one that must be fiercely eviscerated.

Critics have routinely noted that Larsen represents the Black middle class with harsh disdain, as when Helga scolds the norms of the class in *Quicksand*: "Why their constant slavish imitation of traits not their own? Why their constant begging to be considered as exact copies of other [white] people?" (113). What Larsen does is to classify the overall project of the middle class as a desperate quest for "happiness. Whatever that might be. What, exactly, she wondered, was happiness? Very positively she wanted it" (45). Helga adopts the same paths toward happiness as anyone imitating white norms: personal enrichment, travel, culture, and marriage. Early in the novel, though, she learns that both higher education and idealistic values fail as potential avenues to happiness; even as she is slightly not normal, she discovers that her nonnormativity is really within the bounds of normative subjectivity. To escape the trappings of normative Black subjectivity, she begins to believe that a return to an essential Blackness will bring about a state of bliss for herself. Larsen literally changes Helga's path from one of self-education to one of self-racialization to the extent to which Helga relinquishes uplift as a mode to abate anxiety and turns instead to the "radiance" of Blackness in the folk and in the Black masses as other forms of surplus jouissance, if only fleeting ones.

Just as she absconds from the South to Chicago, and upon stepping into the busy "multicolored crowd," Helga pronounces in satisfaction "that she had come home. She Helga Crane, who had no home" (62–63). And just after having been living in Harlem for a year, she finds that "there she had been happy, and secured work, had made acquaintances and another friend. Again she had had that strange transforming experience . . . that magic sense of having come home" (75). Within the context of "home," Helga convinces herself that "she had, as she put it, 'found herself.'" The Black community does indeed provide a sense of home for her just as much as it functions as her next phase of Bildung. By juxtaposing Naxos and Chicago/Harlem, Larsen underscores their similarities, and as might be expected, Harlem—like Naxos and Chicago—must be abandoned. In her second year in Harlem, things turn for the worse, and Helga now finds "life became for her only a hateful *place* where one lived in intimacy with people one would not have chosen had one been given the choice" (84, emphasis added). Helga's yearning for the radiance of Black life seems to have failed, so she no longer feels quite at "home" again—the surplus jouissance has worn out. Her attempt at self-racialization in migrating to Harlem leaves her feeling "horribly lonely . . . shutting her off from all of life around her. . . . In all the climbing massed city no one cared one whit about her" (66). The joy she attributes to the neighborhood disappears: "But it didn't last, this happiness of Helga Crane's" (78). Larsen seems to endow Helga's sadness with the corruption as one with her idea of Blackness as radiance. Take her best friend Anne, for example, who dislikes whites but loves white culture as it is adapted by the Black middle class. She embodies the critique that Helga made of her middle-class peers while still at Naxos: "she aped their [white] clothes, their manners, and their gracious ways of living . . . yet disliked the songs, the dances, and the softly blurred speech of the [African American] race" (80). To escape the good home turned bad, Helga flees to Copenhagen with her inheritance—like a true member of the bourgeoisie! Her Harlem education proves not to advance her self-racialization insofar as family becomes the next source of surplus jouissance to stave off racial anxiety.

Life abroad amuses Helga to the fullest extent with its fancy clothes, elaborate parties, cultural performances, and romance. After just two years of a carefree existence with her wealthy aunt, Helga's unrest and anxiety reemerge, and she ascribes to them, again, a notion of place. She becomes homesick after hearing an African American song and decides that, like her African American father, she needs to be surrounded by "the inexhaustible humor and the incessant hope of his own kind" (122). While Helga regrets leaving Copenhagen and her family, she cannot help but wonder "why couldn't she be satisfied in one *place*?" (123, emphasis added). The idea of a stagnant life perplexes and consumes her. Her adolescent inability to resolve the dialect between "the pale calm of Copenhagen to the colorful lure of Harlem" is called "a trifle ridiculous" by the narrator (125). Larsen alerts the reader that the stakes of Helga's vacillations consist of something more complex and unconscious than a simple choice of setting or a fetish of home or bad identifications. As a form of deflection, Helga interrupts her philosophy of race relations for a more pleasurable worry: her next city and its promise. Previously, Helga had emphasized the spatial dimension of home and race. In her justification for leaving Copenhagen, Helga augments this idea of space to include a cultural dimension: "*these* were her people [African Americans]. . . . She had never truly valued this kinship until distance had shown her its worth . . . [such] ties that were of the spirit. Ties not only superficially entangled with mere outline of features or colors of skin. Deeper. Much deeper than either of these" (125). Helga complicates the notion of a racialized space by demonstrating that "distance" should in no way affect the fact of cultural/biological ancestry. In this regard, Larsen privileges the idea of "spirit" over phenotype, which harkens back to the sense of the "radiance" that Blackness provides in its abstract quality, which appeared at the novel's opening. This raises the question of Helga's mere rediscovery of her own conception of both Blackness and race as historically informed and practiced phenomena. She rediscovers that race is no mere question of skin color but a matter of cultural practices and a rich history. It is this spirit and radiance, now reified into Black bodies, that Helga claims to miss; here Larsen begins to flirt with the idea of Black queer flesh as separate and distinct from subjectivity. The novel must work through subjectivity—uplift in particular—until she discovers that "radiance" (or Black queer flesh) does not operate on the same plane as subjectivity. This incompatibility drives the remainder of the plot as Helga must decide which side she falls upon: Black queer flesh or subjectivity, queer sociality or normative marriage. In addition, Larsen exposes that the quest for the right "place" is another distraction against anxiety—this theme occupies nearly the entire novel.

Romantic relationships and heteronormativity also become forms of surplus jouissance. Critics have long interpreted Helga's sexual life as both a symptom of ephemeral, immature lust and as a marker of a sexuality that cannot be expressed outside the confines of marriage. I want to highlight Larsen's treatment of men here as objects that help keep Helga's fantasies in movement rather than viewing them as underdeveloped characters or as signs of middle-class propriety. I will argue that Helga transforms men into objects along with herself to expose the false dimensions of self-possession and Bildung. This quest will ultimately expose the genre as unable to accommodate the story of Black subjectivity, but at the cost of the reification and destruction of Helga Crane. Men function simultaneously as a distraction from racial anxiety and as commodities that help Larsen bring about the end of the Bildungsroman within the African American literary tradition. Helga's passion for Robert Anderson, for example, is not articulated early in the novel. Does it begin in her resignation meeting, before it, or when she spies Anderson with Audrey Denney or Anne Gray? Larsen crafts an ambiguous point of origin not because love proves nebulous but because that love, too, must be an object that circulates. A serial flirt, Helga manages to seduce James Vayle, who is engaged; Robert Anderson, who serves as a potential affair; Axel Olson through a proposal of marriage; the Reverend Pleasant Green through marriage; and countless other men around the globe in the short span of the novel.

Larsen breaks literary ground by representing Helga's strong sexuality, although she does not fully develop the idea of sexuality in *Quicksand.*

Helga's desires are depicted in constant circulation so they may be deposited and exchanged by the protagonist with each new suitor. After her rejection by Anderson, Helga metaphorically attaches her love to the first man she encounters: Reverend Green. Larsen describes the motility of Helga's love, one that is in perpetual circulation and that settles on Green not because he is an interesting character but because Helga reduces him to a thing to possess: "It [marriage] was a chance at stability, at permanent happiness, that she meant *to take*" (144, emphasis added). Green does not therein register as a minor character but as an object that provides stability, happiness, and revenge. Helga firmly believes that her marriage to Green will injure Anderson and acts accordingly: "he would be shocked. Grieved. Horribly hurt even" (145). Thus Green and the other men function as means to an end for Helga. Even in the case of Anderson, Helga perceives him as a sexual object and nothing more than a romantic partner: "she had wanted so terribly something special from him. Something special. And now she had forfeited it forever. Forever" (136–37). While I am wont to interpret this "something special" as a fulfilling relationship, Larsen does little to allude to romance as an explanatory factor that is integral to Helga's world. All Helga desires is to have sex with Anderson. Marriage and romance are out of the question because he is married, and an affair would not be suitable to his constitution. And like her penchant for commodities, Helga, who believes she has "forfeited" sex "forever," obtains a replacement object in just a few days. In remembering an erotic dream, she confirms the exchange value that men have for her liking: "thinking not so much of the man whose arms had held her as of the ecstasy which had flooded her" (133). In the crudest sense, Larsen thus represents men in the novel for their surplus value.

While in Copenhagen, Larsen stages the consequences of treating male characters as commodity fetishes in her novel. First, an early inheritance from her Uncle Peter enables Helga to journey from Harlem to Copenhagen, albeit from a relative who trades kinship as well as all future relations with Helga for five thousand dollars. The move is disturbing insofar as it illuminates how men, with whom Helga sometimes wants to build relationships, provide no more surplus value for her than surplus jouissance. Such an exchange occurs not in person but in a letter to further emphasize men's alienated status. If we experience sadness on the part of Uncle Peter's gestures, Helga does not, insofar as she merely anticipates and indeed precipitates such a transaction. She regards any one potential husband as "any one of them [who] could give her the things which she had now come to desire, a home like Anne's, cars of expensive makes . . . clothes and furs . . . servants, and leisure" (77). Helga, it turns out, is not a romantic but a burgeoning capitalist! Axel believes he confirms this desire to the extent that he finds just how closely Helga relates to men simply for their value. He in fact refers to himself as an object: "I make of myself a present to you. For love." His wealth enables him to provide handsomely for Helga with material goods, while unwittingly reducing himself to a partner who has no other worth than that of an object with infinite resources. When Helga rebuffs his marriage proposal on the grounds of miscegenation, he retorts at the absurdity of her response, "You have the warm impulsive nature of the women of Africa, but, my lovely, you have, I fear, the soul of a prostitute. You sell yourself to the highest buyer." Axel nails Helga's philosophy quite well when he inadvertently shows how men are nothing more than commodities. An offended Helga attempts to deny Axel's insights when she retorts, "I'm not for sale. Not to you. Not to any white man. I don't at all care to be owned" (117). First, Helga does not deny that men are objects. Second, Larsen blurs the distinction between an object for sale and an object in circulation. Helga cannot be transformed into a commodity by or for men, but she represents herself as an object in circulation, just not one who is for sale. Helga desires to be a commodity without an owner, a piece of public property of sorts. Thus it is not just African American or white men who become commodities. Helga herself participates in the process of exchange and surplus value.

Helga is not "owned" by anyone as she claims, but Larsen does place her in circumstances where she functions as an object of admiration. Her characteristic charm and exotic presentation constitute salient attributes of her identity, ones that also reveal her reification in that they mark her surplus value as a woman. Anderson, for example, calls her performance of self "a lady," and for five thousand dollars, her own uncle purchases his kinship bonds from Helga rather than simply disinheriting or ostracizing her. Besides rendering Helga an object for sale via romance or kinship, Larsen constructs her as a pleasurable object meant for visual consumption. In Denmark, Helga refuses to speak Danish even though she very well remembers much of the language; she prefers to be the object of attention rather than seeking to participate in full conversations: "Intentionally she kept to the slow, faltering Danish. It was, she decided, more attractive than a nearer perfection" (104). While she blames her aunt for her exotification, complaining of "being noticed and flattered," it is clear that "Helga Crane loved clothes, elaborate ones," from as far back as Naxos (104, 51). Helga herself enjoys making herself into an object. If nothing else, Aunt Katrina nurtures Helga's budding sense of style and helps her find love, new friends, and a caring family. Helga interprets this mothering as Katrina's way of showing her off as her exotic creature. Through this savage construction of African Americans, Larsen brings about Helga's transformation into an object.

Through the trope of the savage, Larsen makes known that Helga herself participates in commodity fetishism; she renders herself an object instead of being objectified by others or accepting the prescribed subjectivities she is compelled to adopt. By making herself an object, Helga participates in constructing her own agency. Frustrated that subjectivity will not fully work for Helga, she leaves it behind to perform her own objecthood. Abroad, Helga "felt like a veritable savage. . . . The many pedestrians [in Copenhagen] who stopped to stare at the queer dark creature" (99). Instead of cowering along sidewalks or avoiding the streets altogether, she strolls about the city with her aunt, which to her "felt like nothing so much as some new strange species of pet dog being proudly exhibited." The anti-Black stares do not concern Helga in the least. In those moments, she desires something else from the white masses: "everyone was very polite and very friendly, but she felt the massed curiosity and interest, so discreetly hidden under the polite greetings." At the end of a memorable walk, Helga feels energized from performing the exotic object: "in spite of the mental strain, she had enjoyed her prominence." Later that evening, she readies herself for dinner and puts on "barbaric bracelets." Following the dinner, she positions herself as a talking object: "Helga sat effectively posed on a red satin sofa, the center of an admiring group, replying to questions" (100). Larsen features Helga's treatment in Copenhagen to call attention to her heroine's plight and to inflame readers. Even when Helga might be with relatives, her "exact status in her new environment . . . [was that of] a decoration. A curio. A peacock" (103). She "was, a curiosity, a stunt, at which people came and gazed" (102). Helga transforms from "a lady" of the Black middle class into an object—a curio—amid the refined and elite Danish. There should be outrage, but Helga enjoys performing this role and abandoning subjectivity. She is even ecstatic about becoming a commodity fetish, experiencing delight in the complete erasure of her history, of her Bildung. Though near fluent in Danish, Helga can supposedly only communicate a few words spoken by her new suitor. She selectively translates words that construct her as an object insofar as her "superb eyes . . . color . . . neck column . . . yellow . . . hair . . . alive . . . [were] wonderful . . ." (101, original ellipses). Helga appears "suddenly wild," but then "tameness returned" after Axel's marriage proposal (117). Later Helga describes her own portrait as "some disgusting sensual creature with her features" (119). This sudden transformation into a primitive object also appears to endow her with complete freedom from the necessity of assimilating into white culture (via a middle-class Black subjecthood). At the end of the novel, Helga hastens her conversion into an object via a religious conversion experience. Mirroring Marx's famous line that "religion is the opium of the masses," Helga releases control of what remains of her subjectivity and allows herself to be dominated by God qua Reverend Green and the domestic life he promises to give her. In a church revival, Helga suddenly "began to yell like one insane, drowning every other clamor, while torrents of tears streamed down her face. *She was unconscious* of the words she uttered, or their meaning: 'Oh, God, mercy, mercy. Have mercy on me!'" (142, emphasis added).

Distancing herself from language (Dutch, now English), she finalizes the transition into an object. In Helga's attempt to reject subjectivity—by first turning it into a commodity and then selling it into marriage—she mistakes the handing over of her subjectivity to Reverend Green as its disposal. Instead of being able to self-abnegate and become an object in the earlier examples, she collapses into a depression and is stuck with one subjectivity. She mistook that her "giving" and not selling herself as an object would help her join radiance. She believed radiance was a thing to acquire, and she sought to become similar to it, an object. In uniting with radiance, she believed that she could self-abnegate her subjectivity. Unfortunately, Helga dramatically misses the mark because she plays into the idea of radiance meaning a primitive or savage subjectivity. Instead, motherhood and becoming a wife return Helga to the normative mode of accretive development. She returns to the normative journey of self-formation and thus accidently recovers her subjectivity: she did not self-abnegate. It is impossible to embrace Black queer flesh even though she thought, even if with bad logic, that handing over her subjectivity to join radiance would help her shatter it. Instead, Helga's attempt to render herself an object fails to produce a radically differently ontology: she reproduces instead the ideology of subjectivity driven largely by normative heterosexuality.

Eradicating the Bildungsroman

The Bildungsroman was invented to refine the art of becoming oneself in the expression of white desires. In her appropriation of the genre to represent African American development, Larsen alters the protocols of the genre to her own ends. She stages a Black woman's developmental experiences as a series of cumulative episodes. The opening scene where Helga is surrounded by material goods is the crowning example of the pleasure she derives from those objects that play a more critical role in her life: they protect her from the Black middle class that seeks her complete submission to its culture of gossip, proper decorum, and civilized living. Romantic encounters fail to provide Helga with typical sexual pleasure. Relations with Vayle, Olson, and Anderson evoke feelings of entrapment, which disrupt Helga's sense of individuality. Larsen therefore deemphasizes Helga's desire for men, helping to decipher Helga's reification of the world. Her accumulation of objects and her drive to transform subjectivity into objecthood indicate but also obscure the need for protection from an anti-Black world that robs Helga of her parents and her ability to pursue self-determination and self-possession. It also exposes the Bildungsroman as at odds with the African American experience.

Larsen recognizes that the white Bildung journey cannot be directly applied to or represent Black subject formation. She discovers that her reworking of Bildung to capture the development of Helga—and by extension of African American women—is impossible because it cannot trace the complex historical relationships that shaped the protagonist. Helga moves from one experience to the next without "maturing," repeating the same protocols: serenity, romance, material consumption, anxiety, a supposed epiphany, and finally, a fleeing. This formulaic approach to the novel of female development is anything but progress. Given that Helga reiterates the same drama, but in different outfits and cities, the world she lives in reads more like a picaresque narrative than a Bildungsroman. As previously mentioned, Larsen struggles to craft the African American Bildungsroman only to discover that Black identities have already been packaged according to the dictates of sociopolitical powers. Black subjectivity turns out to be less about the making of identity than the performance of the limited subjectivities available for African Americans. The novel of education exposes how Helga uncovers her prefabricated identity. In *Quicksand,* Larsen tries to give Helga a true Bildung journey, but the historical reality of a limited scope of identities derails the ambitious project. Helga (and Larsen) must repeatedly fail because the genre does not allow for the successful representation of a Black female–defined development or subjectivity.

Larsen represents each episode in an attempt to construct or "fit" Helga into her socially determined subject position. This hidden social realism works in conjunction with Larsen's transformation of Black Bildung into a commodity fetish. Such a conversion helps her reject subjectivity. The reader expects each episode to represent a stage of Bildung instead of simply surplus jouissance. The novel is divided into discrete episodes that include Helga in Naxos, in Chicago, in Harlem, in Copenhagen, back in Harlem, and finally, in the South. Larsen deconstructs the Bildungsroman by turning its episodic form, where Helga appears to undergo a maturing transformation in each episode, into discrete commodity fetishes. Larsen crafts the novel as a series of pleasurable and expected commodities to be consumed by one who wants Helga to overcome her mulatta and orphan background to find love and fortune in a beautiful, "radiant" world. From the opening scene, Larsen gives the reader pleasure but also performs a critical turn with this false pleasure (surplus jouissance) by having Helga relate to the world as if everything were an object in circulation. Larsen introduces reification from the beginning, repeating this social realist mode as a venue to expose the impossibility of Black subjectivity, a fantasy in circulation. She critiques how Black Bildung has become a commodity fetish, one that can only narrate a prefabricated African American subjectivity—the journey of fitting into what is already known and not a journey of unknown adventures. *Quicksand,* for instance, reflects Larsen's desire to borrow a form from white culture and infuse it with a "Black" aesthetic. The novel follows the parameters of the Bildungsroman, yet it reads as if Helga is simply shopping for the right journey to capture her (reified) self-formation. The genre can neither narrate nor define Black self-determination, yet Larsen, as I have argued, creatively works around these obstacles.

2 Nella Larsen and the Emergence of Black Queer Flesh

The making of Black female and male subjectivity through uplift and the Bildungsroman serves to perpetuate the idea that self-formation and subjectivity are the only viable options for thinking about Black existence. By adopting and modifying the Western Bildungsroman, African American authors attempted to co-opt a white literary form, assuming Black subjects should be represented through journeys of self-formation. Although armed with the aesthetics of literary modernism, Nella Larsen and her debut novel *Quicksand* could not fully subvert or write (heterosexual) African Americans into subjectivity. The fantasy of thinking that subjectivity constitutes the normative mode of exercising self-determination, I argue, parades as a surplus jouissance that steers the Black "subject" in the wrong direction. In her first novel, Larsen communicated that Black development was impossible. Critic Fred Moten describes Larsen's rejection of the Bildungsroman and the writing of Blackness as "a refusal of recitation that reproduces what it refuses."[1] To my mind, Larsen exposes how white forms refuse Black adaptation, thereby calling for African American writers to dispense with the Bildungsroman. While Larsen rejects Bildung, other African American authors advance the idea of self-formation, continuing to cover up dispossessed knowledge in the process. By retaining the ideology of self-determination, self-possession, and subjectivity, authors writing in the genre only continue repressing Black queer flesh as an alternative history and existence for African Americans. Adopting the genre of the Bildungsroman, African American writers sought and continue to seek today avenues for writing Black subjectivity into existence. Through this form, they try to imagine a world where African Americans can define themselves, producing a particular model and voice for Black lives. This task seems logical, as the Bildungsroman enabled white Europeans and Americans to follow suit for more than a hundred years, in different countries and sociopolitical contexts.[2]

While remaking the form in *Quicksand,* Nella Larsen uncovered her complicity in reproducing the project of double consciousness. She offered a genealogical recovery in her novel as a way to undo the transcendental homelessness inflicted upon African Americans. The turn toward folklore, "Black radiance," and the primitive attempted, in vain, to assist Helga Crane in resisting commodity fetish and a heteronormative subjectivity. Helga could not reclaim a female subject position by returning to the South, which she mistook as the reservoir of "Black radiance." Larsen's reliance on folklore and an inherited understanding of the primitive created a failed subjectivity while also exposing the falseness of both ideologies. Black women could not develop under any of these fantasies except into their predestined roles. Larsen "corrects" her assumptions about the journey of female development and the tools that seemed essential to helping her achieve those goals. In *Passing,* she adopts a new perspective on the primitive, history, race, sexuality, and gender. In *Quicksand,* Larsen thought she was trying to write a traditional Bildungsroman that incorporated modernism itself as thematic material, but in truth she penned a novel depicting the absolute incompatibility of self-formation and self-determination for African American women. Her art moves beyond this problem in *Passing* by making a synthetic fusion that results in a truly new genre: the narrative of self-abnegation. Larsen revises her relationship to the female body through transcending subjectivity, reworking the primitive, while also embracing deviant sexuality to devise an innovative philosophy of the self.

In *Passing,* the central dilemma involves the return of Clare Kendry to the Black world: after more than a decade of passing for a white upper-class woman, she desperately wants to reintegrate herself (at the price of losing her mixed-raced daughter and white husband) with the African American world. The story's other main contestation relies on an old trope: the love story. Irene's sexual attraction for Clare dominates and also structures the narrative—more so than questions of passing or race.

While many critics find the love story secondary to race, I explore here the dispossessed knowledges that reside underneath Black lesbian love. A handful of scholars have examined the sexual tension in the text, notably Judith Butler and Deborah McDowell, yet I want to go one step further by asking how stopping at a lesbian reading also obfuscates other forms of knowledge. I am particularly concerned with the question of how Larsen moves beyond the optics of sexual attraction and the identification processes that occur in romantic relationships. The text creates a character that everyone—white and Black, woman and man—desires for her exquisite, exotic beauty; the better inquiry is, how can anyone not be attracted to Clare? Within this overdetermined problematic—this dominant narrative of beauty—I locate how Larsen smuggles in her critical project. By turning the raw, primitive beauty of Clare into an expression of Black queer flesh, Larsen exposes the need to abandon subjectivity as a way of achieving this through self-abnegation.

Undominated Woman

In *Quicksand,* Larsen took up the notion of a "Black radiance" as a space and philosophy to emancipate Black women from anti-Black racism and to extricate them from the normative policies of the Black middle class. In an attempt to historicize this folk culture, Larsen played into one of the defining tropes of global modernism: the Black primitive. Helga is viewed as a primitive, thereby eventually performing the primitive. She conflates Black radiance—Black history and culture—with widely held fantasies that equated African Americans to the relatives of African "primitives." To this end, the notion of Black history fails to empower Helga because Larsen, too, fails to grasp the complex history of the idea of the primitive and its application to African American culture. Larsen could not escape "the Negro as 'primitive'—that so strongly dominated the public mind," as critic Amritjit Singh argues about the Harlem Renaissance.[3] This parallels Fabre and Feith's analysis that "if the Negro was in vogue in the 1920s . . . [it was because of] the rather exploitative passion for the primitive and exotic seen in cabarets and revues."[4] The fantasy of African Americans as primitive and exotic sprang from white European consumption of African art earlier in the century, and since this involves a complex history, I offer a brief schematic history of the trope. The nineteenth century viewed "primitive" people—that is, Black Africans—as dangerous, irrational, adventurous, scary, or idealized noble savages.[5] In *Gone Primitive,* Marianna Torgovnick asserts that in the twentieth century, "to study the primitive is thus to enter an exotic world which is also a familiar world."[6]

The idea of the primitive was both a source of fear and also a space for the Western world to deposit its own anxieties, fears, and concerns regarding the unknown. Anthropologists like Franz Boas and Claude Levi-Strauss worked against the notion that primitive Africans (and Asians) lived in simple, developing, and early stage cultures. The idea of the primitive also carried an altered sense of time: "the belief that primitive societies reveal origins or natural order" (46). This cultural fantasy shifted again with Roger Fry's seminal essays in *Vision and Design,* given that his analysis effectively transformed African art—the art of the primitive—into high art in Britain. France, by contrast, experienced a negrophile moment much earlier in the century, starting with the vogue of African art in Paris museums and the work of Picasso; with the 1907 *Les Demoiselles d'Avignon,* for example, the French began an obsession with the primitive. Josephine Baker dominated the cultural scene of 1920s France—"the living embodiment of modern primitivism" with her "J'ai deux amours" and "slave-chic attire."[7] From this perspective, Torgovnick recalls that notions of the primitive become a site for "violence and horror and sexuality" (127). At the same time, notions of the primitive as dark, black, dangerous, and so on continued from the previous century. The Nazis, for their part, represented Jews as primitives in their massive anti-Jewish campaigns (198–99). In European literature, "the primitive becomes a convenient locale for the exploration of Western dullness or degeneracy, and of ways to transcend" (153). Conrad, Lawrence, Eliot, and others critique Western values through the primitive, which is important because Nella Larsen loved Lawrence. While I have no evidence that Lawrence influenced Larsen, literary artists in general inherited this modernist tradition. Adapted for the American context, Larsen embeds her critique of Black middle-class values and norms by having Helga embrace and perform the "primitive." Again, this is an odd maneuver, since, as Torgovnick indicates, "the West's fascination with the primitive has to do with its own crises in identity" (157). This identity crisis for whiteness filters into the cultural imaginations of artists working during the Harlem Renaissance. In performing the primitive, Helga completely escapes the need to assimilate, while she also authoritatively co-opts white identity (or assimilates to it) to such an extent that she takes on its identity crisis.

Josephine Baker spanned European and American notions of the Black primitive.[8] Another bridge is the aesthetic conversation that transpired between African Americans and Europeans. Alain Locke, for one, encouraged Black writers "to imitate European primitivist modernism and to get in touch with their 'African' legacy."[9] Under his guidance, *The New Negro* anthology in many respects formally crystallized the Harlem Renaissance with this philosophy. As historian Nathan Huggins has shown, however, the trope of the primitive adopted and utilized by African American artists "was very romantic and rested on very superficial knowledge of African life."[10] African American intellectuals "had to *learn* to appreciate the value of African art and culture"—most often from white Americans and Europeans (187). Aaron Douglas, for instance, learned the techniques of African art from Winold Reis, a white German émigré. The consequence of African Americans adopting and interpreting the modernist trope of the Black—now African American—subject as primitive can be seen in countless works. The sculptor Richmond Barthé's "treatment of Negro subjects was not merely ethnic but . . . emphasized the primitive" (166). A litany of African Americans living in France during the zenith of French negrophilia could be cited, including Jack Johnson, Sidney Bechet, Claude McKay, Langston Hughes, and James Weldon Johnson. In 1926, Carl Van Vechten, a white patron of many African American and white American writers, published the scandalous *Nigger Heaven*—a novel that played with the idea of the primitive within a quiet librarian and many other versions of the primitive-exotic. Black novelists were not long in responding to Van Vechten's narrative, which had become a best seller, with their own versions of Black life in or bordering Harlem. Rudolph Fisher's *The Walls of Jericho* (1928) and Claude

McKay's *Home to Harlem* (1928) both took up the cultural other—for McKay, using the working class as contrast to the intellectual—as a mode of finding an African American identity.

In essence, "black writers had 'climbed aboard the bandwagon' of exoticism and enjoyed the era when the Negro was in vogue."[11] Besides the literary and visual arts, African Americans in Harlem were exposed to primitive-exotic minstrel shows in Harlem cabarets, or what literary critic Shane Vogel calls the "cult of primitivism."[12] These shows interpreted, reinforced, and challenged stereotypes of African Americans as savage, unrestrained, and simple-minded, to name a few. While the audiences were largely whites from Manhattan, my focus is not on how African Americans served "white psychological needs." Huggins contends that the Harlem cabarets presented "civilized primitives" who could ameliorate whites who felt castrated by bourgeois norms of a cultivated life (89). As Vogel indicates, though, these spaces also provided African American performers a means to redefine themselves through the trope of the primitive—in addition to serving as economic engines for Harlem.

African American authors do not simply inherit these white residues or interpretations. McKay, let us say, moves past the primitive as spontaneous, vital, "exotic, naughty, and quaint" to create men that "are no longer simply primitive-exotics, but [who] foreshadow the radical alienation of the mid-twentieth century," according to Huggins (172, 175). Jake and Ray, McKay's protagonists in *Home to Harlem,* leave civilization instead of agreeing to embody the negative identity that supports white civilization. Duke Ellington, in a complex relationship between economic success, artistic creation, and exploitation of African American identity, composed a "jungle-style" of jazz for his white patrons at the Cotton Club. White patrons sought to experience the primitive they imagined endemic to African American culture. Ellington "had to come up with musical sounds that could be classified [by whites] as 'jungle sounds.'"[13] At the same time that Ellington and the cabarets "sold" the primitive to whites, blues singers appropriated the sexual myth of the primitive to establish agency for African Americans—"Gertrude 'Ma' Rainey and Bessie Smith, who sang openly of sexual relationships, of sugar bowls and deep sea divers—whose double entendres were hard to miss."[14] Literary critic Deborah McDowell points out that Smith and Rainey would have enjoyed singing about sex and the eroticism of their Black bodies in the context of the "Freudian 1920s, the Jazz Age of sexual abandon and 'free love'" (80). In a popular lyric, Smith sings of jelly rolls, which is a barely veiled code for the labia majora:

> Jelly roll, jelly roll ain't so hard to find,
> There's a baker shop in town bakes it brown like mine,
> I got a sweet jelly, a lovin' sweet jelly roll,
> If you taste my jelly it'll satisfy your worried soul. (75)

Gertrude "Ma" Rainey proudly sang "It's Tight Like That": "See that spider crawling up the wall . . . going to get his ashes hauled. / Oh it's tight like that." Bessie Smith also gleefully sang "I'm wild about that thing" and "You've got to get it, bring it, and put it right here" (80–81). While McDowell indicates that Larsen spurned an overt approach to sexuality due to her representation of the Black middle class given their repression of bodily pleasures, I suggest—in a vein similar to McDowell's claim of lesbian desire—that Larsen explores sexuality as an emancipatory agent. While Larsen was unable to directly represent the pleasure of the Black female body, Helga, her character, struggles with her sexual lust for Anderson, making seemingly rash decisions to flee the situation before her sexuality erupts. When Helga does explore her sexual needs, she ends up pregnant and defeated. In a very superficial sense, sexuality dominates Black middle-class women, especially when the Black primitive is understood within the framework of heterosexual culture and practices.

Primitive as Queer Origins

Helga discovered that her attempted recovery of heterosexual Black history did not dissolve the reification of Black women. Throughout the course of the novel, Helga sought to don Black radiance through an adoption of the Black primitive roles circulating in New York and Copenhagen—and in Larsen's own social context. Her attempt to appropriate and reify Black radiance revealed the failed aesthetics and politics of the Bildungsroman to represent—or accommodate or include—African

American women. Larsen revives the trope of the primitive in *Passing,* but as a mere residue of its former self. Larsen sought a different route than Josephine Baker and blues singers like Bessie Smith, who were more capable of critiquing and transforming the primitive myth as exotic, mysterious, dark, and dangerous by appropriating and redefining those fantasies. Larsen instead wonders what might be considered "primitive" in African American women and what a lesbian or Black queer primitive actually entails? Can the sexually emancipated "primitive" like Smith and Baker help release Black queer women from social domination? Larsen responds by returning to the first definition of the primitive, of the sixteenth century: "'original or ancestor' of animals, perhaps of men . . . 'the first, earliest age, period, or stage.'"[15] She returns to the origins of the Black queer woman. This idea of primitive as origins is combined with the definitions of the primitive as applied to the women of the Asia Pacific. The Asiatic primitive of the nineteenth century also expressed the notion of "a return to origins and to find an originary plentitude and wholeness," exemplified in the works of Paul Gauguin, Henry Matisse, and Henry Rousseau. The island primitive in fact conveys the desire to experience simpler social structures and cultural norms that leave room for alternative kinship and sexual practices. Such a definition of the primitive suggests a romantic "recuperability of a primal Edenic idyll and the possibility of regeneration and revivification through unthreatening sensual experience."[16] Larsen imports the Asian primitive but discards the idea of a more simple cultural system. She aims to unravel the history of the domination of Black queer women; she returns to the "origins"—even if a fantasy, but more likely a queer utopia: "that the present and the presence . . . is not enough," as defined by José Muñoz—of when Black queer women were not dominated. The modernist artists still assumed that primitive Asian women were oppressed but that they just lived in "simple" societies. Larsen, on the other hand, wants to delve into the queer utopia of when Black queer women were and are not dominated.

In *Dialectic of Enlightenment,* Theodor Adorno and Max Horkheimer submit that "the domination of nature ensued once man's primal embeddedness in nature was transcended and then forgotten. A radical humanism carries with it the latent threat of species imperialism, which ultimately returns to haunt human relations."[17] Adorno, himself a modernist and susceptible to the trope of the primitive, in a sense falls prey to the idea of the Black subject as exotic-primitive; but he, like Larsen, attempts to excavate the processes that contribute to a damaged life. Before the domination of nature by man, which includes man's own self-domination, he engaged in relationships with nature and other humans through mimesis; a mimesis of the wolf, for example, sought to honor a certain wolf god or to mirror—not appropriate—the hunting skills of the wolf. This form of mimesis does not dominate the wolf for his skills or terrain but acknowledges man's hunting abilities as different from the wolf's. This preserves difference through mimesis. Over time, man manipulated the external world to reach his own subjective—not collective—purpose. This instrumental rationality consequently required the repression of certain desires that could be hindrances to the self—namely, pleasure without restrictions. The unintended cost of this dialectic of enlightenment was the domination of nature (72). In turn, man and woman, too, as parts of nature, become dominated. For Adorno, humankind loses its uniqueness because it no longer honors difference and no longer believes in mimesis: "the countless agencies of mass production and its culture impress standardized behavior on the individual as the only natural, decent, and rational one. Individuals define themselves now only as things, statistical elements, successes or failures."[18] The dominated world rejects difference in favor of the identical.[19]

Larsen exhibits her agreement with this philosophy in her critiques of the disciplining powers of the Black middle class. Helga and Irene struggle to conform to the standards of propriety and "ladylike" behavior, striving for difference but ultimately falling to the interpellative hails to marry and become submissive wives and fertile mothers. Through the process of self-formation and self-determination, Helga and Irene finally fit into the "standardized" mold as dominated Black women. To extricate themselves from this standard mold, Larsen introduces a relationship of mimesis and not replication or standardization for Irene and Clare, and in doing so, Larsen stokes the fires of Black queer flesh to redress the uniformity that comes from adopting subjectivity. Adorno diverges from philosophers such as Aristotle, who thought of mimesis as "the re-creation of the existing object but also changes that were introduced in the process of re-creation—embellishment, improvement, and the generalization of individual qualities."[20] Aristotle believes that the goal of mimesis is to replicate an original but also to consider the augmentations that accompanied that replication process. Adorno is hardly interested in replication with deviations; he wants the process of mimesis to strive toward some honoring of the undominated existence of the referent so that the performer creates from that inspiration point. Also, I highlight that mimicry, when compared to mimesis, lacks the internal or psychological dimension stressed by Adorno. It typically "implies only a physical and no mental relation" (5).

Adorno diverges from theorists like Lukács, who view the role of history as a means to terminate reification for the meta-subject. History should, according to Lukács, eventually allow "a collective meta-subject who could totalize the social world and thereby shatter the illusion of society as second nature [reified]."[21] This unveiling should then illuminate a critical moment—or phase—during which the meta-subject could tear down reification and emerge based upon a new system of labor power. While Lukács and Adorno describe reification in relation to the meta-subject and would disagree with my application of their ideas to individual characters from fiction, their theories provide productive avenues to think through the question of racial formation. For Helga, this journey of historical recovery reveals that she followed a historically white Bildung; yet history fails to shift her present existence. History constituted the reification of race and African Americans as a group, and Black history could be turned against itself to illuminate Helga's seemingly fixed or predetermined social position. For Adorno, reification is not simply the alienated objectification of subjectivity that it is for Lukács. Adorno reminds us that reification is the suppression of heterogeneity in the name of sameness; this reflects the notion that when man dominated himself and nature, he repressed difference for standardization. The end of reification—if even a possibility because of the meta-subject's dialectical engagement with history, culture, and the body, and Adorno is not clear whether reification can achieve termination—must consider the domination of the body and the restoration not only of relationships of difference but also of the bodily drives—in our case, Black queer flesh—that have been repressed and appropriated both by the Enlightenment and the culture industry. Adorno cryptically addresses this when he claims that "all reification is a forgetting."[22] Helga and Irene cannot simply recover a memory or the original meaning or wholeness to undo reification. In many ways, Clare seems to be the perfect recovery of the prehistoric and thus the solution to the domination of woman and race. She is aggressive, beautiful, vivacious, and a bit mysterious, but she is also tormented, traumatized, responsible, and caring. Yet Clare does not constitute the stock figure for wholeness and undominated woman; anti-Black racism dominates Clare, who must pass to survive. Nevertheless, Larsen represents in Clare a possible solution to forgetting and the recovery of Black women before domination and after the end of domination.

In a cryptic statement in *Negative Dialectics,* Adorno elaborates on the methods to combat domination and reification. He reasons that "art is semblance even at its highest peaks; but its semblance, the irresistible part of it, is given to it by what is not semblance. . . . Semblance is a promise of nonsemblance."[23] Adorno is emphasizing how art—or masterly crafted subjects—does not represent a replica of an object, emotion, and so on but is a representation that is mimetic. The artwork fosters a relationship with the referent not of sameness or duplication but of mimesis. Art that is self-consciously aware that it is not self-sufficient but that exists in a mimetic relationship becomes powerful because it reveals a world where domination has not conquered both representation and referent. What is more, this mimetic relationship ensures that the art does not represent itself as whole or complete—it can only survive or impact the world through nonidentical relationships, through difference. Thus realist art might appear to be unique and whole, but its criticality derives from the fact that it is merely paying homage to its referent via mimesis.

Larsen's unwitting manifestation of this philosophy in her work is uncanny. Helga fails in her pursuit of subjectivity in part because she operates without friends. Her closest friend, Anne Grey, turns out to be her rival. Larsen learns from her failure and in a subsequent novel develops a double Bildungsroman through the paired characters of Clare and Irene. Irene embraces standardization; she loves the security of the Black middle class. Clare, on the other hand, is excluded from standardization from an early age as a mixed-race child who lives with her white father. She can never be identical to others in a community that refuses to accept mixed-raced marriages and their progeny. Instead, Clare performs multiple mimetic relationships. First, she (must) pass for white and therefore must learn upper-class femininity and its cultural performance. Unlike Irene, who in the opening scene of the novel forgets that she is engaged in an act of passing, Clare remains incessantly self-conscious of her unstable racial identity and of her inability to represent wholeness/whiteness. She is the "semblance [that] is a promise of nonsemblance." Clare flawlessly passes and provides the semblance of a white phenotype and culture, but she never embraces her own mimesis as the truth. She does so, in the terms set forth by Judith Butler about the performance of gender, by letting white culture speak for her within the performance of race and gender.[24] Clare does not performatively constitute herself as white: she merely performs the tropes of whiteness. Second, Clare does not identify herself as white, but neither is she one of the many other dominated Black women who populate the novel. In marking Clare as occupying a space of limbo—or a space of sexual abjection—Larsen crafts a mimetic relationship to the figure of the prehistoric Black woman before her domination (the referent from above). It is this mimetic relationship with the past that everyone reads as the "primitive" or vital within Clare: her unspoken Blackness is expressed as the primitive because she is racialized as white by most of the characters in the novel.

Clare's vital beauty and charm link her to the primitive. Larsen steers readers to an interpretation of Clare as a more refined version of Helga, who failed to suppress her primal urges. Clare, by comparison, is full of culture and grace. She has poise and elegance, but at the same time, her risk taking, as viewed from Irene's perspective, comes off as animalistic, as in some sense lacking human emotion. Clare's flirtations and too-generous smiles to men frustrate Irene but also align Clare with overly sexualized primitiveness. Irene, at first, perceives Clare as an object of enjoyment—of sexual desire and pleasure. The male suitors, on the other hand, view her as white and exotic with an unconscious importation, as bell hooks has shown, of the idea that Black women are always overly sexualized and promiscuous, inhuman even.[25] While Irene partially traffics in this understanding of Clare, she also confuses Clare's race: neither Black nor white while equally the abject of this form of the primitive—a sexual deviant.

In this respect, most critics tend to agree with Deborah McDowell's and Judith Butler's readings of Irene's queer, as in same-sex desires for Clare, but I want to ask what it means for Larsen to represent this queerness and consider what it prevents us from reading. Irene's obsession with Clare obscures the return to origins, to the primitive prehistorical. Larsen develops a character—however filtered through the perspective of Irene—that indexes the critical momentum of a state before domination. Larsen crafts our view of Clare's character by unfolding a series of mimetic relationships—first with Irene and then later with both male and female African Americans. This accomplishes two tasks. First, the imitations display the social reality of the Harlem Renaissance and the conditions of middle-class Black America. Second, Clare manifests the catalog of characteristics of the imagined prehistoric Black woman free from domination. She demonstrates how natural reality—the body, woman, and Blackness—are transformed by the culture industry while continuing to retain threads of the prehistoric. Forging a character who recovers these fibers and develops mimetic relationships based on the prehistoric can produce a critical moment. For Adorno, this "mimetic moment is intrinsically utopian because it preserved a memory of [wo]man's prehistoric oneness with nature . . . and was thus a prefiguration of a possible restoration of that condition in the future."[26] Clare is out of sync with the time of the novel—she reflects a past moment when women were not dominated by social identities like mother, wife, and even possibly the category of woman. By establishing relationships of mimesis, Clare offers a radical model of Black female development. Thus we must look past the queer relationship to find disavowed knowledges that a normative queer reading would produce.

Larsen, though, must not just work against the cultural fantasy of the primitive to communicate her theory of female development in the context of domination; she must disidentify with the social structures and power systems that uphold African Americans as exotically primitive.

This entails a disidentification with the surplus jouissance she generated by trying to subvert the idea of the Black female as a sexually charged primitive. Like Helga's own unfortunate embrace of the trope of the primitive, Larsen must balance the representation of Clare as the primitive defined by modernism and the primitive from the prehistoric. Either situation can allow Clare to be read as a commodity. In a misreading, she has value only because her attributes—her sensual body and charm—can be exchanged and not because whatever might be regarded as her "essential" subjectivity has value. Thus her use-value—her primitive yet refined beauty—becomes a commodity fetish. And this tendency to fetishize Clare as Irene or others' sexual object erases and reifies the potentiality of the prehistoric. Larsen recovers the prehistoric by demonstrating the necessity of mimetic relationships among African American women. To reveal and nurture these relationships, Larsen destroys Clare's (sexual) use-value in two ways. First, Larsen describes her queer value as her unmarked and untamed queer Blackness masquerading as a white body. Clare is socially constructed as white and can avoid the fate of a racialized mirror stage; her Black queer flesh is not as transformed given that she is misread as one needing to develop a white subjectivity; this fate is how Irene reads her (and conveniently forgets about Clare's upbringing as a Black girl and her childhood best friend). With this slippery constellation of formation, Clare is not always or fully made into a Black woman: forcing Clare into a precarious, limbo state of racialization that opens the door for Black queer flesh. While the first mode of self-abnegation occurs through the eyes of Irene and society, the second involves Clare's own participation. Larsen accomplishes this task by liquidating Clare's social identities and biological features: wealthy woman, mother, white woman, Black woman, wife, and primitive (as overly sexual, as erotic, as that "special" radiance supposedly inherent in Black women). Clare's self-abnegation will help her reach a state of formlessness, occasioning the emptying out of subjectivity itself. Clare self-abnegates not to the prehistoric and a state where Black women are not dominated but to a life with less domination. Clare retains her history and memories of a dominated life and can never be truly free of domination. Unlike a social identity, these memories remain permanently bound to Clare. Irene, on the other hand, interprets Clare as the undominated primitive Black woman, using this model to mimetically relate to Clare. Irene's act effectively evinces not that Larsen's solution is a false utopia of pure freedom from domination but that utopia serves as a critical foundation for initiating social and psychic change. Irene's act embodies José Muñoz's notion of a queer utopia: "the feeling that this world is not enough."[27] The time before the domination of Black queer flesh drives Irene's self-abnegation. These twin journeys of dismantling subjectivity—and not of self-formation—are the progenitors of the narrative of self-abnegation.

Toward No Domination

With this new queer trajectory, the goal of the novel is neither for Clare and Irene to merge nor for Irene to become Clare. A combination of the two or a privileging of either follows the fantasy of the Western Bildungsroman. Rather, Larsen parallels Adorno's argument: "both are torn halves of an integral freedom, to which however they do not add up."[28] The integral freedom refers to the traces of woman before her domination that is part of the history of all Black women—an archive of Black queer flesh. Each character has a different relationship to this freedom. Irene references a socially defined woman—as mother, middle class, docile, civil, proper, hostess, and the ideal Black woman who supports uplift (in name, at least). Clare indexes a womanhood alive before the domination of nature—a primal state of woman before she (and man) dominated herself. In this way, the novel cannot provide a totality of woman—nor does it advocate one definition over another. Woman is multiple, fluid, difference, and occupies a precarious representation, as gender theorist Luce Irigaray might put it. In *Quicksand,* Larsen flirted with the idea that the freedom of women might be achieved by the reconciliation of differences; she discovered that this formulation would be a lie produced by the culture industry. *Passing* demands a constellation of unreconciled desires—of a mimesis of desires that honor the residuals of prehistoric woman.

Clare and Irene do not build up their identities but liquidate them. As a form of *écriture feminine,* Larsen launches Clare and Irene on a journey of mutual self-abnegation. Clare, for instance, liquates the ever-same, the standardization of Blackness and whiteness imposed on her female body. While in *Quicksand,* Larsen investigates how to avoid and extinguish anxiety—by generating surplus jouissance—in *Passing,* Larsen discovers that racial anxiety can be turned back upon the body to shatter ideology and unhinge socially inscribed identities and, in the process, uncovers Black queer flesh. This rechanneling of anxiety occurs in mimetic relationships. Through relationships of mimesis, Larsen represents the disintegration of Black female subjects and their subjectivity that we understand through the notion of domination; the novel provides a new understanding of Black womanhood that is not dependent on racialization and the making of Black subjectivity. To reach this situation, Larsen first undoes gender and race as social constituents of the ego, among many intersectional identities, to return her characters to a queer utopia before—and after—domination.

In *Passing,* the female body remains a site of domination and a site for queer resistance. The novel does not seek to transform women from commodities into subjects because subjectivity is itself another form of domination. Larsen exposes uplift and its sense of liberal humanism as systems of domination and power. For example, to manage Irene's desires, Clare seems to become represented in bits and pieces like a commodity. On the surface, Clare's physical traits, her delightfulness at parties, and Irene's desires become equivalences without qualitative difference. Clare becomes fungible as her "parts" transform into abstract quantities. Any reader will notice that Larsen populates the novel with Irene's observations, primarily, of Clare's body. From their initial meeting, Irene hones in on Clare's smile and laugh: "The woman laughed, a lovely laugh, a small sequence of notes that was like a trill and also like the ringing of a delicate bell fashioned of a precious metal, a tinkling." This tinkling laugh triggers Irene's memory and is the key to her remembering Clare: "I'd never in this world have known you if you hadn't laughed."[29] The laugh, too, contains more than one meaning: "that trill of notes . . . small and clear and the very essence of mockery" (183). Besides mockery, Clare's voice appears to be rather powerful. Irene attributes her decision-making to this voice: "what was it about Clare's voice that was so appealing, so very seductive?" (194). Clare's eyes also "speak" when Irene and Gertrude visit Clare for tea: "in

Clare's eyes, as she presented her husband, was a queer gleam, a jeer, it might be. Irene couldn't define it" (200). As Cheryl Wall remarks, the material of Clare's eyes "symbolize[s] those aspects of the psyche Irene denies within herself."[30] Helena Michie observes that while Irene might identify with Clare's libido, Clare "will not internalize; she draws people in [via the gaze] without allowing them to change her."[31] On one hand, Clare's body seems to "speak" to Irene—conveying messages about queer self-abnegation and queer sexual desires. But what else could Larsen be communicating by describing Clare's every feature in such erotic undertones?

> sweetly scented,
> the ivory of her skin,
> She's really almost too good-looking,
> Clare Kendry's eyes were bright with tears that didn't fall,
> her lips, painted a brilliant geranium red, were sweet and sensitive and
>   a little obstinate. A tempting mouth,
> arresting eyes, slow and mesmeric,
> the caress of Clare's smile, and
> She's so easy on the eyes. (176, 177, 185, 189, 190–91, 230, 249)

Michie critiques McDowell's argument that these abbreviated gazes register a repressed lesbian sexuality. She disagrees that Larsen employs race as a "cover" for sexuality. I find it almost impossible not to read these descriptions of Clare as erotic, as a marker of sexual desire and also about race. The novel leaves no question, in my mind, of the inextricable relationship of race and sexual desire. Part of the problem with these readings is that intersectional approaches to understand race were not popularized at the time, and so either race or queer sexuality had to be the predominant lens of analysis instead of the two—along with questions of gender, parenthood, and class—as contributing factors to the subject positions and expressions of the twin protagonists. By focusing on two intersections, sexuality and race, the novel is quite clear in its exploration of Black lesbian identities.

When Brian creeps up on Irene in her room, she angrily reacts: "in spite, of the years of their life together, [his entering the room unannounced] still had the power to disconcert her" (213). Compare Brian's "noiseless" steps to when Clare "had come softly into the room" and kisses Irene's hair: "Irene Redfield had a sudden inexplicable onrush of affectionate feeling" (225). Irene enjoys Clare's company, and more to the point, she welcomes her into her private space. Larsen reveals how sexuality, race, gender, and class intersect to create this moment of care (or antagonism). But, I underscore another possible reason for sexuality's appearance as the return-of-the-repressed. To expand on McDowell's reading, I consider two scenarios.

First, I argue that Irene reads Clare in bits and pieces because Clare's *white* beauty traumatizes Irene. Irene falls for the passing *white Clare* on the rooftop restaurant. It is only after Irene's lust stirs that this unknown woman reveals her racial history. This subterranean Blackness is only discovered with the erotic tinkling in Clare's laugh. Upon recognizing a desire for Blackness qua whiteness, Irene disembodies Clare—starting with her laugh. This dissonance of desire is placated by the consumption of Clare's beauty in nuggets like her laughter. Irene experiences racial anxiety as she desires a white woman—yet she must also reconcile that she desires the younger *Black* Clare from childhood. In desiring Clare, Irene must process both a desire for a white woman and a desire for a Black woman. To calm her racial anxiety, because she desires a Black woman performing whiteness, Irene turns to surplus jouissance and enjoys only parts of Clare, one sensual and lustful glance at a time. Within this surplus jouissance, though, is the failure of the pleasure and a critical insight into its falseness. At Clare's tea party, as a case in point, Irene chats with the Black Clare and Black Gertrude, but when Bellew, Clare's white husband, enters the context, Clare becomes white—without changing her performance of identity. This shift without shifting raises Irene's consciousness about who she desires. "She turned an oblique look on Clare and encountered her peculiar eyes fixed on her with an expression so dark and deep and unfathomable that she had for a short moment the sensation of gazing into the eyes of some creature utterly strange and apart" (201). Irene witnesses the conversion of Clare into a (passing) white woman—and in the process, her own desires remain the same. Clare's switching from Black to white exposes to Irene how she desires Clare, as lust for a white and Black woman. Larsen grants us access to Irene's twin desires as Irene reflects on the evening: "Irene Redfield was trying to understand the look on Clare's face as she had said good-bye. Partly mocking, it had seemed, and partly menacing. And something else for which she could find no name. . . . A slight shiver ran over her . . . [she] was close to tears" (206). Irene elicits surplus jouissance as "tears" as a way of refusing to unravel her desires for a blonde white woman she knew as the Black Clare. The emergence of Black queer flesh must be stopped with tears.

Clare in Bits and Pieces

The novel struggles to articulate—at least through Irene's narration—Black queer flesh. The illegibility of Clare—both in her letters and in her racial identity—cascades into the narrative as a major disruption to the process of character formation; it queers self-possession, self-determination, and subject making. Irene can never read Clare all at once, nor can Larsen present Clare as a legible subject. This reflects two facets of the genre: Clare's position as a subject self-abnegating and the impossible representation of cohered Black queer flesh. On one hand, this violent reading practice forces Clare's body into a sort of containment. Irene traps and preserves Clare as an assemblage of eroticized body parts. Each one can be controlled or contained, whereas Clare as a whole cannot. Examining the critical moment within this controlling maneuver illuminates the crux of my argument and the second reason for Clare being in bits and pieces. Each part of Clare—from her tear-filled eyes to her luscious lips—underscores the need for domination, implying that Clare is partially free from domination; Clare performs the freedom that African Americans desire, a freedom from legibility and coherence that constitutes her Black queer flesh, one that rebuffs an organized unified subjectivity. Through a confusing visual structure, Clare possesses the freedom denied to African Americans because of her veneer and historical racial formation as white. But as a Black woman, she should be conquered and mastered; her freedom threatens the mold of African Americans as a dominated people. This logic is expressed from the perspective of Irene, who views Clare not simply as passing but *as a Black woman who is not dominated by anti-Black racism*. Even Clare, as a Black woman, appears haunted only by her own doing and not by anti-Black racism—in part because the world has interpellated the adult Clare as white. This confusing state of seeming undomination draws Irene into admiring Clare all the more and precipitates Irene's mimetic interpretation of Clare's state of freedom as an undominated Black woman. From this experience, Irene learns to disintegrate her social and moral obligations; if Clare exists as undominated, Irene, too, can model herself on this condition.

The most prominent example of this undominating mimesis leading to disintegration happens when Irene follows Clare's ability to "throw anything away." After convincing herself of Clare and Brian's affair, the narrator reports, "Yes, life went on precisely as before. It was only she [Irene] that had changed" (251). On the next page, Larsen provides an example of this change. Irene discards her identity as a mother: "the boys! For once she'd forgotten them" (252). She continues her disintegration by imagining her life without Brian and no longer functioning as a wife: "Time with Brian. Time without him. It was gone, leaving in its place an almost uncontrollable impulse to laugh, to scream, to hurl things about." She accepts that her function for Brian is not even wife but reduced only to asexual mother, which she has already abandoned in forgetting about her children: "she didn't count. She was, to him, only the mother of his sons. That was all. Alone she was nothing" (254). At this critical juncture late in the novel, Irene has stealthily shed her identity of wife and mother as she moves toward being "nothing." She accomplishes the disintegration by neutralizing her surplus jouissance. The pleasures of security found in normative modes of Black woman and motherhood are crushed by the thought of an affair. This conflict slowly erodes the powers of pleasure and launches Irene into a fit of panic, of unmediated racial anxiety. Irene literally shaking and shivering, Larsen demonstrates how this psychic disturbance helps Irene disinvest from her core identities because she refuses to stop them with surplus jouissance.

I want to turn the screw once more—and soon enough—so I can reach the penultimate piece of the journey of self-abnegation in Larsen's brilliant novel. Clare in bits and pieces does not merely evoke Irene's need to contain, to control the utopian possibility of Black women as undominated. The process of relating to Clare in fragments illuminates the vectors of domination and at once allows Larsen to enact a disidentification with the idea of Black flesh as theorized by Hortense Spillers. Returning to Clare and Irene's first adult encounter, after falling for the white beauty of Clare—and I want to account for double consciousness that makes the desire for whiteness seem natural—Irene fails to recognize Clare Kendry; I do not think she ever recognizes Clare Bellew, a white upper-class woman, in the novel. Only with the jingle of her laugh does this beautiful white woman transformed into Clare Kendry reenter Irene's life: Clare Bellew, after all, refuses to provide her name when Irene thinks of her as white. Clare only materializes once Irene knows the woman before her as Black. Encoded within the laugh, possibly its constituents, as I will return to in the final chapter, is the thing that enables Irene to locate Clare Kendry—not Ms. Bellew—within the archive of Black life; up until this moment, Irene has been flirting with an anonymous white woman, and conscious recognition beyond lust does not occur. In *In the Break,* Fred Moten observes that phonic substance can underlie laughter, and in this situation, a specific form of Black queer flesh gives rise to this sonic materiality.[32] When Clare laughs, the Black queer flesh of Irene and Clare mingle and improvise and find within their dancing a lost love affair. It is this ensemble of queer love that precipitates—performatively constitutes—Clare Kendry, the undominated Black woman of the past, back into existence. In this way, Black queer flesh can be sustained but unrecognized by Irene during their interactions: it is Irene who unwittingly abnegates Clare's subjectivity as a white woman and allows Clare to embody Black queer flesh. The novel, then, begins with Clare as Black queer flesh, but Irene must work through self-abnegation to recognize flesh; Clare, on the other hand, must also retrieve her Black queer flesh.

In this context, I do not mean Black skin or bodies as they have been racialized into specific subject positions. Drawing on the model put forth by Moten, I understand Clare and Irene's interaction as the mixture, the ensemble of the sonic dimensions, of Clare's laughter and Irene's silent desires. Emerging from this ensemble of lesbian love is Black queer flesh that gives materiality to Clare's voice and Blackness and Irene's drive that reaches toward Clare's undominated flesh. In this moment—in this radical break of subjectivity—Irene tears away her subjectivity so she can engage with Clare's undominated Black queer flesh. At stake in this encounter is the emergence of Black queer flesh and the dissipation of surplus jouissance and identity. Instead of the eruption of Black queer flesh into the Symbolic and its immediate containment or defeat by surplus jouissance, the breaking of Clare into bits and pieces and sexual attraction enable Larsen to let Black queer flesh sustain itself for longer than a moment: for longer than an hour, Irene loses track of time (the Symbolic) as she shares herself with Clare. The novel opens, too, with a letter from Clare—before we are given this rooftop encounter. The first paragraph reveals an impatient Irene waiting to read a letter from Clare; she savors the letter and its contents as her final item to read for the day. Clare mails herself—the oversized and nonstandard paper of the envelope, its audacious purple ink, and its nearly illegible handwriting all mark or embody Clare—to Irene. In this way, Clare circulates around Irene just as Irene cannot but be drawn toward Clare, unable to touch her and the envelope at first. Irene must approach Clare only after careful study, but once she opens the letter, the feelings come rushing through, and Irene cannot stop herself. Larsen, in this first paragraph, alerts us that Clare as Black queer flesh circulates around Irene as a psychic drive—and is not dominated by subjectivity. The metaphor of circulation becomes rewritten from *Quicksand,* and Larsen sets the challenge of deciphering that Black queer flesh is the psychic drive from the beginning. To reiterate, Larsen makes clear that Clare lacks subjectivity—from Irene's point of view—and instead we must, or Irene must, reconcile why she keeps Clare in bits and pieces as Black queer flesh.

The Rise of Black Queer Flesh

This opening scene rewrites the introduction of Helga in *Quicksand.* Helga sits alone, like Irene, but what surrounds her is not Clare but material objects: fancy lamps and rugs, books, and expensive clothing. Larsen thematizes her protagonist as just another commodity in circulation. In *Passing,* on the other hand, Larsen hints at the commodification of Blackness and love objects, but we soon read within the illegible handwriting that it is Black queer flesh in circulation—one that is individually crafted and hardly a commodity. First, the missive, envelope, and stamp represent pieces of Clare in motion and not ready for consuming or appropriation by Irene. Clare as something unreadable hints at an ontology of Black queer flesh, which attracts Irene. The only legible transaction, lesbian desire, itself a taboo, deflects from our reading of flesh as we read and become scandalized by the prospect of queer love. Irene in the opening scene visibly shakes and appears in full racial anxiety; we think the answer lies in repressed lesbian desire, but this quick answer—or simply that she is furious—functions as surplus jouissance. By fixating on Irene's lust (or annoyance) for Clare, we fail to acknowledge another critical circuit. Black queer flesh parades in the novel underneath Irene's sexualization of Clare, so we must work through queer desires to excavate Black queer flesh. Thus the narrative provides us Irene's thoughts and desires, and we often encounter pieces of Clare's body. We should be reading the surface, to recover queer desires that a heteronormative reading disavows, and its underside, to recover what homonormative readings disavow: Black queer flesh.

The Black queer flesh I am evoking is not limited to that theorized by Spillers and her interlocutors: Fred Moten, Amber Musser, and Michelle Stephens. For them, Black flesh seems to exist without the expression of sexuality itself but rather the traces of white patriarchy's brutalizing torture, rape, and dehumanization of African Americans within, mostly, a matrix of heterosexuality, deviant or otherwise. Nella Larsen modifies, through disidentification, the notion of "straight" Black flesh; she makes it queer as in nonnormative and same-sex love, doing away with flesh becoming the grounds for subjectivity. While Black flesh records the unrecorded and abject history of the Black experience, Black queer flesh has been further marginalized within the archive and rendered largely unthinkable. Larsen empties Black flesh of its heterosexual origins and augments the concept to include pleasure, excitement, and queer sexual interactions and queer sociality.

What is queer about Black flesh? While the Real, or Freud's land of the id, might be polymorphous and lack cultural inscriptions of "sexuality"—and I do not want to naturalize same-sex love to a mere biological argument; I want to understand Black queer flesh as the foundation—the citation must be recognized and created after the fact, a queer utopia, to perform queer Blackness, for queer African Americans who have lived in this anti-Black, homophobic, misogynist, transphobic, ableist world. As mentioned in the introduction, Black queer flesh changes its function in relationship to subjectivity. I employ queer as both same-sex love and nonnormative within this argument. First, same-sex attraction does not seem to make it into Spillers's notion of the painful past. Queer African Americans could rarely express themselves within the Black community, let alone in dominant society. This painful experience of the closet and the need to repress queer desire need to be acknowledged and somehow positively represented in culture and not as mere gay sidekicks in pop culture. Black queer flesh documents this erased and neglected history of queer sexual abjection that the heterosexual articulation of Black flesh omits.

Second, Larsen disidentifies with Black flesh in order to constitute Black queer flesh and, in doing so, extends its functions. Instead of limiting flesh to serving as some sort of opaque historical record, Larsen queers this idea and makes Black queer flesh the center of her critical project. Most prominent, she makes Black queer flesh hypervisible. By reading Irene's behaviors in the novel as allegories for closeted, repressed, or open desires for Clare, the potentiality for Black queer flesh stops with specific bodily configurations and relies on our fixed understanding of Irene trying to commodify Clare's beauty just like everyone else. In reading Clare as overly sexual and erotically "primitive," we galvanize our interpretations onto sexual pleasure—and that is it. In doing so, we read Irene's cataloging of Clare's body on every page as cheap reproductions of repressed lesbian desire, and we stop reading for the critical moment. Larsen tells us in *Quicksand* that sexuality offers more than just sexual pleasure or practices; we must do more with Black queer bodies than enjoy them through consumption. The reproduction of Clare all over the novel can be understood as postmodern widgets that mean nothing beyond the surface: the appropriation of Black female bodies for pleasure. She is literally everywhere in the novel, and we become accustomed to consuming her on each page as Irene's desires spiral out of control.

At this point, I want to return to Adorno's idea of the work of art to make the final turn in my interpretation of Clare in bits and pieces. He describes it as "semblance is a promise of nonsemblance."[33] Adorno does not want to embrace replicas or reproductions as art. With this in mind, the critical moment becomes the disidentification with Black queer body parts. Adorno suggests art should engage in mimetic relationships. Building a relationship with the object compels us to create and to reflect. In the case of Larsen's *Passing,* she renders each presentation of Clare's body as if it is identical to the next queer desire, which can confuse readers into believing that Clare functions as a commodity of racial beauty or Irene's repressed lust. Instead, Larsen crafts each description of Clare as a complete work of art: the semblance to desire, to sexuality, to race, produces a relationship of mimesis, namely, Adorno's nonsemblance. The supposed fracturing of Clare into objects disidentifies with the commodity: Clare is not in circulation or a reproduction. This queering of Black women's bodies enables Irene to relate to Clare at the level of Black queer flesh. Each piece of Clare is really Black queer flesh masquerading as a commodity—it is the drive exposed, and this exposure includes the disbanding of subjectivity. Larsen's critique of this seemingly floating Black queer flesh is that Irene is trying to relate to all of Clare's flesh, trying literally to study it to know it better for her own mimesis.

In this way, Larsen provides an alternative hermeneutics to read Black queer flesh. *Passing* is a project of getting Clare and Irene to engage in mimetic relationships with each other's flesh so they can both appreciate and step out of subjectivity: they are learning to self-abnegate. Irene cannot know Clare all at once, so she slowly crafts her mimetic relationship—taking care not to master Clare all at once, otherwise she, too, would dominate Clare. By slowly engaging in mimesis, Irene and Clare learn to undo their identities as modeled by the other, but never appropriating or copying.

Mimesis and Self-Abnegation

When Clare reenters Irene's life, she frames their friendship as an imitation of their close bonds during childhood. By calling Irene "'Rene," Clare creates a relationship out of sync with the present. Irene, too, mirrors

Clare's locution; she and the narrator refer to Clare not as Clare Bellew but as Clare Kendry. These appellations pull the past into the present. They rekindle the shards of their primitive, or "original" (in the sense of relating to origins), past. The reminders of their shared childhoods allow them to reexperience the feeling of freedom prior to domination by adulthood and the solidification of double consciousness. Reclaiming the past in the present implies that the future can be made into a state of difference. Midway through the novel, before the phrase makes complete sense, Larsen instructs readers that the rekindled relationship between Clare and 'Rene/Irene is "something that left its trace on all the future years of her existence" (253).

In addition to forging a mimetic relationship to the recent past and demonstrating the impact of mimesis on the present and future, Clare engages in a mimetic relationship toward Irene at the level of the unconscious and Black queer flesh. On numerous occasions, Irene remarks that Clare predicts or is "aware of her desire and her hesitation" (187). The narrator agrees with Irene that Clare appears to be a mind reader: "as if she had been in the secret of the other's thoughts" (185). Clare models aspects of her personality on a study of, and homage to, Irene. She rejects, for example, Irene's invitation to accompany her to a popular Black summer resort in Michigan because of a deep empathy. As Clare declines the offer, she tells Irene, who is thinking the same thing, "Don't think I've entirely forgotten just what it would mean for you if I went" (186). Larsen distinguishes between identification and mimesis (the nonidentical that preserves difference) in this example. Were Clare truly selfish, she would agree to go on the weekend outing. Clare does not "identify" with Irene; her language also reveals that her declining the invitation stems from a knowledge of the past—not of the present: "don't think I've entirely forgotten." Clare is not identifying with Irene in the present, but rather, her mimesis functions in alignment with a myth or memory of Irene from the past; Clare modulates her behaviors according to an idea of 'Rene—though not the Irene of the present. 'Rene as a child and now as an adult—not Irene the adult—can be Black, and this past-present continues to haunt Clare as a source of her own Black queer flesh.

Irene enjoys a taken-for-granted radical freedom, from Clare's perspective, of being an openly Black woman; Irene can "parade" and perform as a Black body, taunting while also eliciting the Black queer flesh in and of Clare. In addition to the rare initial act of passing that she casually (and successfully) performs in the novel's opening, Irene can express her Blackness (especially in Harlem and Southside Chicago) at any moment without much fear. This freedom from domination, from Clare's perspective, elicits her racial anxiety. Larsen describes an episode of this racial anxiety during Clare's childhood: "'Rene, how, when I used to go over to the South Side, I used almost to hate all of you. You had all the things I wanted and never had had'" (188). Irene interprets this "having" attitude as the need for money and a middle-class nuclear family. She misses the intimation that Clare desires precisely what Irene takes for granted as an innate condition of sociopolitical life: her ability to be (or be racialized as) an African American woman. The children play and openly socialize with each other as Black children (a halcyon scenario Clare attempts to re-create in her subsequent tea party!); in their neighborhoods and homes, their race is not prohibited, and Clare, unconsciously, interprets this to mean the practice of Black queer flesh. This rejection from community and extended kinship networks causes Clare to experience racial anxiety. Clare re-creates her childhood dream by inviting Irene and Gertrude over for a real tea party. This desire shatters when John Bellew enters the apartment; Clare begins to fracture, even though it is Irene who appears the most disturbed. After the party, Clare writes to Irene, conveying how "excitingly happy" it was to play. The letter concludes with the postscript "*It may be, 'Rene dear, it may just be, that, after all, your way may be the wiser and infinitely happier one*" (208). Through a mimetic relationship with Irene, Clare begins to unhinge her decision to pass and to create a white family. By reaching into the past for inspiration, Clare's tea party and Bellew's intrusions help her disidentify with subjectivity to follow a queer-of-color journey. She begins to discard the present in the hope of a better future when she, too, can flourish in a radical freedom of Black queer expression.

Irene initially rejects building a friendship that would assist Clare (and herself) in her journey of self-abnegation. Two years pass before the arrival of Clare's second letter, and Irene refuses to answer it. In the time that has passed, Clare has been churning over their encounter and stewing over the possibility of Black freedom. She writes to Irene,

> For I am lonely, so lonely . . . cannot help longing to be with you again, as I have never longed for anything before; and I have wanted many things in my life . . . You can't know how in this pale life of mine I am all the time seeing the bright pictures of that other that I once thought I was glad to be free of. . . . It's like an ache, a pain that never ceases

and

> And it's your fault, 'Rene dear. At least partly. For I wouldn't now, perhaps, have this terrible, this wild desire if I hadn't seen you that time in Chicago. (174)

Clare has been in anxious ruins without Irene. Until their encounter in Chicago, Clare had successfully repressed the desire for and knowledge of racial freedom. Isolated in a white world, she could not socialize with middle- and upper-class African American women; she refused a Black maid for fear of being discovered and of being forced to experience the other woman's freedom. Now, Clare feels the ceaseless ache of racial anxiety after forging a mimetic relationship with Irene. Critics have noticed how Larsen presents the second reunion in highly sexualized terms, which reinforces the deep, mimetic relationship Clare established with Irene. Larsen portrays Clare's angst over not hearing back from Irene as the jilted lover. Clare describes her waiting as if "an illicit love affair and that the man had thrown me over." Like a heartbroken lover, she stayed up "half the nights . . . awake looking out at the watery stars—hopeless things, the stars—worrying and wondering." When Irene dodges an explanation, Clare continues the lover's discourse: "You mean you don't want me, 'Rene?" (225). While Clare speaks, Irene even lights the symbolic phallus, a cigarette, which she refuses to give Clare. Still smoking the cigarette, Clare reiterates her letter: "If it hadn't been for that [Irene's visit and the reestablished relationship], I'd have gone on to the end, never seeing any of you. But that did something to me, and I've been so lonely since! You can't know. Not close to a single soul. Never anyone to really talk to" (227). Clare shifts the framework from that of a lover to that of kinship. In her white upper-class world, she cannot complete an utterance as a Black woman. Her speech as a Black woman is all unidirectional because she lacks anyone who can hear and respond to her language and her performance of Blackness. As language philosopher Mikhail Bakhtin indicates, a complete utterance needs a respondent who can understand, interpret, and respond—including to its political and racial dimensions. Clare exists in a state of empty speech, save the moments when she has become a white woman, I would argue. Her Black queer flesh, before reuniting with Irene, had no one with whom to interact: it had to let subjectivity run her life.

After twelve years of passing, which is almost all of Clare's formative years as an adult, her performed racial and political identity has had to cite white femininity. I assume that she speaks with her white friends and husband and gets recognized as a white woman. But, since Irene's visit, Clare can no longer confine herself to performing whiteness. At this juncture in the novel, Clare does engage in racial passing but also remains barred from a normative or Black queer subjectivity. She feels her domination of herself as a socially, materially bound white woman-mother; Clare cannot just unpass and try to assume a Black identity without essentially destroying her daughter's life and future. This stress aggravates Clare, but it is her conscious understanding of her domination as a Black woman and her lack of freedom to perform her Blackness that drive her to literal tears. She confirms this, weeping, "'How could you know [of her anxiety]? How could you? You're free. You're happy. And,' with faint derision, 'safe'" (227). The last element is spoken with irony, because Irene is so free that she can fabricate a condition of unfreedom to occupy her boredom. In this moment, and in the second letter, Larsen depicts Clare beginning to self-abnegate her white subjectivity. She can only enter full speech with Irene if she is a Black woman; this requires the abandonment of her whiteness—the irony, of course, is that Clare is mixed raced. Thus, through a mimetic relationship with 'Rene, Clare begins to disintegrate her social and racial identities.

Larsen endows the character of Clare with a scandalous choice. As Clare disidentifies and self-abnegates from her whiteness, she must also sever the ties associated with that identity; separating from a white history comes with a high cost. Irene anticipates a divorce, but she does not expect Clare to destroy the white mother–daughter relationship. Unlike Helga, who allowed motherhood to limit her existence, Clare believes that the mother–daughter relationship is also subject to the risks of life. She states "that being a mother is the cruelest thing in the world" (227). Irene challenges what she views as Clare's immoral risk taking; Clare cannot unpass, otherwise Margery would be motherless and rejected by her father. Larsen concludes Irene's scolding about seeking a divorce with "it's a selfish whim, an unnecessary and—'" (228). Irene is interrupted, and the conversation changes topic. Not until near the tragic end of the novel does the topic of motherhood return. Margery is enrolled in a European boarding school, and when Irene inquires about her, Clare must repeat Margery's name as if she has forgotten her own daughter. I contend that this moment signals Clare's disinvestment from her "white" daughter. At this point in the novel, Clare is ready to give up her entire life so she can achieve freedom. Even though she attributes her not moving to Harlem as loyalty to Margery, Clare has already sacrificed her daughter—in her "having" way: "I haven't any proper morals or sense of duty. . . . why, to get things I want badly enough, I'd do anything, hurt anybody, throw anything away. Really, 'Rene, I'm not safe" (240). Clare understands the difficult choices that must be made in the journey of self-abnegation. The path is unconventional and challenges the limits of moral behavior and ethics. Larsen suggests that Clare acknowledges her severed ties with her white daughter when Irene suddenly breaks off with, "and as for your giving up things—" (241). Clare then bursts into tears upon realizing she has given up her white identity and her daughter. Clare must be focused and committed if she intends to follow a journey of self-abnegation, but she is not the only one engaged in self-abnegation.

Irene launches her journey of self-abnegation upon her second friendship with Clare. She abnegates by forging a mimetic relationship with Clare, including her risk taking, Blackness, and whiteness. Larsen presents Irene's racial anxiety as a reaction to Clare's performances of her undomination. Her taboo body and social identity as a white mother yet simultaneously a potential Black lover recall the traumas of a queer world after domination. Irene cannot tolerate Clare's commitment to her own desires; she describes the younger Black and present white Clare as having "no allegiance beyond her own immediate desire. She was selfish, and cold, and hard" (172). This dedication to desire stokes Irene's repression of her own desires and manifests as an obsession with security and control—these forms of surplus jouissance attempt to block mimesis and self-abnegation. Unlike Helga, who struggled to master and accept middle-class norms, Irene jumps over the requirements to become middle class. She adopts the norms so much that she becomes a panopticon for the rules and in turn exercises the power of these social norms upon everyone in her circle. This embrace of standardization effectively quells all of Irene's desires, and the pursuit of Black queer flesh (via desires for Clare) is the ultimate form of racial anxiety: Irene's entire lifestyle and practices work to repress Black queer flesh, namely, undominated Black life, and any critical moment of reflection.

Larsen presents Irene's pleasure in security as a form of surplus jouissance. She illustrates the calming effect of this security: "She was aware that, to her, security was the most important and desired thing in life. . . . She wanted only to be tranquil. Only, unmolested" (276). Irene enjoys controlling the lives of her guests, her husband, and her sons. But Larsen allows readers to surmise that this is all a show to keep Irene from exploding, from following her desires to self-abnegate like Clare. Adorno offers a similar explanation when he explains that "the culture industry replaces pain, which is present in ecstasy no less than in asceticism, with jovial denial. Its supreme law is that its consumers shall at no price be given what they desire: and in that very deprivation they must take their laughing satisfaction."[34] Surplus jouissance exposes the constructedness of socially mediated relationships. It helps articulate or unrepress the real inequalities hidden behind apparent equivalences, behind the use of pleasure. Larsen capitalizes on (anticipates) these formulations by demonstrating how Irene crafts a mimetic relationship with Clare after learning that her pleasure contains a pearl of falseness—that it is not security she desires but aspects embodied in Clare and ultimately the comingling of her Black queer flesh with Clare's.

When Clare insists on attending the Negro Welfare League ball as a single lady, Irene objects—both verbally and with racial anxiety. Besides voicing her need for security—"all I'm concerned with is the unpleasantness and possible danger which your [Clare] going might incur"—Irene must get up from her seat, rearrange flowers, and "her hands shook slightly, for she was in a near rage of impatience and exasperation" (230–31). Larsen displays the corporeality of racial anxiety—the need to dance with Clare at the ball. Even though the danger is targeted at Clare, Irene frames everything around herself: "I shouldn't like to be mixed up in any row" (231). Irene eventually capitulates to Clare's request and thus welcomes the supposedly dangerous Clare back into her life. She knows the dangers of letting Clare return and goes against her own surplus jouissance situated around security. By placing herself in Clare's position—of being the possible prostitute and, more important, of being exposed by Bellew or one of his associates—Irene begins to empathize with Clare. This start of a mimetic relationship helps Irene embrace her own abject status as a Black and (lesbian) desiring woman. She interprets Clare's "futile searching and the firm resolution" as a positionality of abjection. Irene then aligns herself with what she considers the abject and begins to erode her normative identity. Likewise, this new deviant position still generates surplus jouissance because Irene creates another threat to her security. She takes cynical pleasure in "the disagreeable possibilities in connection with Clare Kendry's coming among them loom[ing] before her in endless irritating array" (232–33). Clare's inclusion guarantees "endless" pleasure, repression, and also self-abnegation for Irene. Being associated with scandal will help erode Irene's connection to middle-class norms. Literary critic Helena Michie offers a complementary analysis, arguing that Clare "forces Irene to look at herself and the constructedness of her marriage, her sexuality, and her racial position." While I agree that Irene changes because of a relationship with Clare, I think it is through a complex mimesis and not simply from an "exchange of gazes" that involves identification as sameness.[35]

Larsen illustrates Irene's mimesis of Clare (as an undominated Black lesbian). A good example arises when Clare provides a post office box address. Irene is frustrated that Clare does not find her wise enough to avoid being indiscreet. Irene, in a fury, thinks, "Having always had complete confidence in her own good judgment and tact, Irene couldn't bear to have anyone seem to question them" (222). This insight partially explains Irene's misstep—her lack of good judgment and tact—when attempting to manipulate Brian into taking their son abroad for school. She deals with her "fear which crouched, always, deep down within her, stealing away the sense of security," not in a wonderfully elegant manner, as she had done before Clare's return, but by antagonizing Brian about the sexual and racial education of their children. She loses her tact because she has begun a mimetic relationship with Clare; she abandons patience and, like her accusation of Clare, has "no allegiance beyond her own immediate desire" (172). The manner in which Irene approached the conversation was "unsafe" with "certain unpleasantness and possible danger" (172). This is the same language used to describe Clare; Larsen portrays Irene mirroring Clare, but without the same results—Margery is in boarding school in Europe, and Irene fails to send her children abroad. The episode highlights Irene's subtle differences and interpretations of Clare. She does not identify or exactly copy Clare's behaviors but incorporates interpretations of specific attributes—particularly acting as if not dominated by social conventions of propriety, a small but important act of self-abnegation. By emphasizing mimesis, Larsen retains a difference that is lost in pure mimicry. Irene learns not to make Clare the standard but to practice versions of Clare's behaviors and desires. In the process, Irene reads the prehistoric, undominated aspects of Clare, and while discovering undominated Black queer flesh, in particular, Irene unknowingly begins to release it herself; releasing it requires deactivating the surplus jouissance that typically prevents Black queer flesh from operating except in the drive or eruptions of anxiety. At the same time, welcoming Black queer flesh requires self-abnegating subjectivity. Moreover, her acts of self-abnegation become more distinct and important as the novel progresses.

At the ball, Irene gains an immense excitement—this time not from the surplus jouissance of controlling Clare but from openly desiring Clare and having the scandal associated with herself. Irene tries on the outfit of the undominated Black woman expressing herself and sets aside her heteronormativity; Irene practices self-abnegation at this dance with Clare by her side. Clare's attendance excites both positive and negative attention. This gesture requires that Irene absorb the risks. In this manner, Irene abandons her security and models herself after Clare, taking on the risk-taking qualities of Clare—but with slight modifications. Irene, like Clare, begins to "shut away reason as well as caution" as she develops their friendship (231). This includes the dismantling of her need for security—at least temporally. Near the end of the novel, Irene's mimesis becomes more transparent. In another fight with Brian, she loses her patience again: "She must not work herself up. She must not! Where were all the self-control, the common sense, that she was so proud of?" (264). Because of her mimesis with Clare, Irene has learned to abnegate her self-control and common sense.

Ethnic solidarity, although at times a source of frustration, seems important for Irene—proud to support uplift and proud of the skin color of her husband and children. She weakly claims an extended kinship with Clare because of their past and because of their racial sisterhood. Supposedly Clare does not care about the African American race but merely belongs to it. This formula frustrates Irene, who remains silent about Clare's secret out of a supposed commitment to their shared race. She thinks, "She couldn't betray Clare . . . she had toward Clare Kendry a duty. She was bound to her by those very ties of race which, for all her repudiation of them, Clare had been unable to completely sever" (212–13). While critics such as McDowell and Cheryl Wall describe Irene's rationally articulated sense of duty as a smoke screen for her erotic desires, Ann DuCille offers a more provocative perspective: Clare is Irene's "alter libido."[36] Following this logic, I could argue that the vicarious thrill of Clare's passing is what keeps Irene attached to Clare.

I will propose instead that this scene does indeed provide a thrill for Irene, but I want to add another—not necessarily divergent—facet of interpretation. Irene's obsession with assisting Clare falls under the rubric of the Bildungsroman: helping a friend maintain her secret so she can advance or develop. Returning to the previous example, Brian wants to educate his children on sex, lynching, racial slurs, and "the race problem" (263). Irene rejects this approach in favor of a philosophy of Bildung: "I want their childhood to be happy and as free from the knowledge of such things as it possibly can be" (263). Larsen emphasizes the alignment of Irene with a "raceless" middle-class childhood; she subscribes to the journey of development, and as a parent, she wants that journey to be "smooth," that is, without the horrors of race. At this point in the novel, Irene has already begun to fracture and self-abnegate, but she also partially mends those wounds. Larsen introduces this confrontation as a way to expose the unreality and impossibility of Irene's notion of Bildung for African Americans. Brian wants to fracture the children's sense of reality with a "proper preparation of [Black] life": lynching, violence, and anti-Black racism (264). This demand for racial consciousness in Irene does not entail embracing a politics of racial uplift but rather a consciousness that the subjectivity of African Americans has been corrupted by anti-Black racism, which contributes significantly to the making of raced subjects. She must leave the room and is "seized by a convulsion of shivering" (264). To quell this anxiety, Irene begins to suspect that Brian is having an affair with Clare. The fantasy of the affair becomes the surplus jouissance for the latter anxiety and not the affair. More strikingly, Irene is unconsciously attracted to Black queer flesh—and not just the sexiness of Clare's physical features. In negotiating with Brian, Irene must balance her newfound mimesis with Clare and the idea of Black women as undominated and her commitments to "the race" and her family. Further exposure to Black queer flesh, though, will unhinge Irene's identity and subjectivity until nothing remains—including her bonds to her family and to the normative aspects of her "race."

Achieving Self-Abnegation

The novel ends with a confusing twist: does Irene push Clare to her death, or does Clare jump out of the window? Critics have long been divided over this issue. Considering the role of self-abnegation, I contend that actual death is a viable option—and metaphorically required—for narrative closure with self-abnegation; complete self-abnegation followed by the "death" of the initial subjectivity becomes one telos of the genre. Resolving if Clare jumps or not, then, is quite significant for understanding if self-abnegation is truly achieved. That is, if Irene murdered Clare, then no "self"-abnegation could be completed: the question remains if complete self-abnegation is possible. By examining Irene's ethical dilemma—whether to tell of her encounter with John Bellew—I turn to examining the ending of the genre's refusal of a happy ending and the mandate for resolution.

After Bellew discovers that Irene and Clare are Black women passing as white women, Irene enters a state of ecstasy. Larsen structures Clare's outing as pleasure; Irene had hoped to remove Clare from her life, and "as if in answer to her wish, the very next day Irene came face to face with Bellew" (259). This turning point in the novel acts as the intersection of multiple plots. First, this moment works to undo the racial anxiety Irene felt about the (pre)historical freedom she traced in Clare's body. This jouissance derived from Clare's being caught, and the end of her "passing" allows Irene to return to her "normal" state of security. Previously, Irene had partially severed her connections to her secure life by engaging in a mimetic relationship to Clare's supposed state of freedom. The trace she located in Clare, of a time when Black women were not dominated, propelled her to abandon her Black middle-class norms and, more radically, her identities as wife and mother.

Through this dialectic of identity, Larsen demonstrates that Clare and Irene must completely self-abnegate their identities. Irene engages in a relationship of mimesis with Clare, but she does not fully self-abnegate her identities like Clare has done. If Bellew were to divorce Clare, she would remain in Harlem and thus threaten Irene's security. While a surface reading suggests that Irene would be most anxious at the prospect of being abandoned by Brian, Larsen reveals that Irene's racial anxiety arises from that fact that Irene would inevitably be led to a state of formlessness; her mimesis of Clare entails her emotional, moral, and psychic disintegration. Larsen clues readers in to this logic: "If Clare was freed, anything might happen" (268). It is Clare's imagined freedom as a passing woman that evokes Irene's racial anxiety, and if Bellew destroys that freedom, Irene might be "happy." As many critics have proposed, Larsen seems to attribute Clare's death to Irene; the murder would restore her security and prevent her from experiencing Black queer flesh and, more important, achieving complete self-abnegation.

A second interpretation emphasizes how the act of withholding information more fully articulates Larsen's theory of queer-of-color self-abnegation. In wanting to discard Clare—to destroy the possibility of freedom for African American women—Irene "wished, for the first time in her life that she had not been born a Negro" (258). The desire to discard Clare qua race translates into Irene's desire to do the same via being born—not just passing for white. She claims to be torn between an allegiance to "the race" via Clare and to her own happiness. This seems like a counterintuitive exchange, because Irene's desire for whiteness provides her the freedom that she wants to extinguish in Clare. She wants to achieve Clare's state of undomination by dominating Clare, by becoming Clare, instead of preserving a difference through mimesis. The switch to domination and the binary of identification/refusing identification suspends Irene's self-abnegation and her mimesis. Contrary to self-abnegation, Irene returns to heteronormative Bildung and attempts to add—not subtract—layers to her identity. All is not lost with this hiccup: Larsen reveals that Irene has not fully given up a mimetic relationship to Clare but merely had a temporary lapse.

Irene returns to an undominating mimesis—thereby supporting Clare's quest for self-abnegation—after Clare acknowledges Irene's outing of herself. Shortly after Clare's arrival at the final party, Larsen plants numerous clues for us to decipher. First, Clare "kissed a bare shoulder [Irene's], seeming not to notice a slight shrinking." Then, Irene cues Clare: "Philadelphia. That's not very far, is it? Clare, I—?" (265). Irene and Clare both understand that John Bellew would mostly likely return from his short business trip in Philly the same day as his departure. Next, Irene observes that "Clare didn't notice the unfinished sentence." Irene refuses to speak, but she does make a statement; Larsen ends the confession that she ran into Bellew with a question mark. This unfinished question demands a response from Clare; she must locate the question within Irene's cryptic behaviors—and after all, Irene provides the only full speech, as defined by Bakhtin, in which Clare has been able to engage as an adult; the messages must be clear. The "shrinking" shoulder, for example, should alert Clare to Irene's repugnance and dismay; this greeting, when compared to the other times Clare enters, is extremely different. And, if Clare really "knows" what Irene is always thinking—as so often proven in the novel—Larsen wants us also to know that Clare understands Irene's unspoken messages, which plague their awkward interaction. Like Clare's scribbled writings, Irene has mastered Clare's "feminine," wordless communication through Black queer flesh; her discursive intention indeed reaches Clare, as the two women can communicate beyond ordinary language. Larsen exhibits Clare's reception of the message in her answer to Irene's unfinished question regarding what she would do if Bellew were to discover her secret. Even Irene seems to register the answer, although she represses her awareness of it: "That smile and the quiet resolution of that one word, 'Yes,' filled Irene with a *primitive* paralyzing dread. Her hands were numb, her feet like ice, her heart like a stone weight. Even her tongue was like a heavy dying thing. There were long spaces between the words as she asked: 'And what should you do?'" (265–66, emphasis added). The resounding and primitive yes answers Irene's earlier, yet unspoken confession-cum-question.

Clare speaks from a state of near-abnegation, so the "I" that she enunciates is slightly confusing; as she learns of her impending fate, she gathers the strength to finish self-abnegating from both her white and Black lives. In a space without identity—she becomes Black queer flesh that is merely decorated by an elegant dress and shawl—Clare communicates with the authority of the primitive, of a time and space when queer African American women were not dominated. Larsen even indicates Irene's acknowledgment of Clare's transformation. The "long spaces between the words" are what Lacan would call eruptions of the Real and the "voice" of the unconscious. In this context, the long spaces should be read as Black queer flesh beginning to play with language, to test itself in the Symbolic. As Irene pauses, she corresponds—here I evoke Fred Moten's rupture to propose that the Black queer flesh between Irene and Clare improvises and ultimately learns to create an ensemble of discourse that speaks through sonic materiality, the pauses, the em dashes, rather than formal language per se—her warning and feelings for Clare. Larsen has previously established a queer form of communication between Clare and Irene early in the novel, and when it appears to queerly fail at this juncture, readers understand that this is not simply a gap in the narrative but a critical maneuver where Black queer flesh can be sustained, can speak its own language. This new form of discourse, at first, scares Irene, and she quickly represses this knowledge: "Clare Kendry had always seemed to know what other people were thinking. . . . Well, she wouldn't know this time" (266). Irene's surplus jouissance tries to shatter the bonds of Black queer flesh and Clare's roaring yes to her unspoken question.

After reestablishing her mimetic relationship—conscious or not—Irene no longer relies on the surplus jouissance of Clare's removal to calm her racial anxiety. She exchanges this pain for her old form of surplus jouissance, namely, the security of her middle-class nuclear family. In this exchange, Irene feels "this absence of acute, unbearable pain," which is "unjust" (267). She tastes the failed moment in surplus jouissance, which reveals that her fears about Clare and security are both equally artificial. In this moment of not feeling the trauma of her self-induced pain-pleasure, Irene self-abnegates her identity as a loving wife: "She couldn't now be sure that she had ever truly known love. Not even for Brian. He was her husband and the father of her sons. But was he anything more?" (268). She realizes that her marriage is a sham and her heterosexual love has only led to her domination. Irene views Brian as merely a social position and function; she finally self-abnegates her identification with wife, lover, mother, and middle-class "lady." She will pass as a mother and wife just as Clare passes as a white woman. This ultimate self-abnegation is the key element of the novel, and as Irene's case demonstrates, enacting self-abnegation rather than flirting with the idea or establishing mimesis does not come easily: Irene must work through not only surplus jouissance but also the desire to feel normative by retaining ties to her family. Self-abnegating an identity is not just a process of ease or perlocutionary declaration; the work includes ups and down and many unsuccessful attempts—and even temporary returns to comfort, as Irene has made.

Through Clare's death, Larsen represents another process of this queer narrative: a redoing of the African American self so as to preclude double consciousness and the internalization of anti-Black thought. Larsen seeks, as a form of rebirth so prevalent during this time period, some way of recovering Black queer flesh and making it the central organizing system for queer African Americans: can Black queer flesh somehow become the basis for an emancipated sense of self? As Clare self-abnegates more and more of her identities, she approaches a state of formlessness—of existing as a self-without-subjectivity. More important, Clare returns to a place before subjectivity was installed, to the location of Black queer flesh. Clare relinquishes her social and political identities over the course of her unpassing. The remaining attachments are psychic and emotional. Irene is the last connection Clare maintains in the world, and she seems to betray Clare. Larsen strongly implies that Irene desired Clare's death and pushed her out of the window. An earlier moment, when Irene drops the teacup at one of her parties in rage, mirrors the ending: a fragile white thing smashes to the ground, and Irene obscures the cause (254–55). Returning to the final party, "Irene finished her cigarette and threw it out [the window she'd opened], watching the tiny spark drop slowly down to the white ground below [snow]" (270). The red flame drops to the ground just as Clare in her red dress will fall to the earth. Larsen relies on less subtle imagery when Irene has reached a point of openly wanting Clare out of her life and imagining her dead (261). It seems that Irene terminates her friendship with Clare, but as critics have noted, in killing Clare, she acts out of (sexual) passion. I want to closely examine the scene of Clare's death to pinpoint Irene's role in it and elaborate on the process of Clare's undoing of subjectivity: how will she reconstitute the self upon relinquishing the strong arm of subjectivity forced upon her?

The spatial configuration of the characters in this scene provides insight into Larsen's theory of remaking the self-without-subjectivity. When Bellew enters the apartment (indeed, he returns from Philadelphia the same day he left, as Irene foretold), he rushes through the line of men and toward the seated Clare. As he shouts at her, three events simultaneously occur: the men approach him, Felice (the host) warns him, and Clare moves from a chair to the large picture window that Irene had recently opened. As Clare stands at the window with "a faint smile on her full red lips and in her shining eyes," this smile "maddened" Irene. She runs across the room, bypassing her husband, Felice, the line of men, and Bellew, to place herself between Bellew and Clare. Irene seems to be the only person protecting Clare, acting as a shield from Bellew, yet Larsen offers a different vocabulary: "Before *them* stood John Bellew . . . beyond *them* the little huddle of other people" (271, emphasis added). The paragraph describes the configuration of the room, but as I have shown, Larsen provides a detailed map of everyone's location before this two-sentence paragraph repeats the information. What this paragraph adds is Larsen's description of Clare and Irene as a singular unit: "them." How does Irene move from a point of mimesis to a coupling with Clare?

This dyad forms as a consequence of Irene's recognition that Clare stands before the party as if "the whole structure of her life were not lying in fragments before her. She seemed unaware of any danger or uncaring" (271). The fact that Clare does not become visibly emotional but remains calm and poised befuddles Irene. Similarly, she makes readers conscious of Clare's self-abnegation by articulating the fragments that Clare has shed: her identities are literally trash fragments on the floor. Clare is a self-without-subjectivity. Then Irene recognizes Clare's freedom shining through in the smile that appears on her mouth and in her eyes. Irene reads on Clare's body the signs that announce her achievement of self-abnegation and the reemergence of Black queer flesh—with all but one identity evaporating. Irene rushes to Clare's aid and thinks, "She couldn't have Clare Kendry cast aside by Bellew. She couldn't have her free" (271). While the freedom Irene references presumably recalls a divorced Clare living openly as a Black woman in Harlem and seducing Brian and Irene, Larsen indexes a radically different set of meanings. First, Clare is in a state of formless Black queer flesh. Through the process of self-abnegation, she has dislodged her social, political, and psychic identities from her body and ego. In this process, Clare has moved closer to a state free from domination—in a process that mirrors how Irene understands Clare's existence. If, at this point, Clare is "cast aside," Bellew transforms her back into an object by reconstituting her identity as a divorcée and *a dominated Black woman* and effectively turns her entire journey of self-abnegation into a waste. He would transform a formless Clare and in effect reinstigate normative racialization and subjectivity. Bellew could redominate Clare, only this time as an African American woman. Irene refuses to have Clare available—"free"—for reracialization, for domination. The radical freedom Clare achieved must be the launching point for remaking the self out of Black queer flesh.

At this point in the sequence of events, Bellew might force subjectivity back onto Clare, Clare could somehow remain as Black queer flesh or die, or Irene might join her as flesh. Larsen indicates that the latter occurs by creating the dyad structure. Irene and Clare become united. As a loving friend, Irene assists Clare in crafting a new identity. Remember that Irene did not fully betray Clare by being seen by Bellew with her Black friend and that she unconsciously informs Clare of her impending outing by Bellew through a conversation facilitated by Black queer flesh. Clare's sole remaining psychic bond is with Irene. The stage is set for the emergence of a new sense of self, a rebirth of Black queer flesh. The window and jump serve as wonderful images of the womb, but the question remains: whose womb, and why does it need to be a maternal space and image? Earlier, Irene opened the window and launched a red flame out of it. Now, Clare occupies the same space and initiates a queer sociality with Irene. When Irene rejoins the space, the two women—as Larsen alludes to with the unified pronoun—animate a new sense of self. In this second self-making process, Clare can model herself off of Irene's love and care in a mimetic fashion. Clare understands that her lover is a healthy and vital Black woman comprising Black queer flesh and queer love. Instead of Black queer flesh being restricted by subjectivity, it can flourish when bodies self-abnegate, and thereby it does not need to become repressed, uninhabited, or rejected, as is the case with subjectivity.

To get rid of her last cathexis, Clare disinvests from Irene and trusts that the "them" undoes Irene as an object to which she attached and thus places Clare in a true state of formlessness. Clare, now completely self-abnegated, can establish a primary mimesis—and not identification—with Black queer flesh without interference from anti-Black racism or Black heteronormativity. Irene has proven a caretaker and defender of Clare, has assisted her in reentering the Black world of Harlem and now this protective dyad. First, Clare can read queer flesh in Irene—as had been established earlier that evening—and can model herself on the histories contained within queer Blackness; she has complete access to Irene's Black queer flesh in the dyad: she reads and interacts with the queer love, the queer bond, and the queer history and practices expressed by Irene's Black queer flesh. Because this relationship and sense of Black queer flesh exist outside normative discursive modes, there is no problem of translation and no problem with access. In primary mimesis, Clare can model herself on this new apparatus without fear of retribution, anger, or hostility—unlike the heteronormative mirror stage that constitutes the subject out of lack and fear; she is not taking but crafting a primary relationship to Black queer flesh that is already "herself" within this dyad.

As she proceeds to secondary mimesis, Clare must imagine—no, she knows with certainty—what her love desires: Irene desires Clare to be free, to enjoy a life without domination (or as little as possible). For the entire novel, Irene has relished the desire of life without domination by men, by society, by heteronormativity, and especially by racial uplift politics. Clare can now begin inhabiting her Black queer flesh without domination: remember, it is only Irene who believes Clare to be undominated, because she "sees" past subjectivity into Clare's Black queer flesh. Irene's Black queer flesh can sonically speak to Clare. At this point in her transformation from subjectivity to flesh, Clare is not Clare Kendry or Clare Bellew but the entire history and experience of Black queers. Unfortunately, we do not get a chance to interact with this new person, as "Clare" dies moments after gaining complete freedom from subjectivity and remolding themselves through Black queer flesh. We are granted some insights into the afterlife of subjectivity in the final pages of the novel.

The last few pages of the novel seem anticlimactic after Clare's harrowing death. Irene appears to be in a state of shock from her murderous act. I propose that Larsen continues Irene's journey of self-abnegation in the aftermath of Clare's arrival to Black queer flesh. Clare, the love object, has been destroyed. Although death does not equate to a psychic abnegation, Larsen suggests that Irene will negotiate the category of woman through living as Irene discovers, too late, that the person pushed from the window was not Clare but a newly structured self: without a psyche or subjectivity. Irene's shock stems in part from this new knowledge and Irene's attempt to reconfigure her mimetic relationship to this new self, this new Black queer flesh. She, too, must try her hand at recovering flesh. Larsen resumes Irene's self-abnegation from her identities. When Irene wants to comfort Brian, she is "helpless, having so completely lost control of his mind and heart" (274). Unlike her earlier vacillations, she remains true here to the abandonment of security and of her identities as a mother and wife. The marriage bonds are gone. Larsen confirms this when Brian provides Irene a "soothing gesture" and gives her his coat. Instead of feeling warmth, she reacts with anger and sadness, as when Brian enters her room unannounced: "She began to cry rackingly, her entire body heaving with convulsive sobs" (274). She cries for Clare and rejects Brian's attempts at comfort.

In the psychic register, Irene can easily self-abnegate from her love attachment to Clare after she asks, "Is she—is she—?" and convulses, namely, using grief to decathect her love from a dead object. Clare is not only dead; their subjectivity was destroyed, and they died only as Black queer flesh—refusing to reconstitute a subjectivity. Irene need not fear self-abnegating love bonds to Clare because she saw that Clare is no more. Furthermore, Irene cannot complete her final utterance of the novel because no one can understand her. As she informs the police that Bellew did not push Clare, she says, "I'm quite certain that he didn't. I was there, too. As close as he was. She just fell, before anybody could stop her. I—" (274). Irene lets Bellew off the hook, but she cannot articulate her own actions. I contend that when Irene does utter the penultimate sentence, her illocution re-creates the dyad. The lone "I" performs the perlocutionary act of offering Irene's end, her last moment of existence. The single "I" impresses upon readers Irene's slippage into Black queer flesh, because she no longer exists as a coherent subject; she is now a self-without-subjectivity. Thus her "I" refers to an impossible subject, and the sentence cannot be completed, as there is no longer the same subject who speaks. Irene is, after all, still the "them" from before; this "I" is false. The next two paragraphs of the novel, I believe, confirm this advancement.

Larsen describes the scene as Irene's "knees gave way.... She moaned and sank down, moaned again. Through the great heaviness that submerged and drowned her she was dimly conscious... then everything was dark" (275). These experiences repeat Clare's falling and the movement into a dark space of the womb/flesh. Irene, too, falls and is covered with the same darkness involved in Clare's death. When Irene awakes from her rebirth "centuries after," Larsen leaves readers with an odd last word to the novel spoken by the police: "Death by misadventure, I'm inclined to believe. Let's go up and have another look at that window" (275). The window, as womb, recalls Clare's rebirth and now Irene's. Larsen wants us to remember the womb/window as a reminder not of Clare's defenestration but of Clare and Irene's recent emergence into Black queer flesh. In addition, "centuries later" recalls Clare and Irene's quest to re-create a time-space where Black queer women were not dominated. This radical and primitive freedom existed eons ago, centuries ago, and it is apropos that Irene emerges from Black queer flesh dazed. They just returned from that ancient past where Black queer flesh was not dominated. Irene returns to the space of the novel not as a new subject; she returns as Black queer flesh undominated—by subjectivity and by society. Unlike the new Clare, Irene commits to exploring life as a Black queer self free from the psychic constraints of anti-Black racism. They must continue to negotiate anti-Black racism in the social and political spheres, but they are no longer dominated by a socially imposed psyche or subjectivity. Although Clare dies at the conclusion of her journey of self-abnegation, Larsen encourages her readers to look into the window that they opened together and to follow Irene's journey, to conceptualize the queer utopia that Irene now occupies. The novel ends, then, with neither Clare nor Irene as neophyte subject with freshly crafted psyche but with both as selves of Black queer flesh that resist organization and legibility.

Irene's and Clare's complete self-abnegations inaugurate lives constituted on, through, and by Black queer flesh. Larsen proposes that the self extricated from subjectivity embraces Black queer flesh. This movement away from normative models of self-making allows Larsen to celebrate the disavowed knowledges within Black queer flesh. The latter drove the process of self-abnegation and helped to dismantle subjectivity and the psyche. By extricating Black queer flesh from subjectivity, Larsen opens the door to a new set of possibilities for Black queer life. I argue that Larsen is unable to narrate Irene after becoming flesh for two reasons. First, they are a new person that should not be written: Bellew tried to rewrite Clare, and Larsen would not let that happen. Subjectivity and subject positions are what allow for the naming and descriptions of personality. As Black queer flesh, these categories that exercise power have been successfully rejected. No doubt others might try to apply them to their bodies, but Larsen models how not to enact this violence against Black queer flesh by refusing to narrate.

Narrative closure for the queer-of-color Bildungsroman does not simply demand the production of a self-without-subjectivity who can and must remove subjectivity but also asks Black queer flesh to govern the self without domination. In effect, Nella Larsen creates a journey of self-abnegation and argues for the emergence of Black queer flesh as the principal matrix for Black queer bodies. Her masterpiece thereby not only undoes the Bildungsroman but also forges the first uniquely queer literary genre. Although she never publishes another novel, Ralph Ellison, Richard Wright, and Saidiya Hartman, among others, have taken up the call to dismantle subjectivity and make way for Black queer flesh.

3 Queer Underworlds in Ralph Ellison

Disability and the Archive

The temptation to embrace self-formation and subjectivity through the Bildungsroman endures long after the Harlem Renaissance. Chief exponents of protest literature Ann Petry and Richard Wright adapt the Bildungsroman to convey the inequities of Jim Crow and racial discrimination with the aim to create new forms of self-determination for African Americans. The remonstrance against a seemingly natural, indelible world order relies on the assumption that African Americans possess limited agency that can, to some degree, effect personal—rather than social—change for themselves; the protest tradition exposes social structures, attempting to alter them so as to shift this assumption. The representation of African Americans as constructed beings, a major tenet of the Naturalist aesthetic, creates friction as it adjoins a plot of self-determination: the tension of self-formation and the idea of being socially and psychically constructed come to a head in protest literature. In this way, the surplus jouissance of Bildung carries forward from the modernism of the Harlem Renaissance into protest literature and one of the final works of Black modernism: Ralph Ellison's *Invisible Man.* Although an intellectual interlocutor and close friend of Richard Wright, Ellison distanced himself from the protest aesthetic—yet this style undergirds drafts of the novel and the published "Battle Royal" chapter, which revived and reconfigured a queer-of-color modernist aesthetic. He resumes Nella Larsen's project from *Passing* by beginning and ending his novel with a self-without-subjectivity and telling the story of self-abnegation through his male,

punk, and disabled protagonist, which intersectionality and disability studies will help me explicate given my argument that Ellison purports to obliterate subjectivity.

The intersectionality of racial and disabled identities has a long and contentious history. Historian Josh Lukin convincingly shows that colonialists forged this nexus to oppress enslaved and free Blacks.[1] With the dissemination of slavery, Dea Boster in *African American Slavery and Disability* traces the myriad cultural practices and implicit laws that further coupled the phenomenon of race with disability.[2] The history of slavery and the making of African American identities in fact became indelibly entwined with each other, and with disability as well. Everyday anti-Black whites were not the only purveyors of this fantasy, however. The Union Army, too, relied on the trope and campaigned to "cure" African American men of their disabilities. By advertising Black bodies as "inherently defective, [as bodies] afflicted with 'deformity' and disease," the Union Army ostensibly proposed that they could be transformed into able bodies, that is, into "rehabilitated black bod[ies]," by joining the fight for freedom.[3] Proper masculinity would practically be bestowed upon those Black soldiers who risked their lives for the war; their white counterparts could decouple the link between race and disability, and often did, whereas Blacks could not do so. Jennifer James, another key voice in this discourse, reveals how, in the medical model of disability, in which disabilities are presumed to need a cure because they are erroneously viewed as inferior to able bodies, one glimpses how African Americans found ingenious ways to circumvent these ableist models. Nonetheless, ascribing disabilities to African Americans due to race shot not only through white America like a surge of electricity but also through material culture.

As might be expected, African American artists and community leaders took issue with this link and did all they could to decouple race from disability. Whether disabled or not, African Americans could nevertheless be indiscriminately labeled with forms of disability. The cultural practice was by all intents and purposes ableist and racist. Literary scholar Tyler Dennis traces how twentieth-century novelists such as Charles Chesnutt, Frances E. W. Harper, Jessie Redmon Fauset, and James Weldon Johnson continued in the fight against the representation of African

Americans as disabled, in literature as in life. Dennis observes that even though no character in these authors' novels explicitly debates the trope—because of the myth's wide acceptance in the social imagination—they do represent characters with disabilities "to counter the enduring myths of African Americans as innately disabled and to reveal disability itself as constructed."[4] Ralph Ellison, in particular, critiques the social construction of disability insofar as he indicates how whites with disabilities view themselves akin to able-bodied African Americans, and in doing so, he makes visible in his work an often overlooked intersectional identity. Ellison will circumvent ableist models of identity by capitalizing on the logic that African Americans with disabilities simultaneously await able bodies and access to subjectivity. Not fearing the ideology to be neither able-bodied nor a subject, Ellison celebrates African Americans with disabilities and spurns the need or pursuit of a cure: he disavows the medical model of disability. Instead, I submit how Ellison moves to describe and represent an ontology of Black disability—while recognizing the vast diversity of differences under the broad terms of *Black* and *disabled.* By representing the experiences of those with disabilities, the author will explore not only their relationship but also their embodiment as Black queer flesh.

The recent access to the Ralph Ellison Papers at the Library of Congress gave scholars entry into the components that went into the making of the American masterpiece *Invisible Man* (1952). Early drafts reveal discarded characters and plotlines as well as an expunged social protest aesthetic abandoned in the published novel. Purged scenes include Invisible Man working alongside his queer uncle and the adventures of characters living at Mary's boardinghouse. Although I cannot cover all of these extratextual chapters, I do want to focus on a reoccurring theme in the archived materials: Ellison's attempt to represent the lives of nonnormative African Americans salient for my project. I understand nonnormative as marginal intersectional social locations and queer sexuality. Uncle Charles appears to be a fairy—a third sex from the early twentieth century—while Mary transforms into a voodoo-practicing, nonagenarian orderly who rescues Invisible from hospital experiments.[5] The archive houses photographs taken by Gordon Parks for Ellison's article

"Harlem Is Nowhere," originally scheduled for publication in *'48 Magazine of the Year* before it closed, and most of the images fell into obscurity. Jean-Christophe Cloutier found some of these lost images in the Ralph Ellison Papers.[6] This photojournalism article, published with new photos, narrates mental illness in Harlem, which includes an image of sexual deviance.[7] Within the archive are a trove of stories of African Americans with disabilities: gays and fairies who were viewed as mentally ill until 1973; we get a glimpse there, also, of infirmity; visual impairments; and cognitive disabilities.[8] Disability, speaking quite generally, reflects a range of physical and cognitive differences that from the 1930s to 1940s encompassed the overdetermined category "handicap." The Goodwill Industries, in its annual report of donations to fund activities for those with disabilities, grouped together a variety of differences, such as "Blind, Deaf or Defective Speech," "Mental, Emotional or Social Handicaps," "Handicapped by Age or Infirmity," and "Orthopedic or General Health Handicaps."[9] Placing this information on billboards and advertisements, especially around the holidays, in part reflects how the public understood and categorized the magnitude of this category. Disability historians such as Longmore and Umansky contend that "disability has never been a monolithic grouping" and includes "people with a variety of conditions, despite considerable differences in etiology."[10] Rosemary Garland-Thomson even unravels the tendency to essentialize the category of disability when she explains that "a blind person, an epileptic, a paraplegic, a deaf person, and an amputee, for example, have no shared cultural heritage, traditional activities, or common physical experience. Only the shared experience of stigmatization creates commonality."[11] Alongside this collective, shared stigma, Ellison takes up and complicates disability through coarticulations with sexuality and Blackness. I now want to think through these intersections and their consequences to understand conceptions of the liberal human subject in the middle of the twentieth century.

Delving into these intersections, I seek to understand how disability, race, and sexuality modulate one another, which leads me to draw from various analytical methods that are sometimes at odds. Derrick Bell, the civil rights activist and legal scholar, once opined that disability studies should be referred to as "white disability studies."[12] Thus normative methodologies and assumptions about disability cannot simply be extended to African American culture and experience. Alison Kafer and Robert McRuer, for instance, have shown the limits of extending normative disability studies to (white) gay and lesbian culture and experiences by developing new analytical methods to account for the intersection of experiences of disability and queerness.[13] How, then, can we explain the fluctuating multiplicities of identity given that current theories do not encompass the varied range of experiences and histories of intersectional difference? I would like to consider these questions, especially the constellation of disabilities as inflected through race, by analyzing a chapter that did not make it into the published novel before proceeding to explore Ellison's writing of self-abnegation through disability, sexuality, and race.

In "Wheelchair," an excised chapter from *Invisible Man,* Ellison writes about Invisible Man's relationship with Margaret Vevers—a white woman with a disability—and his protagonist's subsequent negotiation of that relationship within intersecting elements of disability, racial politics, gender, and class. Here Ellison confuses traditional social hierarchies when he introduces individuals who find themselves living with disabilities. When Invisible Man first meets the hostess and his employer for a charity gala, he summons a normative sociality in which a white woman relates to a young Black man as hypersexual, as a potential rapist, or as a docile servant. Angry about his paltry wages after working tirelessly in her kitchen, Invisible Man is aghast when he accidently startles Miss Margaret Vevers in her courtyard. Assuming that she deems him a brute—instead of a stranger wandering about the house—he immediately seizes upon her fantasy. He balls up his dollar bill (his salary for working the party), tossing it into her lap, which she automatically catches. Invisible Man is quick to tell her "that's a present, but don't expect more, I've shot my wad, see?" Clearly he thinks that she sexually desires-fears him, so the idea that she caught his "wad" gives him "a malicious pleasure."[14] Thinking he has not only preempted but actually exposed the dynamic that must exist between white women and (attractive) young Black men, Vevers loses no time in deflating his twisted volley.

Vevers, however, disrupts Invisible Man's assumptions as he proceeds to clarify that her relationship to him is far from sexual. She makes known, moreover, that her gesture is simply one of deep empathy for him as an African American: "You've been hurt. We've hurt ["injured" appears as a handwritten correction] you badly." In this unexpected gesture, Vevers acknowledges that whites have somehow assailed the lives of African Americans like his. Even though she is unable to complete the sentence that explains how African Americans have been hurt because of her pedantic affect, she does end up upsetting him in the end: "What I had done should have frightened her . . . produced no less than a riot call." Vevers's refusal to occupy a normative white femininity, and one that should be scandalized by such a sexual interlude, perplexes Invisible Man. He does not understand how to relate to disability, so his first reaction finds him enacting an ableist (or should I say, an uplift?) positionality. To the injurious claim of hers, he adamantly retorts, "I'm a responsible man! Can an injured man present presents? . . . Do the injured offer gifts? Tell me, tell me!"[15] While his pronouncement does not make sense on the surface—since Vevers herself was "injured" by a fall from a horse that left her paralyzed from the waist down, and she aids African American causes—Invisible Man highlights in this encounter not just disability but its intersection with race and gender. Invisible Man replies to her unstated idea that he is disabled—this so-called hurt or injury—by indicating that he can indeed work, earn money, and buy gifts. In doing so, he equates being able to give a gift and being "responsible" with having an able body that can work, "properly." He suggests that if he had a disability, he would not be able to work, declaring that he is not lazy. At stake in Invisible Man's protest is the question of whether he is disabled or able-bodied and whether he controls his subjectivity (feigned as the rapist and then as able-bodied) or Vevers does.

Through the character of Margaret Vevers, Ellison explores the larger white cultural fantasy that all African Americans are somehow disabled: Vevers is "hurt" and "injured," indicating that disability is somehow inherent to the Blackness constructed by normative culture—a racist and ableist standpoint indeed. At the same time, Ellison wants to find a critical moment or a disavowed set of knowledges within this flawed reasoning, asking if in it there could indeed be an axis of resistance that is overlooked by immediately denouncing the possibility that African Americans could have disabilities. How do we in fact account for African Americans with disabilities if their existence is erased or made impossible for a larger political project? Invisible Man could—and does—have a body with disabilities, but his quick reaction eliminates this possibility. Vevers suggests an alternate in a problematic world that lies at the intersection of gender, race, and disability—a world that Invisible Man himself contemplates.

Vevers evokes the long history of whites rendering African Americans as inflicted with a variety of disabilities, while Invisible Man begins to understand that he might just be "injured" from racism and that some African Americans might have bodies with disabilities and not just those projected onto the race at large. The terms "injured" and "hurt" each evoke a deficit model of disability that is highly problematic because it establishes able bodies as normative, while also relying on the language of the superior, the undeformed, and the pristine. In this way, disabled bodies are seen as lacking something, succumbing to a deficit model and the medical model of disability. These perspectives, according to Alison Kafer in *Feminist, Queer, Crip,* occur when a person "expects and assumes intervention but also cannot imagine or comprehend anything other than intervention" (27). Yet Ellison becomes a much more nuanced thinker about disability and one who critiques this sort of ableism in other discarded chapters as well.

Ellison explores the possibility that Invisible Man might have automatically dismissed a disability. One senses this in Vevers's first words, as when she hears Invisible Man's sad laughing: "'Well, well! But aren't we happy' she said quite musically. . . . What *we* did she mean?" Beyond the formal use of "we," Vevers immediately creates a bond between the two as she inserts herself into his psychic universe. The pronoun itself reveals Vevers uniting her white body with a disability along with his disabled Black body to create a sort of intimacy or collectivity. (While Invisible Man ponders that "we" might mean a commonality in terms of disability, he weakly rejects it by claiming the ability to work, and thus communicating that he is not disabled.) The setting of their meeting, too, reveals Ellison's larger project: "a regular little private garden of eden. We went past an apple tree."[16] The courtyard garden transforms into an Eden in which the two figures will create a new society. Eve, if citing the dominant story of creation, is brought to life from Adam: Vevers's disability is cut from Invisible Man's own disability. Ellison furthers this solidarity between the two because of their shared disability. When Invisible Man pushes Vevers out of the mansion complex down a busy hill and into a shopping district, there is no mistaking that the two are seen as a unified blur running-wheeling through the town. Their bodies become conjoined as he pushes the wheelchair at high speeds, which constitutes a way of exploring how the two might be linked via a broadly constructed representation of disability. Invisible Man even indulges in the fantasy by buying Vevers her favorite flowers—transforming his wad into a slightly romantic gesture. They appear to be getting along by this point because of some similarly perceived injury.

After accepting the flowers and Invisible Man's apology for essentially kidnapping Vevers, he understands her sympathy for the new Adam; he understands that she views him as one who embodies some sort of disability. He vehemently denounces this association, screaming at the top of his lungs, "Can't you see me? Do you think its no more than a crippled leg!!!"[17] It becomes apparent that Vevers has been viewing Invisible Man and his race—the "its"—as a "crippled leg." In trying to hone his understanding of the relationship between white forms of disability and the African American condition, Ellison struggles to solidify the nature of their socially fabricated bond. He writes the following line in three different ways to emphasize the assorted arrangements that could exist between race and disability:

> "You're no cripple and you know it," I yelled, "And you think you're like us. Why, we have to keep moving while you sit on your wheel chair. Getup from there!"[18]

and

> "You're not cripple and you know it," I yelled, "And you think you're one of us, while we have to keep moving and you sit on your wheel chair. Get up from there!"[19]

and

> "You think you're sharing our experience when you rest on your wheel chair and we have to keep moving! Get up from there!"[20]

With these statements, Ellison tries to theorize the relationship of white disability with the cultural myth that views African Americans as disabled merely because of race. The first example employs a simile, "like us," to preserve the differences between the two groups, but also to signal a refusal to make the two equivalent. The primary argument of the line reveals that the two systems of disability operate in a similar fashion and create subjects that also share qualities—albeit distinct ones. In the second example, Ellison seems to play with the idea that white disability, here Vevers's actual physical disability, falls into the same family of disability as the myth of race as disability. The two may not be equivalent, but they are part of each other and indicate some kinship: "You're one of us." The boundaries between race and disability in this formulation are porous and interchangeable. In the final example, Ellison goes a step further in his attempt to define race as the index value for trying to understanding disability. He writes that "you're sharing our experience" to indicate that Vevers (including her physical disability) attempts to appropriate or co-opt something that is essential to African American culture, namely, "our experience." By establishing that all disabilities are similar, Ellison exposes Vevers's belief that she can appropriate and experience Black disability because hers is already equivalent. In this way, Ellison reveals how race becomes inflected, policed, and constituted by the category of disability. To help explain this argument, I avail myself of Garland-Thomson's critique: his formulation of disability as one that encompasses many different bodies. Through this framework, Ellison might explain why two experiences could be viewed as similar given that the definition of disability encompasses both. Garland-Thomson reminds us that power structures have allocated different bodies into the larger category of "disabled"—a collapsing of differences that creates a false community that allows for false linkages that were nevertheless practiced in everyday life (see the Goodwill Industries and its construction of "handicaps"). Borrowing from this cultural phenomenon, Ellison exposes ableism as both an ideological category that collapses many differences and also one that reveals how African Americans, regardless of bodily experience, were considered part of the larger family thought constitutive of the disabled. In making this connection for readers, Ellison establishes the extent to which an intradisability conversation has been missed within Black studies. More poignant still is that African Americans with disabilities, as conjured within the aegis of disability, have produced disavowed knowledges about identity and the making of the self. This neglected conversation is what Ellison seeks to recover, seizing upon this project from the very beginning: from his early forays into what would become his magnum opus.

The various draft endings of "Wheelchair" span a number of directions and seem to negate much of Vevers's claims, yet all the endings seem to keep open Invisible Man's own understandings of Blackness as engaged in some sort of relationship to disability that is not authored by whiteness. Ellison contemplates the parameters of Black disability as defined by Black culture instead of by and in relationship to white disability. In the preceding dialogue, Invisible Man frames disability in a number of ways, but the ends of the sentences are all the same: he forces Vevers to get out of her wheelchair for her to walk. This ableist act, though, yields a surprising result: Vevers can indeed walk, which raises a number of consequences given this miracle. In two separate endings, Invisible Man sexualizes Vevers, and these gestures both distort the initial relationship of Adam and Eve and restore the normative sexual dynamic between white woman and hypersexual Black man. When she walks, Invisible Man's own words become erect: "'Oh woman; Woman; WOMAN!' I said amazed that she had walked, amazed at her womaness." With the neutralization of disability from race and gender, Invisible Man can now embody a more comfortable sociality with Vevers as the sexualizing Black male: he is more comfortable assuming a normative subject position. With Vevers now occupying an able body, she will not reiterate that African Americans are like her via a shared family of disabilities; this might be a success for Ellison, as his hero can now begin to define Black disability for himself and without the aid of white interlocutors. In another ending, one can almost hear him whistle as she regains the ability to walk: "I glared at her shapely legs. 'You're just a woman.'"[21] Without her disability, Vevers embodies merely gender. Much like her "womaness," Invisible Man emphasizes gender, because the intersection of gender, whiteness, and disability tended to make the latter hypervisible. He wants the same logic applied to himself as he not only catcalls at Vevers but also remakes himself into a heterosexual man appreciating a "WOMAN." This shift cloaks—or poorly changes the focus: that the entire chapter framed Invisible Man as disabled and returns him to the identity he had originally elicited: the predatory Black man instead of the Black man with a disability who is "legitimately," in Vevers's perspective, a man—an Adam who can mate with her. Miscegenation can be transgressed to the extent to which their shared abject positionality as disabled allows them to be equivalent. The rest of the chapter narrates his fleeing from the police just after they are alerted about Vevers's disappearance.

The final exchange between Vevers and Invisible Man remains consistent throughout the various drafts. As she regains the ability to walk, Vevers acknowledges her relationship to disability, claiming, "Perhaps I am a fraud. If so, I think I'll accept it gladly. But you. . . . When will you accept . . ."[22] The final clause that should contain "your handicap" cannot be spoken. The ellipsis mirrors the same ellipsis at the beginning of the story—again in a line that remains fairly unchanged beyond a few tense shifts: "We've hurt you badly . . ." In both instances, Vevers does not dare provide the perlocution that would performatively constitute a real disabled body, and instead Ellison burdens Invisible Man with defending the race from her assumptions and with contemplating how her unspoken words might be true somehow, how what she fails to say helps him uncover dispossessed knowledge about a marginalized portion of African Americans. Invisible Man must explore how African Americans with disabilities experience themselves and, in particular, how they construct identity categories at the margins and with limited input from white influences. In this journey, he must also sort through socially imposed experiences and representations of disability.

In fact, Ellison exposes two sources of ableism in *Invisible Man*: anti-Black racism and racial uplift. While Vevers illustrates the former, the Battle Royal scene, originally published separately in 1947 before the publication of the novel in 1952, explores the intersection of white able-bodied men exploiting young African American men for a night of revelry.[23] Unlike the encounter with Vevers, who offers a more indirect approach to aligning race and disability and proposing a new world crafted out of disability, the white men in the Battle Royal explicitly aim to make or enforce that African American men especially embody disability. While the historical record is clear on how whites policed Blacks to relegate them to a state of disability, the record fails to address how Blacks themselves, through the ideology of racial uplift and respectability politics, unwittingly participate in ableist ideologies. In the Battle Royal, Ellison critiques the uplift philosophy that Invisible Man mobilizes in his defense to prevent him from being cast as disabled. In a counterintuitive maneuver, Ellison also suggests that Invisible Man reconsider the valences associated with disability and how disability itself might be a productive route to understanding his experiences and identities. While Invisible Man rejects anti-Black racism's framing of African Americans as disabled, Ellison emphasizes that Invisible Man needs to recognize his own bodily differences. By giving representation to Black characters with disability—and showing the complexity of their lives from their own perspectives—Ellison provides a theory of Black disability that rejects the parameters of subjectivity. He lays bare that queer African Americans with disabilities have long followed Nella Larsen's call to self-abnegate and reject subjectivity—individuals that abound in his novel and whom no scholar to date has explored.

Histories of Disability

While metaphorical blindness by whites is the most striking instance of the novel's formulation of race, it may well surprise us to find that disability is present everywhere in *Invisible Man*. Ellison registers broader cultural trends in America that align African Americans with persons with disabilities. In the 1940s and 1950s, America experienced one facet of the effects of massive war efforts in their production of a huge number disabled bodies. During the Second World War, more than half of the soldiers injured suffered nonfatal wounds, leaving approximately 671,846 disabled veterans. Additionally, the war efforts at home produced nearly 8.5 million disabled workers.[24] After the war, the country underwent transformations not only in its physical geography and politics but also of its biopolitical landscape, which now included millions of citizens with disabilities. While Goodwill Industries (and other agencies) employed people with disabilities, more often than not, those with disabilities were deemed vagrants, as they were typically unemployed—probably due to discrimination, hostile workplace environments, or employers who offered no accommodations, as they were not legally mandated.

The term *disability,* as we now understand it, did not yet exist in Ellison's period, so he employed the language of "handicap" or "defective" and "invert" in keeping with the discourse of his historical context. That is, he used the term quite broadly across many forms of handicap, while he simultaneously specified conditions as they arose. Rather than try to map his matrix of what was considered a "handicap" in the broad sense of the term, I draw upon our understanding of the wider field of disability. One exception to this logic concerns my discussion of gay people, who, prior to the advent of modern queer identities, constituted the expression of a "mental handicap." Until the recent past, in fact, gay sexuality was thought of as a handicap or mental deficiency; so, apropos this history, I reference gay identities as a form of handicap in keeping with the historical context, even as I recognize the pitfalls of how "handicaps" play into the medical model of disability. Ellison reverses this logic by asking us what knowledges we have missed by thinking about people with disabilities as either handicapped or restricted because of this bodily difference.

The Goodwill Industries was late to the game of stigmatizing the disabled by way of national institutions, since the practice had begun much earlier in the nineteenth century with the "Ugly Laws." Cultural critic Susan Schweik uncovers how these Ugly Laws operated in the nineteenth and twentieth centuries, writing that in addition to removing disabled bodies from the streets, the laws immediately extended beggars into the category of the "disabled" or "handicapped." The 1867 law, initially aimed at disabled and able-bodied beggars, quickly spread to cities and states throughout the nation and took hold in the first half of the twentieth century. Chicago's revision of the law sought to remove "any person who is diseased, maimed, mutilated, or in any way deformed, so as to be an unsightly or disgusting object, or an improper person to be allowed in or on the streets . . . or public places in this city, shall not thereon expose himself to public view."[25] Besides focusing on persons with physical and intellectual disabilities, these Ugly Laws targeted and transformed beggars into the disabled, many of whom did in fact possess visible impairments. Schweik makes the linkage of how able-bodied beggars (males, females, and fairies; Black and white) were read as handicapped due to their co-contamination of the public sphere—their improper occupation of the street instead of places of work.[26] High unemployment rates among whites combined with the influx of African American beggars, job seekers, and street performers to urban centers during the Great Migrations reinvigorated the racist fantasy that African Americans must innately be handicapped; according to Schweik, "any black might be assigned unsightliness," and an increased representation as the unemployed or those engaged in street work further exacerbated this logic.[27]

Before the Ugly Laws, official records were used to distort and literally deform African Americans into people with disabilities. Michelle Jarman uncovered that in the 1840 census in Worchester, Massachusetts, the town of 151 residents recorded 133 insane Black paupers. There, she illustrates how anti-Black whites manipulated medical discourses and census data "to promote baseless connections between blackness and cognitive inferiority."[28] Clearly the history of conceptualizing African Americans as people with disabilities runs deep and wide in the American landscape and should not be thought of as a rarity or anomaly that appears in Ellison's work.

In 1948, Ralph Ellison visited the Lafargue Psychiatric Clinic in Harlem. In an essay pursuant to this visit, Ellison aimed to demonstrate that the intellectual disabilities of African Americans required immediate attention and that the clinic had "become in two years one of Harlem's most important institutions."[29] In a letter to Richard Wright, Ellison even explained his work on the clinic as "a piece . . . describing the social conditions of Harlem which make the clinic a necessity."[30] While in the clinic and in Harlem, he observed that the Great Migration—the massive influx of approximately four hundred thousand Southern African Americans to the urban North—created a great strain on African Americans. Ellison attributes African Americans' vulnerability to emotional stress and to psychic breakdown to anti-Black racism. He argues that "in the North he [the African American] surrenders and does not replace certain important supports to his personality." This occurs because "segregation and discrimination" both produce "Negroes that have no stable recognized place in society." Moreover, these intellectual disabilities arise no less in part because "the major energy of the imagination goes not into creating works of art, but to overcoming the frustrations of social discrimination."[31] His biographer Arnold Rampersad claims that "no single task honed more sharply Ralph's ability to depict Invisible's experience in Harlem and New York City" than his own experiences with the Lafargue Clinic.[32] Ellison's resulting familiarity with disabilities would subsequently help him give representation to those with disabilities.

In the United States, homosexuality was officially regarded as an intellectual disability until 1973. The American Psychiatric Association's *Diagnostic and Statistical Manual of Mental Disorders* removed it from its list of all mental diseases in that year. But the concept of homosexuality has a long and somewhat celebrated history in America. Historian George Chauncey has shown that the term *homosexual* did not exist in American English until around the 1930s to 1940s—the time when Ellison began writing *Invisible Man* and was domiciled in New York. Chauncey indicates that during this time, gay men were classified into numerous categories instead of merely under the umbrella category of "homosexual" deviant or "disabled" person. Gay men who behaved effeminately were commonly known as "fairies" or "inverts" and were popularly cast as an intermediate sex (a "third sex") between male and female. They were often associated with transvestism, but that designation did not entirely define them. Fairies usually performed a conventionally feminine role, yet they were sexually aggressive in soliciting men for sex. Fairies were attracted only to men and usually performed the passive sexual role. Men who behaved in a conventionally masculine manner but who had sex with fairies were grouped into two main categories at the time: "trade" and "wolves." The former were men who had sex with both women and fairies. Fairies were a legitimate and sometimes preferred substitute for female prostitutes. Often military men or immigrants would sleep with fairies because they viewed them as another sex—not as men—and they were thought to be sexually passive, like women of their imaginations. Wolves (also known as "husbands" or "normal"), on the other hand, acted in a masculine manner and slept exclusively with fairies or "punks." A punk, on the other hand, was "often neither homosexually interested nor effeminate, but was sometimes equated with women because of his youth and his subordination to the older man," the wolf. The wolf assumed the active position and seduced both fairies and punks. With the latter, wolves often provided "money, protection, or other forms of support."[33] These gay sexualities enter into the fabric of the novel and continue the articulation of disability as a means of evoking racial anxiety as inherently taboo.[34]

With this brief history of how race and disability intersect under different guises and within the same nomenclature, I want now to turn to the Battle Royal to point out the dialogue happening there between the two systems of ableism—anti-Black racism and racial uplift—and the enormous impact surplus jouissance has on our ability to read the scene, one that theorizes disability, race, gender, and sexuality. The scholarly accounts of *Invisible Man* have not addressed disability, and as I hope to demonstrate, this opening chapter of the novel—excluding the prologue—is replete with images of disability. And more important, I want to illustrate how our understanding of uplift serves as a vehicle for surplus jouissance, that is, one that obscures this salient thread by emphasizing the brutality of anti-Black racism, which misses how this system of power relies both on ableist rhetoric and white heteronormativity. In essence, scholars and readers have overlooked the centrality of disability in Ellison's masterpiece and his general critique of ableism and racial uplift. This misreading also obscures how Ellison seeks to represent the alternative epistemologies offered by African Americans with disabilities. This initial scene, I argue, frames the novel as one that seeks to recover the experiences of African Americans with disabilities and does not call for us to read, necessarily, for uplift and anti-Black racism's representation of disability.

Cripping the Battle Royal

The chronological narrative of *Invisible Man* begins with the terrifying Battle Royal, where the narrator partakes in a series of brutalizing and humiliating rites of initiation into the world of Black male adulthood. Ellison published the Battle Royal separately from the novel in 1947, and critics immediately recognized his brilliant portrayal of Jim Crow race relations, yet there was no mention of disabled bodies. Even today, the pugilism and the dancing blonde remain key images that overpower any reading of disability. The placement of the Battle Royal as the first episode of Invisible Man's adult life—in distinct contrast to him as a Black child—serves to introduce the main themes of the novel. Although easily eclipsed by the vivid imagery of trauma, Ellison rehearses his critique of ableism within anti-Black racism and uplift.

As Invisible Man prepares for the boxing match, the white men blindfold him and create the allegorical blind Black man—anticipating the arena speech and giving the reader a Black man blinded from a fixed fight while also alerting us to notice the insights of Reverend Homer Barbee, who offers an alternative ontology of Blackness not caught up in uplift. This fledgling blindness parallels the arrival of consciousness: "Blindfolded, I could no longer control my motions. I had no dignity."[35] Invisible Man registers the negative social and corporeal dimensions of disability at the same time that he learns that African American men—not boys—experience new forms of oppression. Foreshadowing Tod Clifton's demise as he sells dancing Sambo dolls, the boys themselves "dance" in the boxing ring, humiliating themselves for the entertainment and aggrandizement of whites. Forged from the image of Black street performers, the young Black men become disabled street performers (violently) hopping around for donations. Invisible Man does not launch an attack against the white men who blind and abuse him but rather develops (or reinforces) a desire to become able-bodied: "I wanted to see, to see more desperately than ever before." The violence against Black bodies and the conversion of Invisible Man from able-bodied to disabled trigger the pursuit of normalcy: for uplift and its compulsory able and female-desiring body. Only when he regains part of his sight—recovering an able body—does Invisible Man feel comfortable in the ring: "With my eye partly opened now there was not so much terror" (23). Feeling comfortable after discarding his disability, he proceeds to pummel his blind peers. Even affects seem to fall under the jurisdiction of able-bodiedness. Ellison codes the return of sight as a triumph and appears to legitimize a coming-of-age narrative that rejects disabled bodies; does disability inhibit the journey associated with a novel of education? The boxing ring sequence inaugurates Invisible Man's entrance into a world where Black masculinity signifies social and corporeal disabilities. Yet, at the same time, Ellison demonstrates how the other boxers take ownership of their blindness. For example, they all know to exit the ring at a prescribed time and to perform their blindness for a five dollar payment. In a scene of disidentification, for the Black men who do not subscribe to racial uplift, blindness functions not as a hindrance but as a strategy for survival. At the same time, their exploitation of disability produces financial gain and sustenance and fails to expose the ableism. Instead, their playing into the power structure, even with glimpses of subversion and survival, reinforces ableism and the need for uplift to lift up these poor men. In both cases, the reader is distracted, given surplus jouissance, in the form of a simple protest against the exploitation of Black men. The question of how they are exploited and transformed into disabled and blind beggars is overlooked by protest and the spectacle of the scene.

The next amusement for the evening, the electrified rug, casts the Black men as doubly disabled. The white men cover the rug with coins and bills and interject mendicancy discourses: "come on up here boys and get your money." The men are forced to beg for money just as the street beggar must obey the donor—one white man even uses the language of the disabled beggar that will reappear at the end of the novel to encourage Invisible Man to beg for the coins: "that's right, Sambo" (26). Upon reaching for the coins, the now begging men are violently and repeatedly electrocuted. With convulsing bodies, the image conjures up intellectually disabled men receiving electroshock therapy and foreshadows Invisible Man's electric lobotomy to cure him of his disabilities. Invisible Man attempts to defy the situation by crawling away and throwing a white man onto the rug. By switching places, he attempts to make the white man the beggar and intellectually disabled and himself able-bodied; he wants to occupy the normative position. In this scene, he relies on an uplift model of able-bodiedness to reject Blackness as a social disability. Here we notice how uplift tries to distance itself from the idea of African Americans as inherently disabled. By adopting "white" middle-class values, uplift also adopts its able-bodiedness and ableism. Invisible Man, subscribing to uplift, unlike his fighting partners, wants to return to an able body. Ellison wants his hero to stop fleeing from disability and to create an identity out of this experience, instead of negating it for uplift.

With the introduction of the blonde dancer, Ellison not only summons heterosexuality and the predatory Black male stereotype; he also queues gay desire as a sexual disability. Surrounded by bare-chested Black men, Invisible Man redirects his gaze from the spectacle of the nude blonde, not to the erections of the white men but to Tatlock's erotic body instead: "wearing dark red fighting trunks much too small to conceal the erection which projected from him." In contrast, when Invisible Man describes the sexual reaction of a white man, he relies on unflattering language: "drooling," fat, bald, "posture clumsy like that of an intoxicated panda," and with an "obscene grind[ing]" of hips (20). Invisible Man narrates the bodies of the Black men with trepidation and with positive remarks, thereby directing whatever homoerotic gaze upon their bodies. The white male body, even with its erections, serves for Invisible Man as a source of disgust; in an early disidentification, the white men might be able-bodied yet lack sexual appeal. From the positionality of a disabled gay man—even if he refuses to acknowledge it at this point in the novel—Invisible Man desires Black men and consequently begins to undo hegemonic readings of Blackness.

In the final scene of the Battle Royal, Invisible Man delivers a graduation speech—one in which Ellison reverses his protagonist's newfound disabilities. With blood filling his mouth, Invisible Man draws from Booker T. Washington's 1895 Atlanta Compromise speech. As the white men heckle him, he commits a parapraxis, spouting "social equality" rather than "social responsibility," thereby angering the audience. They retort, "we mean to do right by you, but you've got to know your place at all time" (31). In that instant, they require him to be in the right "place," as a disabled Black man, and he simultaneously tries to proclaim his allegiance to uplift—with social equality and responsibility—to contest the making of his disability. By moving toward one version of uplift rather than the other, Ellison confuses the reader to think that the various flavors of uplift are what is at stake. Instead, the focus on competing philosophies temporally erases gay desire, begging, blindness, and intellectual disabilities from the text. Invisible Man's conversion from a disabled Black boy into an able-bodied African American man usurps the narrative, and the critical moments emerging from the intersection of race, sexuality, and disability recede into the background. The surplus jouissance involved in performing uplift calms any sense of racial anxiety on his part, in this situation in particular, the embodiment of disability.

The Battle Royal forces the African American men to perform specific disabilities, and the white men do not distinguish between them; the larger condition of being disabled, regardless of the particular experience, enacts the coconstruction of disability, race, and gender. As a response, Ellison also ignores the differences between specific disabilities and asks what type of community and cultures African Americans with actual disabilities create. In a sense, Ellison answers Vevers's call for a new Eden based on disability but instead asks what critics have overlooked within Black disability itself as a critical apparatus and sociality. The world of Black disability operates with different values than the uplift worlds from which they are excluded, and Ellison need not invent but record. A major project in *Invisible Man,* then, is to excavate these dispossessed communities, practices, experiences, and characters so that Invisible Man can create bonds with them rather than trying to subscribe to modes of Black identity, racial uplift, and Black communism that continually performatively constitute him as able-bodied and heteronormative.

Disidentifying with Uplift's Philosophy and Methods

The normative reading of *Invisible Man* places the novel within the typical vein of the Bildungsroman, one in which the naive character learns the lessons of life, although in this context, within a particularly traumatic and racialized one. Critic Kenneth Burke compares the plot of *Invisible Man* to Johann Wolfgang von Goethe's *Wilhelm Meister's Apprenticeship,* the first Bildungsroman, and its unfolding does indeed bear a similarity to that prototypical example of the genre. The narrator leaves for college, gets expelled from school, migrates to the North, and undergoes a variety of "learning" experiences in New York. In the city, he literally blows himself up, starts a riot, becomes a national political figure, and eventually hibernates in the sewers of Manhattan. Valerie Smith claims that the narrator seeks "an appropriate identity," while John Wright interprets the quest for Bildung as a picaresque event. In each reading of the novel, no scholar has attended to the fact that nearly each major and minor African American character—save for Bledsoe—has a disability. Normative reading practices exclude disability because they are reading for anecdotes of racial uplift. The nexus of race and disability cannot occur in the context of uplift and the surplus jouissance it ushers into the novel. At the same time, the sexuality of Invisible Man is limited to his bad heterosexual encounters with white women. Alternative readings of gay life—not to mention the queer universes that openly exist in the draft chapters—cannot be represented or acknowledged. The critical scholarship has refused to tackle the queer identities within the novel and how they critique the heteronormative cultures with which Invisible Man is forced to align himself. Daniel Kim explores the white men's desires for the Black men at the Battle Royal, but even this reading theorizes the closet and looks past Black men loving other Black men.[36] Attributing this lack of inquiry amounts to challenging racial uplift and the methods of Black studies that are predicated on this philosophy.

I propose to apply the methods of queer failure and queer-of-color disidentification to the normative readings and narratives surrounding *Invisible Man,* including the concept of Blackness as apprehended by racial uplift philosophies. In particular, Invisible Man, to borrow from José Muñoz's framework in *Disidentification,* will revalue Black disability from a position of abjection into a fundamental, positive experience. To put it another way, Invisible Man assumes a "positionality that has been rendered unthinkable by the dominant culture."[37] By disidentifying with the heteronormative readings of the intersectional identities produced at the juncture of race, disability, sexuality, and age, we can celebrate the queer and disabled Black cultures and characters that have been erased from the historical record and effectively effaced from Ellison's project. By diverging from the expected reaction—uplift's demand that we say race and disability do not have a "real" relationship beyond anti-Black racism's successful attempt to make it impossible to extricate the two—Ellison can inquire about what other life might appear at these intersections of identity. Underneath the desire to keep disability invisible, Ellison finds, in the words of Judith Halberstam's *The Art of Queer Failure,* a world filled with queer "knowledges disqualified, rendered nonsensical or non-conceptual."[38] Furthermore, by retrieving these disqualified histories and experiences, Ellison honors African Americans with disabilities for their creativity, for their distancing from subjectivity, and for their production of Black culture; moreover, their supposedly abject voices and histories become visible by bringing their dispossessed histories to the forefront of the text (and by text, I mean the novel and its archived and excluded chapters and notes).

While African Americans with disabilities are not actually abandoned by mainstream Black society, Ellison highlights the consequences of silencing and excluding African Americans with disabilities from participating in the making of "Blackness." The forging of hegemonic Blackness arises from an elaborate system of power that operates both from anti-Black whites and heteronormative Blacks advocating uplift. And African Americans with disabilities primarily contribute by serving as the abject who reinforce the racist position of defining Blackness as the abject; they also serve as a cautionary tale to able-bodied African Americans who might question uplift. As a primary project, Ellison wants to illuminate the self-production of disabled African American communities and experiences, and as a secondary project, Ellison disidentifies with the assumed worthlessness of that culture from the perspective of uplift and anti-Black whites.

As I mentioned previously, a disability excludes an African American from being a subject as defined by racial uplift. To follow uplift requires an able body that can be seen in public spaces, in a good way, and able to work (or retain a job because there is so much discrimination against those with visible disabilities). Since most African Americans with disabilities cannot integrate into society at this time, they are excluded from it and the ideological protections guaranteed by uplift and its normative subjectivity. I am most concerned with how those excluded from uplift are also not granted deviant subjectivity. Ellison responds to this categorical judgment by complicating appropriations of Black culture and bodies.

If African Americans with disabilities are barred from Black subjectivity, then, as Ellison reveals, there is an opportunity not only for subversion but also for a different set of parameters for world building. Subjectivity, for example, does not hold as much sway over the shaping of African Americans with disabilities, and Ellison narrates their alternative mode of being. With limited appropriation of this form of Black culture and limited policing of these bodies—besides their exclusions from systems of privilege and not the forcing of their bodies into normativity—Ellison shows how these communities have, in Fred Moten's phrase, "non-value," suggesting that the abject create objects, such as culture, that are not recognized as such because they need not be reproduced to the likes of hegemonic powers.[39] Ellison represents this non-value culture that readers have missed and overlooked—not by way of complicated close readings or difficult excavations of Ellison's avant-garde aesthetics but by refusing to acknowledge that each Black character has a disability and alternate worlds. Unconscious ableist reading practices have trained generations of readers only to read the text through the optics of race—and, more recently, gender.

By bringing the methods of queer failure to bear on African American normative systems that define what counts as Black, Ellison asks what other forms of Blackness might be available outside of the strictures of racial uplift. When normative Blackness is made to queerly fail, what other histories can emerge? Ellison experiments with communism and reveals its problematic relationship to race while he also makes fail the worlds of Africana America assembled by advocates of racial uplift. If the membership to Blackness is expanded, what does it mean for Blackness and Black sociality to include persons with disabilities? Ellison does not seek some sort of reconciliation or the inclusion of African Americans with disabilities within the heteronormative matrix of Blackness. Instead, he pushes for a more radical project by asking what sort of Blackness and Black community have been created (not merely a quest for a utopia in the future) when we examine African Americans with disabilities.

Ellison uncovers a way of living that precludes, yet simultaneously includes, subjectivity. With a more diffuse and inconsistent enforcement of subjectivity upon bodies with disabilities, Ellison locates a Black existence without the imperative or chance to be individually bounded and obsessed with the self-organizing powers of the ideologies of self-determination and self-possession. African Americans with disabilities, as far as Ellison is concerned, create complex worlds in plain sight without being noticed, without being taken seriously. Long ignored in the public sphere and in the scholarly literature, African Americans with disabilities have been existing as Black queer flesh rather than as Black subjects per se. Invisible Man, for instance, keeps trying to don the mantle of Black subjectivity (via uplift and its nemesis Black Marxism). Ellison wants his character with disabilities to embrace his Black queer flesh and abandon his quest to become a normative or deviant subject. Thus Invisible Man's adoption of disability leads him to the main quest of the novel: the self-abnegation of his subjectivities if he is to join the world of flesh and disability.

While Larsen's Irene Redfield eventually becomes a self-without-subjectivity at the conclusion of the novel, Ellison's portrayal of this mode of being becomes typical for a subset of African Americans with disabilities. In particular, Ellison emphasizes how these characters inhabit the trickster figure to slip out of subjectivity. Recall that in African American folklore, the trickster is a figure that challenges and subverts oppressive systems from within. This subversion also includes the creation of a new way of living that is in direct defiance of the prohibition of agency, recognition, freedom, and world building. The trickster manages to do all of these. Ellison channels these attributes into his characters with disabilities—mostly Reverend Homer Barbee, Jim Trueblood, and Mary (from the originally conceived hospital episode). The outcome is a theory of Black disability and Black queer flesh: the problem is that normative reading practices skip over these subversive worlds. Most prominent, these trickster figures pretend to don subjectivities when in fact they have refused the entire enterprise.

Invisible Man, then, must learn from these characters with disabilities—must forge mimetic relationships—so that he, too, can inhabit Black queer flesh. They advocate not the making of subjectivity but self-abnegation that leads to the recovery of Black queer flesh. Ellison drops this hint early in the prologue (when the narrator has already become a trickster and talks to us as a self-without-subjectivity). In trying to articulate the quintessence of Blackness, a preacher during Invisible Man's descent into an alternative spacetime matrix delivers a text titled "Blackness of Blackness." The preacher tropes on the oft cited binary that "black is . . . an' black ain't" to offer an idea of the parameters of Black identity. A controversial moment ends the sermon when the preacher proclaims that "Black will make you . . . / Black." The second capitalized "Black" signals the proper noun and proper Blackness that is uplift. The preacher then advocates to his congregation "or black will un-make you," to which the congregation replies "Ain't it the truth, Lawd?" This church explodes as "a voice of trombone timbre screamed" and asks Invisible Man, "Is you ready to commit treason?" (10). The lowercase "black" requires treason against uplift and entails the unmaking of Black (uplift) subjectivity. The process of self-abnegation works against uplift and heteronormative forms of "Blackness." To arrive at the blackness of blackness, then, requires not just wading through normative Blackness but ablating it to recover dispossessed knowledges, practices, and histories that are recorded and lived by African Americans with disabilities who thrive in Black queer flesh. Ellison does not just provide the turnkey to understanding his project of self-abnegation at this juncture but prepares the reader for this key scene; in the prologue, he instructs the reader that "the end is in the beginning and lies far ahead" (6). In the prologue, we find Invisible Man as a self-without-subjectivities. It is only in chapter 1 that the Bildung portion of the novel begins and we gain a sense of the narrator. The narrator of the prologue does not convey much about himself, his desire, his hopes, his dreams; instead, Ellison narrates Invisible Man's daily activities and not the man himself because he has, at this point in the story, the near-end, slipped out of his subjectivity.

While Invisible Man will encounter many characters with disabilities and gain many opportunities for self-abnegation, he struggles down this nonnormative path. Surplus jouissance returns as a hindrance to the process of abnegation. When Black queer flesh does become readable by Invisible Man, surplus jouissance arises as the urge to feel heterosexual and able-bodied "normal." As such, Invisible Man returns to the typical Bildungsroman that involves building a subjectivity, not undoing it. In each episode, Invisible Man will begin a friendly engagement with a character with a disability, only to have the connection cut short. As Fred Moten observes, Invisible Man suffers from "the inability to linger and the rationalization of that inability."[40] Invisible Man needs time to forge mimetic relationships with the characters so as not to quickly replicate and dominate and commodify them through sameness. Lacking the ability to "linger," his own Black queer flesh cannot come out to play and to help him rupture his subjectivity. Only when Invisible Man lingers with Tod Clifton for about a third of the novel does Black queer flesh have a chance to unfold, while simultaneously precipitating the deterioration of subjectivity. In the following sections, I provide examples of Invisible Man's disidentification with subjectivity and his subsequent attempts at self-abnegation, until he finally achieves this by embracing his bodily differences.

Old School Lessons from the Infirm

While an explosion at Liberty Paints constitutes a memorable scene in the novel, I want to draw attention to Invisible Man's disgust toward the aging, decrepit, and disabled Lucius Brockway. As Invisible Man descends into the basement, he sees a short, "small, wiry and very natty" man with a head covered with "cottony white hair" (207). Lucius's withered old frame, his extreme Blackness amplified by the soot and grease, and his slavery-era hair repel Invisible Man: "I was so disgusted to find such a man in charge that I turned without a word and started back up the stairs" (208). Importing stereotypes from the Ugly Laws, Invisible Man socially constructs Lucius not as an Uncle Tom, as most critics simply assume, but as an African American male disabled by infirmity. Invisible Man details the contours of an infirm body, yet Lucius is old but not exactly impaired by age, because he has operated the boilers since the onset of the factory. Ellison even constructs Lucius's gauges as impaired to drive home his point; they fail to register the correct pressures; he operates by sound and not their readings, and this alerts us to the fact that Lucius might be a trickster. Lucius transforms the entire underworld of the factory into a space where only his old labor can be effective. His impairments—decrepitude of body, dark skin darkened further by layers of soot, and disabled labor—disrupt uplift ideologies of those who can work, while his running of the factory suggests an alternative mode of being within disability.

Lucius begins instructing Invisible Man about the advantages of being disabled—Invisible misses this, of course—by discussing his survival at the company: sole knowledge of the resin process. More important, Lucius cryptically reveals how to be Black during Jim Crow: "*we the machines inside the machine*" (217). The machines and boilers appear to do all the work, but it is Lucius's disabled body and mind that transform the resins into paint. The metaphor, again provided shortly thereafter, exceeds a critique of modernization. Evoking the imagery of a disabled body relying on a prosthetic device to function, pass, like an able body—such as a prosthetic leg or arm or, in Lucius's case, teeth and youth—Ellison represents Black disability as a source of knowledge residing within the appearance of Blackness. The image returns to the sermon in the prologue about the blackness of blackness. Uplift readings place Lucius in a die of disability as negative, while Lucius himself regards his infirmity as creating an entire underworld unnoticed and undecipherable by able-bodied Black (and white) people. Lucius points out that the quintessence of African Americans resides not in able bodies and their "good" labor but rather within Black disability.

After Invisible Man misses the point, Ellison proceeds to endow him with temporary disabilities during a fight with Lucius to make him realize the power within disability and to invoke his own disabilities, which he refuses to recognize. Invisible Man legitimates the violent fight because he views Lucius as disabled, surmising that he does not merit deference, protection, or sympathy like the elderly yet able-bodied African American men from his childhood. Invisible Man partially loses his sight during the fight: he can only see Lucius as a disfigured "black blur" (225). Furthermore, he cannot see Lucius's prosthetic teeth embedded in his shoulder, so he assumes that he has been stabbed. What is more, Invisible Man loses the ability to hear; Lucius's cries of surrender do not register until the precipice of Invisible Man's final punch, which dislodges Lucius's prosthetic teeth. When Invisible Man begins "feeling suddenly the older" and responsible for the disabled Lucius with a caved-in face, he wants to save Lucius. As temporarily disabled himself—his body generates a new way of knowing through being unable to hear and see and infirm—he can empathize with Lucius, but before lingering in the new positionality, the boilers explode, because Invisible Man fails to heed the advice of a disabled man.

While surplus jouissance from viewing Lucius as infirm and incapable of running the factory excites Invisible Man, he eventually works through this false pleasure supplied by ableism. After speaking with Lucius and building up some camaraderie, Invisible Man can begin to build a mimetic relationship with Lucius. He feels "the older" because he begins trying to imagine Lucius's body and the world he has created; he can embody disability and a new sense of Black queer flesh. Unfortunately, Invisible Man cannot linger in this space and has literally blown his chance at discovering a world forged by Black disability. He actually explodes and destroys this world. The lesson of the chapter: a disabled Black man survives, while Invisible Man, with his insistence on being able-bodied, lands him in a hospital psychiatric ward. At the end of the episode—or beginning of the next chapter—Invisible Man is transformed into a person with a mental illness. The white doctors seek to cure his cognitive disability (the assumption that African Americans are intellectually deformed) and thereby cure Blackness itself via the deficit model; even after an experimental lobotomy, Invisible Man refuses to acknowledge that whites view him as disabled and as one who requires medical cures.

This factory episode highlights the slippery slope Ellison takes when discussing disability. Disabilities can manifest as corporal, social, political, and sexual, and he places them on the same circuit board. He seems to make equivalent, for example, Lucius's infirmity and prosthetic teeth with Invisible Man's experimental lobotomy and temporary blindness. It does not matter that the decayed teeth impair speech in a much different way than infirmity affects the body. And that Lucius is read as infirm when he is not necessarily physically disabled by age does not matter to Ellison. Racism makes Lucius disabled: kept out of sight in the basement, he is made infirm by the white world—and Invisible Man. For Ellison, all of these manifestations of disability are in circulation, and all are wielded, indiscriminately, to oppress African Americans by whites and Blacks following uplift. It is this commonality that he exploits rather than a subscription to a hierarchy and separation of disabilities. Responding to power's wholesale grouping of disabilities into a strategic discourse to oppress African Americans, Ellison takes this essentializing categorization and reveals the multiple cultures it creates.

Stumbling in the Dark: "Blind as Bats"

As Invisible Man begins his initiation into the Brotherhood by adopting and reproducing their ideology, Ellison just as quickly rebuts this lineage of self-determination by transforming him into a blind person. The Harlem arena scene seems to give birth to fledgling blind Blacks—Invisible Man and Harlemites. As Invisible Man enters the locker room, he pauses by a dilapidated poster to discover that the arena played host to the creation of a blind African American athlete: "a popular fighter who had lost his sight in the ring. It must have been right here in this arena" (334). A fixed fight ends with the boxer going blind and living in a home for the disabled. This barely veiled foreshadowing announces Invisible Man's downfall within the Brotherhood, because his journey and identity have been predetermined—fixed—by racist attitudes. Invisible Man will fight with words in the arena, but he, too, must become blind and end up in a hole for the disabled.

Before unraveling the Black queer flesh within experiences of being blind, Ellison primes the reader by introducing two additional types of disability. First, Invisible Man encounters an unsightly and diseased unhoused Black man exhibiting syphilitic sores. Appropriately, the man lives in the shanty behind the arena, and Invisible Man imagines coming "up to the street only to beg money for food. . . . In my mind I saw him stretching out a hand from which the fingers had been eaten away." The imagery of the diseased, isolated, and disabled Black beggar rewrites Invisible Man's own resurfacing in the prologue as a person with a disability too; in alignment with the Ugly Laws, Ellison overlaps a sexual disability, unsightly disease, race, and mendicancy. Back at the arena, Ellison preps Invisible Man by introducing old age; as Invisible Man leaves the disabled and diseased beggar, he feels "very young and inexperienced and yet strangely old, with an oldness that watched and waited quietly within" (337). In this moment, Invisible Man recalls lessons from those disabled by infirmity: Lucius, Mary (from drafts), a blind man in the rain (from drafts), and the evicted couple, the Provos. The advanced years Invisible Man experiences conjures Black old age as disabled as well as folklore images of an ancient Black culture that remains resilient while being disabled. This feeling of "oldness" also recalls a series of budding mimetic relationships that have been removed from the novel. The draft chapters involving Mary and the wonders of her boarding house present her as an elderly African American woman. In those chapters, Invisible Man and Mary become much better friends, and he begins to listen to her advice—unlike in the published novel, where he tends to dismiss her and where Ellison renders her a flat character.

These two encounters—with the blind boxer and the beggar—help Invisible Man combat the uplift ideology he was about to espouse as a new spokesperson for the Brotherhood. Ellison wants him speaking from the positionality of disability and Black queer flesh before he reaches the stage; the Brotherhood needs him able-bodied and touting their virtues. On stage, Invisible Man returns to their normative position by persuading African Americans to ally with the Brotherhood. He advocates a new kind of subjectivity—the ideology and culture of the Brotherhood—that further suppresses Black culture in favor of communism. As indicated, though, Ellison combats this compulsory able-bodiedness by reactivating Invisible Man's disability in public. As he walks onto the stage, the spotlights blind him, and in two subsequent moments, "the light was so strong that I could no longer see the audience" (341) and "I couldn't see them [the audience]" (342). Invisible Man delivers his speech seeing only the blinding whiteness of the lights and no Black bodies—in essence, Blackness is being covered by whiteness like the coal covered by optic white paint. This imagery conjures both subjectivity's ideology and Marxism as white-influenced modes of Black existence. Ellison wants the model proposed by Lucius: mobilizing Black queer flesh.

During the speech, Invisible Man—speaking as if he were a blind man—disidentifies with normative ideas of being disabled and articulates Black disability as a source of strength and as an existing, vibrant culture.

He shouts, "They [whites] think we're blind—*un*-commonly blind. . . . They've dispossessed us each of one eye from the day we're born. . . . We're a nation of one-eyed mice." Ellison drives home the metaphor: "If we aren't careful, they'll slip up on our blind side and—*plop!*—out goes our last good eye and we're blind as bats!" (343). While the speech serves to indoctrinate African Americans into the Brotherhood, it also ensures their exclusion as disabled bodies. Invisible Man transforms an entire arena of, I will assume, mostly able-bodied Blacks into disabled bodies—disabled bodies that can escape the ideology of subjectivity. Unlike in his fight with Lucius, Invisible Man does not want the restoration of individual sight—no prosthetic glass eyes to make African Americans pass as able-bodied Bledsoes (Bledsoe being the only minor African American character that is able-bodied in the novel). The hegemony of the visual register, as the title of the novel gestures toward, seeks to define Blackness through sight, through the privilege of able bodies and the hermeneutics set forth by racial uplift. Instead, I would like to suggest a different way of reading the title as "Disabled Man." Invisible Man suggests that African Americans remain disabled to reestablish a sense of community—to end the myth of uplift as an individual process and its obsession with self-determination, self-possession, and self-formation. He advises the audience to join hands as blind people to create a new culture around a shared impairment, to reclaim Black history and live in Black queer flesh. Political action becomes a collective Black and disabled enterprise distinct from uplift and communism. By not advocating the restoration of sight and able bodies, Invisible Man draws from the political resources in Black disability, telling the audience, "Did you ever notice . . . how two totally blind men can get together and help one another along? . . . Let's get together, uncommon people" (344). Within the sociality created by Black disability—these "two totally blind men"—Invisible Man implores Blacks to stop fighting uplift and instead to embrace an already existing culture of Black disability. Ellison, then, sutures a heterogeneous Harlem by introducing the basis of community within the nexus of disabled Black bodies. Blindness becomes a powerful mode not of reclaiming Blackness as uplift but of relinquishing subjectivity to join each other in Black queer flesh. As soon as Invisible Man leaves the stage, and not ironically, as he simultaneously regains his sight, the Brotherhood strips him of this radical pedagogy of disability and reasserts the mask of uplift coterminous with sight and an able body.

While this example of Black disability might require a more subtle reading, in the draft version of the hospital scene, Ellison more explicitly expresses the role of disability in Invisible Man's life. After escaping the hospital and making his way to Mary's house for the first time, Invisible Man encounters an infirm blind man who asks for help crossing the street. Invisible Man fails to hear and see a car that nearly hits the couple—again temporarily becoming disabled, like in the fight with Lucius, or blind, like on the stage. The man does not get mad; instead, he kindly gives a good-bye, saying, "Well, a young fellow has to keep moving . . ."[41] Invisible Man mistakenly associates the phrase with his grandfather and Bledsoe, but he begins unraveling its message, unlike in the published novel, where the saying haunts him. Ellison embeds the lesson of self-reflection within the words of an elderly, blind, and African American man. The blind man calls upon Invisible Man to critically reflect on his life, to slow down and engage with the world to which he has access—Black disability—and not keep rushing after the Bildung of uplift, "to keep moving" after a false dream. Ellison confirms that this scenario marks a failed lesson to inhabit and embrace Black disability. In the next chapter, titled "At Mary's," Invisible Man returns the next day to find the blind man and to retrieve the missed lesson: "a blind man who seemed actually to have led *me* across the street."[42] He begins to acknowledge that alternative forms of knowledge and experience exist within Black disability—that Black disability allows one to see and hear differently—and when he misses it, Invisible Man retreats to the surplus jouissance offered by following racial uplift and communism.

The Insane Asylum

After visiting the Lafargue Psychiatric Clinic in Harlem, Ralph Ellison, along with photographer Gordon Parks, documented the dramatic rise in number of African Americans suffering from what would have been considered mental handicaps. Brother Tarp's phantom limp serves as a prime example in the novel of the physical manifestation of the conditions documented in "Harlem Is Nowhere." Ellison's resulting familiarity with psychological illness—figured as mental disabilities at the time—helps him imbue characters with the fortitude to suffer through the "'maze' of psychological dispossession" in the North.[43] He did not just visit the clinic with Gordon but also helped to found the clinic in 1946 with Richard Wright, Dr. Fredric Wertham, and others. As David Alworth notes, Ellison "spent considerable time at Lafargue in the 1940s" and thus was fully immersed in the psychiatric needs of the Black community in Harlem.[44] He embeds an alternative world of disability that is rooted in psychiatric disability with the insane veterans. The term *insane,* now derogatory, encompasses a wide spectrum of disabilities. During the writing of the novel, the term *insane,* however, could be used interchangeably with another now derogatory phrase: *mental handicap.* These categories encompass what we now consider intellectual, cognitive, learning, and psychiatric disabilities; acquired brain injuries; posttraumatic stress disorder; and mental disorders. Additionally, homosexuality, no longer considered a mental disorder, fell under the rubric of a mental handicap.

The veterans enter the novel as a collective form of public contamination, littering the streets with their unsightly and inconvenient bodies: "The disabled veterans . . . hobbling down the tracks on crutches and canes; sometimes pushing the legless, thighless one in a red wheelchair" (35). The reader must negotiate between psychiatric disability and orthopedic disabilities along with race and masculinity; the draft chapters also include a gay veteran among the crowd of veterans with disabilities. While the insane veterans are typically dismissed because they are believed to lack able-bodied minds and thus the ability to craft coherent subjectivities, Ellison complicates this reading by endowing Burnside with the residues of medical knowledge, and the reader begins to imagine him as a subject until encountering his disability. At that point, Ellison dramatizes how persons with disability are not considered to possess subjectivity but only illnesses. The former physician who now suffers from an unknown psychiatric disability appears to accurately assess and prescribe a remedy to the psychological maze forced upon African Americans. Burnside lectures that the social world has blunted the narrator's "humanity" and "emotions" to create a "mechanical man" (94). Ellison emphasizes that uplift nurtures the development of a Black subject that is a controlled, disposable, and mechanically reproducible Black "automaton." When Invisible Man does not make the connection that his subjectivity is not really unique but a reproduced commodity, Burnside adds an enigmatic statement rather than a clarification: he labels Invisible Man "a black amorphous thing" (95). He suggests Invisible Man abandon his mechanical self and become a text that resists writing, a blank Blackness without structure, namely, Black queer flesh. Finally, Burnside reiterates Lucius's advice: "Look beneath the surface . . . learn how it [racism] operates, learn how *you* operate" (153–54). The call to look beneath subjectivity and find Black queer flesh fails to register with Invisible Man because he writes off Burnside as disabled and thus lacking knowledge. Burnside, though, explicitly evokes that African Americans with disability exist as Black queer flesh, namely, "a black amorphous thing."

In draft versions and excised chapters, on the other hand, Burnside's philosophy of rising consciousness seems to have been attained by our hero early in the novel. At the Golden Day, Burnside introduces a conundrum that launches Invisible Man into a more critical mindset: "Perhaps our standard of measurement is in error. Perhaps somehow the men downstairs [the insane vets] have blundered into the fundamental reality and, recognizing it, have refused to leave it."[45] Ellison clearly lays out his project to celebrate the culture of African Americans with disabilities: the marker of insanity can catapult African Americans to a realm where Black queer flesh thrives. By being stripped of the option to organize themselves into and by subjectivity, the veterans reject the normative world and create their own. In the draft chapters, Invisible Man figures this out by engaging in a mimetic relationship with Burnside and heeds his advice to embrace his own disability. For instance, Invisible Man understands that the factory doctors view him as mentally and emotionally disabled because of the stereotypes associated with African Americans. In the published novel, Invisible Man resists being socially constructed as disabled as he is driven by the ideologies of uplift and communism. In another draft episode, Invisible Man wants to critique the Black bourgeoisie to Emerson, but hesitates: "I remembered the Vet's advice to learn the rules of the game," and he performs the nexus of Black disability for whites.[46] Finally, in an entirely excluded plotline, Invisible Man trains as a waiter under the tutelage of his queer uncle Charles. After watching Charles negotiate and manipulate white diners for bigger tips, Invisible Man recalls the more radical version of Burnside: "It was like the vet had said, I had lived and breathed and had understood or felt very little."[47] These alternative plots contain an already self-conscious hero who understands himself as an African American with a disability—a disability of feebleness and mental inferiority inflicted upon all African Americans through the Ugly Laws and stereotypes reproduced by anti-Black racism as well as a queer sexuality. In these earlier imaginings, Invisible Man wields his mentor's powerful skepticism and understands that his uncle camps up the fantasy that African Americans have intellectual disabilities and thus must beg for larger tips and handouts from whites. In these alternative worlds of Black disability, Invisible Man, his uncle, and the insane veterans exist on the same page of Black queer flesh. In this plotline, he embraces Burnside's lessons to accept his disability and to join in building and participating in an unseen universe of Black disability and Black queer flesh. In the published novel, on the contrary, Invisible Man refuses to believe a person with a psychiatric disability possesses wisdom—referring exclusively to Burnside as "insane"—or can orchestrate a viable life, let alone an entire world of people living without being organized by subjectivity. Instead, Ellison transforms the published novel into a series of encounters in which Invisible Man—and thus the reader—must be taught how to achieve this (archived) radical self-consciousness by embracing the Black queer flesh that flourishes within, through, and among African Americans with disabilities.

Punk Sexuality: Inviting Invisible Man to Step Out of the Closet

Disability, race, and queer studies scholars often overlook the multiple modes of being gay in the first half of the century. Though rarely discussed, Ralph Ellison was immersed in New York gay culture: two of his mentors, Langston Hughes and the sculptor Richmond Barthé, were closeted and openly gay, respectively. Ellison also worked and resided in the gay centers of the city: the West Village and Harlem (whose Faggots Balls were immensely popular). Ellison lived with Barthé in the former and at the Harlem YMCA, which historian George Chauncey in *Gay New York* traces as a hotbed of gay Black life (250). Ellison biographer Lawrence Jackson reports that a gay dean, the possible inspiration for Bledsoe, had sexually harassed Ellison at Tuskegee.[48] Ellison, according to Barbara Foley's intellectual history of *Invisible Man,* initially described Bledsoe as a "passive and feminine leader, who *is* homo."[49] Needless to say, Ellison operated in an intimate world filled with gays and lived with an openly gay man for a number of years.

In the larger cultural context, as I argued previously, homosexuality was regarded as a mental handicap until 1973 by the American Psychiatric Association. Beyond clinical definitions, the wider public from the late ninetieth century to the time of Ellison's arrival in New York viewed gays as infected with sexually transmitted diseases or with corrupt morals, at the very least. These gays were subject to public and criminal policing via the Ugly Laws' inclusion of not only visible disabilities but also invisible gay ugliness; the laws name "any person who is diseased, maimed, mutilated" as disabled. As Schweik points out in *Ugly Laws,* the laws would have directed their force upon gays who "flaunted" their deviant, diseased bodies. The Ugly Laws passed in Columbus, Ohio, Omaha, and New Orleans, for example, included "improper dress," such as public nudity and "wearing clothing of [the] opposite sex," as an indicator of disability.[50] In "Harlem Is Nowhere," for example, Ellison included a photograph of what appears to be a fairy in a princess gown as an example of a mental-sexual disability. During this period, as queer studies scholar Siobhan Somerville has also argued, "racial and sexual discourses converged in psychological models that understood 'unnatural' desire as perversion."[51] These "unnatural" queer desires existed when America understood there to be three sexes and many more forms of gay life.

Chauncey has written that the term *homosexual* did not exist in American English until around the 1930s to 1940s—the time when Ellison began conceptualizing and penning *Invisible Man.* As discussed earlier, before this time, gay men were classified into numerous categories instead of through the binary of homosexual–heterosexual. In his working notes, Ellison reveals his familiarity with these categories by characterizing the flamboyant Woodridge as "a disillusioned, *inverted,* cynical man."[52] These lost gay sexualities, the invert, and third sex, integral to Ellison's storytelling, help the reader to better understand our hero. I argue that Invisible Man is gay, more specifically, a punk.

Scholars such as Daniel Kim argue that there is a "latent homophobic logic" to the novel, while Douglas Steward in "The Illusions of Phallic Agency" restricts gay desire to white men desiring Black men.[53] Michael Hardin goes further by suggesting that Invisible Man and possibly Ralph Ellison himself are homosexuals in "Invisibility, Race, and Homoeroticism." Instead of speculating on Ellison's sexuality, my reading focuses on the disidentification with the social processes of racialization that attempt to label African Americans as possessing mental and sexual disabilities. Roderick Ferguson, for instance, argues in *Aberrations in Black* that Woodridge exemplifies that the "queer of color subject can both trace the workings of interpellation and inspire other subjects to defy its operation."[54] In this vein, I argue that queer characters and their disabilities "inspire" Invisible Man in defying uplift and his quest for subjectivity by embracing punk desire. To be more precise, Ellison allows Invisible Man to "linger" with gay characters and accomplish a mimetic relationship such that he achieves self-abnegation by exposure and attraction to Black queer flesh and its normative representation as racial anxiety. Besides a sexual interlude with a white female supporter of the Brotherhood, a brief and failed liaison with Cleo (a young boarder at Mary's who calls out Invisible Man as potentially gay), and a brief mention of a possible girlfriend at Tuskegee, contemporary compulsory heterosexuality demands us to account for Invisible Man's desire (or lack thereof) for women while also forcing us to refuse the evidence supporting his gay desires. We should reconsider the evidence from the archives and novel itself through the prism of the Ugly Laws and Chauncey's findings of gay life in New York to help us explore where Invisible Man directs his desire. The answer: Black and white men.

In an excised encounter with Woodridge, a literature professor at Tuskegee, Ellison continues introducing Invisible Man to an alternative world he can join, but this time from the point of view of a fairy. After the

Golden Day debacle, Invisible Man unconsciously stumbles into Woodridge's dormitory apartment and thinks, "I had always avoided his quarters" because of "certain rumours whispered about Woodridge." Invisible Man demeans Woodridge for being weak, yet finds himself seeking Woodridge's advice. His advice arrives in the form of a riddle: "If you belong to the lady of the races, isn't it all right to become a 'lady.' . . . A man is automatically a woman. . . . Why don't you ask yourself whether it is possible for the lady of the races to produce a man?" As Roderick Ferguson has shown, Woodridge offers a queer-of-color critique and disidentifies with Robert Park's social construction of Black masculinity as the "lady of the races." Furthermore, Woodridge plays into the sexual pervert by overexaggerating his perceived disability. With humor, he informs Invisible Man that he is neither "dangerous, wicked" and that "I don't really hurt little boys."[55] By adding the historical category of the fairy—a third sex and not a woman or man—and Invisible Man's punk identity to Ferguson's insights, Woodridge does more work than protesting and rewriting gay identities as positive. Woodridge transforms his perceived mental-sexual disability into a conduit for productive dispossession. He camps up how his supposedly diseased body strips him from being read as able-bodied, and as a consequence, he does not need to assimilate to subjectivity and cover up his knowledge of Black queer disability history and culture. For Ellison, Woodridge might be read as marginalized, geographically and socially, at the college, but he does not abide by the social conventions that should oppress him; he remains the only teacher on campus able to transmit the Black experience to students—via a disabled pedagogy.

At one point, Ellison reveals Woodridge's pedagogy as a transparent directive—but scratches it out for being, I assume, too direct and not educational. Woodridge chastises Invisible Man for unconsciously swallowing uplift: "You believe the stuff, *any* stuff." Reversing course, Woodridge conveys his pedagogy in more abstract terms: "All you need to deny it [uplift] is humanity, self-acceptance, which is what you need more than self-reliance." Woodridge dismisses the quest to find some authentic (white) American self and ethos from Ralph Waldo Emerson's treatise. Instead of learning to reject conformity to follow personal desires, as might be gleaned from Emerson, Woodridge calls for the self-acceptance of being male, Black, disabled, and a punk. Like the performance of Black disability by the other characters in the story, Invisible Man frames his relationships through identification rather than trying to learn about the other person and craft authentic, mimetic relationships. Invisible Man "believes the stuff, any stuff" taught by the "strong" heterosexual professors in lieu of building a queer sociality with Woodridge.[56] Ellison decides, for reasons I assume parallel his dismissal of Invisible Man's critical awareness that was forged through a bond with Burnside in the drafts, that Invisible Man cannot "linger" with Woodridge but only taste a glimmer of Woodridge's disidentification with heteronormativity and gender binaries. While Invisible Man misses the point of Woodridge's advice, Ellison keeps this plotline alive: a white wolf continues teaching Invisible Man about queer communities.

At first glance, the young Emerson functions as a stock figure adapted from the image of Carl Van Vechten or James Weldon Johnson's patron in *The Autobiography of an Ex-Colored Man* as the bored, wealthy wolf who helps struggling African American punks. Besides the overt sexual predation of the encounter, Ellison's rationale for creating Emerson reveals his hope that disability—as a cohesive yet diverse community—could enact political change. Initially, he imagined a white female secretary delivering Bledsoe's letter to Invisible Man out of a sense of pity but decided that a character with a similar disability would best relate to Invisible.[57] In his archived notes, he explains this rationale:

> Just as IVM enacts universal problems in terms of their relevance to Negro experience, I must have [a] white character obsessed with [the] same problems on a slightly different level; thus he will be a psychologically crippled white man . . . who is grappling with his personal flaws—which can be homosexuality, a stutter, physical ugliness, etc.—come[s] to identify himself with Negroes.[58]

Emerson, as "psychologically crippled" from diseased homosexuality, can speak with Invisible Man, a punk and "Negro," because they embody parallel (or shared) disabilities. Make no mistake, Ellison aligns queer sexuality as a form of disability—"psychologically crippled"—in this note. Emerson's main purpose is to jolt Invisible Man, as Ellison writes in his notes:

"Emerson is a messenger who brings news *which destroys* 'IM' changing him from believer into questioner."[59] Queer sociality should initiate Invisible Man into a new world of gay (disabled) life and should help him self-abnegate. Ellison needed a gay white man, according to the biography by Jackson, "who would move outside of at least some of the textures and patterns of normative behavior to help Invisible Man" accomplish this task (387).

Emerson approaches Invisible Man as if their relationship were that of wolf and punk. He protects Invisible Man from Bledsoe's wrath, offers financial stability as a valet-lover, checks out Invisible's sexy physique, and, lastly, arranges for a job at Liberty Paints. Emerson is not the only character expressing gay sexuality in the exchange; Invisible Man masters gay discourses and bodies. For instance, upon encountering Emerson in the published novel, Invisible notices Emerson as "the figure out of a collar ad: ruddy face with blond hair faultlessly in place, a tropical weave suit draped handsomely from his broad shoulders, his eyes gray and nervous behind clear-framed glasses" (180). The descriptions focus not only on Emerson's attractive body but also on his marks of handicap (from that era): the invisible gay nervousness that registers as defective speech. Next, as Invisible Man walks into the office with Emerson, who enjoys a view of Invisible's athletic backside, Invisible Man listens, "sounding the tone of his words for a sign" (182). Since Invisible Man believes Emerson to be a secretary, the sign Ellison evokes is gay desire and not some approval from a boss. Gay African Americans would commonly refer to being "in the life" as a passcode to verify safe spaces for gay bodies to come out. And Emerson unleashes a torrent of not-so-subtle signs of being in the life: Club Calamus (Walt Whitman's section of gay love in *Leaves of Grass*), *Totem and Taboo* (Freud and homosexuality), and phrases such as "but fellows like you" and "I'm afraid my father considers *me* one of the unspeakable" (both phrases reference coded language for queer).[60] Invisible Man finally acknowledges the signs given by Emerson. He asks Emerson, "What kind of man are you, anyway?" (189). This question asks if Emerson is in the life; is he a punk, wolf, trade, normal, fairy? Ellison repeats this same question when a white man propositions Invisible Man for sex in an alley (in the original hospital scene)—and it is Invisible Man's way of coming out of the closet to the reader in the know. Thus Invisible Man rejects white gay sexual advances while at the same time alerting the reader to his comprehension of gay culture.

This ability to read gay Black culture appears in the "Uncle Charles" chapter along with the Battle Royal and the Golden Day. In the latter episode, surplus jouissance works overtime trying to obscure and repress queer desires, particularly Invisible Man's lusting after Supercargo. As the attendant of the veterans, Supercargo has left the men alone to visit a prostitute, and in his absence, the men tear up the bar. Hearing the commotion, Supercargo emerges from a room of a prostitute and stands upon the balcony with Invisible Man looking up with hunger in his eyes: "I saw a huge black giant of a man, dressed only in white shorts, swaying on the stairs. It was Supercargo, the attendant. I hardly recognized him without his hard-starched white uniform" (82). Freud could not have summoned a better example of displacement: Supercargo's physicality and the "hard-starched" clothing betray Invisible's lustful gaze upon the throbbing, erect penis much as he glared at Tatlock's in the Battle Royal. Next, five vets charge Supercargo, and Invisible Man records, "I saw the giant bend and clutch the posts at the top of the stairs with both hands, bracing himself, his body gleaming bare in his white shorts" (82–83). In a final push down the stairs, "I saw Supercargo snap suddenly erect and grab his forehead, his face bathed in whiskey. . . . I saw him wave, rigid from his ankles upward" (83). The barely veiled sexual images hark back to the narrator's recent visit to Jim Trueblood. The descriptions of Supercargo present the erotic: his "giant" manliness, his "gleaming" bare skin, the question of what is underneath the white shorts, and his multiple body parts becoming erect. Supercargo's rigid members preoccupy Invisible Man's gaze.

While the imagery speaks for itself, I want to focus on the emergence of surplus jouissance in the form of a literary style that attempts to suppress the narrator's desire. Two competing styles overwhelm the scene: a sharp, crisp narrative of the veterans' attack juxtaposed with a naturalistic aesthetic with an erotic tone. The latter produces a feeling of passive calmness as the narrator articulates minor details of the story, such as "Supercargo got set to swing his leg again. It was a narrow stair and only one man could get up at a time. As fast as they rushed up, the giant kicked them back. He swung this leg, kicking them down" (83). Even though the narrator should be in complete anxiety because Mr. Norton, the white trustee of the college, sits at the center of this bar fight, the report reads as if the narrator has no concern about Mr. Norton. Instead, every movement must be recorded to hinder the reader with inconsequential information: essentially, Supercargo fell down the stairs. The meticulous attention to detail translates Invisible Man's sexual desire from eros to boredom. Invisible Man catalogs each movement of Supercargo's stiff or erect leg, posture, hands, head, face, ankles, feet, eyes, and ribs—everything but the erect penis that the shorts barely conceal. Early in the published novel, then, Ellison alerts the reader to gay desire but successfully diverts that reading. Surplus jouissance erupts as boredom.

This gay desire cannot remain legible for an extended period of time at this point in the novel. The heterosexual and insane Black men destroy the gay icon by cutting his body with beer bottles, dragging him down the stairs, and mutilating Supercargo's body.[61] A vet "aiming a shoe at the attendant's head . . . the flesh above his right eye jumped out as though it had been inflated. . . . Men were jumping upon Supercargo with both feet now and I felt such an excitement that I wanted to join them" (84). The narrator joins the heterosexual men in disfiguring the sexual beauty of Supercargo. Their brutal attacks ensure Supercargo's body will no longer excite gay lust by deforming the object of desire; Ellison even reveals that Black queer flesh is forced out of Supercargo's erotic body when the vets slash it open. The Black queer "flesh . . . jumped out" and remains floating in the atmosphere of chaos, and Invisible Man, while drawn to it, forces himself to look away by joining in the attack of Supercargo. The surplus jouissance afforded by compulsory heterosexuality helps Invisible Man reject an encounter with Black queer flesh. An alternative version of our hero depicts Ellison's denunciation of compulsory heterosexuality wherein his narrator is on the verge of becoming an openly gay protagonist.

The original hospital episode that appeared in 1963 as "Out of the Hospital and Under the Bar" reveals Ellison's intentions to construct a protagonist who is out. Instead of the paint factory explosion, Invisible enters the hospital from eating too much southern food. He also meets Mary, now an elderly orderly, who helps him escape his entombment in an experimental machine with unknown purposes. Besides constructing Mary as disabled due to infirmity and unable to bear children (due to cervical cancer), Invisible crafts a story—or recalls a memory—to convince Mary to aid in his escape: his false narrative involves fleeing the police after beating a white man who accosted him for sex. Supposedly a white man, carrying a loaf of bread, a microscope, and a bottle—all too easy phallic images—chases Invisible Man into an alley. The man performs an illocutionary act—one that Invisible Man repeats with Emerson in another gay encounter: "Look at me, black boy, what kind of man am I?"[62] Invisible fails to reply "a wolf" and utters only "a white man." Frustrated, the man rephrases the question: "But what *other* kind of man am I?" Again, Invisible Man stumbles, so the man reverses the game: "So I'm a white man, and what are you?" (254). The perlocutionary response should be Invisible confessing "punk." Since both men hold back the correct response, Ellison narrates gay desire by having the white man perform deviance and his disability: facial tics. These bodily gesticulations, similar to Emerson's nervousness and planned stuttering, and their messages of queerness as a disability, allow the man to approach Invisible. Within arm's length of Invisible, he resumes the discourse of the punk–wolf relationship: "You're supposed to do whatever I say. . . . I want you to stand still while I put this twenty-dollar bill in your pocket" (254–55). The roles for the sexual encounter become transparent, yet Invisible Man refuses the money and claims, "I didn't do anything to earn it." The man continues the sexual encounter: "You don't have to worry about that. That's my worry" and "You don't *have* to do anything, you know that" (255). After establishing that they are both "in the life," Invisible finally utters the correct response—"yes, sir, I know it"—and the wolf initiates the sexual encounter with a whisper: "It won't take but a minute" (256).

While Mary might be left in the dark about the sexual content of this conversation, Invisible describes in perfect detail an interracial sexual encounter between a Black punk who receives financial incentives and protection (refusing to out Invisible to the working-class men in the adjacent bar and getting money) from a white wolf. The series of questions about the type of man and the coy refusals turned acceptance signal not only Ellison's fluency in the discourses of gay life but also Invisible Man's desire to imagine being sexually touched (and penetrated) by a wolf. His medical treatments for his gay or Black disability seem to fit the context (versus the novel's lobotomy). Mary, though, assumes his Blackness as disability is what excites the white doctors in their experiments, as she has witnessed a number of African Americans being experimented upon.

The original hospital episode records Invisible Man's active participation in gay relations. Ellison reinforces that the sexual encounter was not simply a tall tale for Mary but rather an episode from Invisible Man's lived past. In two separate scenes from the archive, Ellison frames this punk–wolf narrative as a repressed memory rather than fiction. While telling Mary the story, Invisible was "suddenly gripped by a feeling that I was relating an actual happening, something that had occurred sometime, somewhere, in my past."[63] In one of three deleted episodes involving Mary's boardinghouse, titled "At Mary's," Invisible recalls the story again as a memory: "I started making it up but somehow it seems true though I don't remember when it happened."[64] The crafting of Invisible Man as an out punk character seems to permeate the archive, but it also, as I have shown, remains in the published novel. The shortcoming with these previous examples involves too short of an encounter with other gay men; Invisible Man lacks the ability to develop mimetic relationships in these fleeting situations. It is not until a friendship with a member of the Brotherhood that a true mimetic relationship can flower.

Queer Love and Mimesis: Tod Clifton

Invisible Man finally forges a prolonged queer friendship. Unlike his encounters with the Black young men in the Battle Royal, Supercargo, Uncle Charles, the man in the alley, and Emerson, Invisible cannot come to grips with his sexuality as it is a form of disability; he continues to insist on his able-bodiedness that drives his quest for some combination of uplift and communist subjectivity—but subjectivity nonetheless. With Tod Clifton, the story line shifts from repression to open punk desire: from able-bodied to disability. Tod enters the novel with a rush of sexual excitement launched by a sigh from a female and sustained by Invisible Man's long, erotic gaze, which I quote at length:

> I saw that he was very black and very handsome, and as he advanced mid-distance into the room, that he possessed the chiseled, black-marble features sometimes found on statues in northern museums and alive in southern towns in which the white offspring of house children and the black offspring of yard children bear names, feature and character traits as identical as the rifling of bullets fired from a common barrel. And now close up, leaning tall and relaxed, his arms outstretched stiffly upon the table, I saw the broad, taut span of his knuckles upon the dark grain of the wood, the muscular, sweatered arms, the curving line of the chest rising to the easy pulsing of his throat, to the square, smooth chin, and saw a small X-shaped patch of adhesive upon the subtly blended, velvet-over-stone, granite-over-bone, Afro-Anglo-Saxon contour of his cheek. (363)

Ripped from the pages of a Harlequin romance, the descriptions vacillate between a feminine and masculine binary beginning with a woman's gasp and then with Tod's ultra masculine "easy Negro stride." The descriptions appear to be filled with masculine objects—a statue, bullets, knuckles, stiffness, wood, stone, and granite—that grossly conjure an erect penis. At the same time, the description wavers between hard and rigid objects to soft and lush ones: shadow/light, Black/handsome, chiseled and marble/flesh, bullets/barrel, arms outstretched stiffly/sweatered, muscular/curving, and granite/velvet. The oscillation reflects not items in tension but rather a unity—the punk. When read through a punk lens, there is no repressed desire or confusion or binary: Invisible Man openly expresses sexual attraction. Only from a post-1940s perspective where the categories of heterosexual and homosexual have become standard binaries would this passage—and the novel as a whole—be read as repressed homosexual desire. On the contrary, the novel should be read as a queer text when we account for its historical production and the different ways of being gay that no longer exist and therefore are difficult to read.

The scene concludes with the narrator focused on the beauty of Tod's cheek and the "x," which serves not only as the stain of sexual desire but also a conduit to Black queer flesh. The x created by the bandages—the literal x that marks the spot—converges punk desire and race onto Tod

Clifton's body. The x mark draws our attention to the taboo and that which must be x-ed out if we follow uplift. The bandage marks not the healing of the body but gay desire embedded within Tod—just as desire marked Supercargo's body—and the possibility of Black queer flesh seeping out. In this first meeting, Ellison positions Tod and Invisible Man as potential lovers and friends.

Their queer bond blossoms as the two run around Harlem promoting the Brotherhood and doesn't end with Tod's murder. They fight Ras (and Marcus Garvey supporters) and spend their working and nonworking hours together. Invisible Man extends his queer care to Tod in an endearing example. He hangs the "After the Struggle: The Rainbow of America's Future" poster that features Tod right next to his desk. He also organizes Tod's funeral. By engaging in a mimetic relationship with Tod—both during and after the Brotherhood and in his death—Invisible Man can face racial anxiety and self-abnegate his heteronormative and uplift identities. He turns away from surplus jouissance and falls into anxiety.

After disappearing from the Brotherhood, Invisible Man finds Tod working the streets—he becomes triply disabled: queer, Black, and begging. Invisible Man witnesses Tod's death-by-cop and organizes a funeral march through the streets of Harlem to mourn his lost love object. He stays up for seventy-two hours organizing and delivering the memorial. Without losing consciousness for sleep, Invisible can remain connected to Tod without short-circuiting his gay sociality and love. The funeral isn't merely a political protest that Black lives matter or a refutation of the Brotherhood but a direct manifestation of his care and mourning for Tod. This love work enables Invisible Man to express and to accept a punk identity—along with his conscious and self-directed transformation into a character with a disability. As a consequence, he also places his subjectivity into a precarious position, risking its dissolution for unknown Black queer flesh.

By embodying his punk desire for an uninterrupted period, Invisible can discover what lies within the realm of Black disability: the lowercase Blackness advocated by the many Black characters with disabilities. For example, during the funeral march, an African American man marked as infirm, "worn, old, yellow face," leads the crowd in a slave sorrow song.

Under the surface of his disabled music, Invisible hears "the shattering stroke of my heart" (453). In the music that originates from an infirm man, Invisible feels gay love for Tod and seemingly rehearses a modern coming-out narrative: "I had known it too and had failed to release it out of a vague, nameless shame or fear." Following this transition from an able-bodied straight man to a punk and disabled body, the proud and out hero proceeds to deliver a public punk-Black-disabled eulogy. He begins with a description of his love object, Tod: "tall and some folks thought him handsome. And though he didn't believe it, I think he was" (455). Instead of reminiscing about Tod's work in Harlem, Invisible focuses on Tod's beautiful body (face, hair, lips, smile, eyes, hands, heart) in the first quarter of his address. While remembering the physical body begins the work of mourning, Invisible emphasizes Tod's leadership as a revolutionary African American in addition to his sexuality. In particular, he focuses his speech on the distortion of Blackness by racism—in this case, the white cop's racist beliefs manifested in killing Tod.

Invisible Man concludes the eulogy with a call to political action—a riot that metaphorically mirrors his internal upheaval. While Invisible feels betrayed by the Brotherhood for their refusal to mobilize into action against the police, Ellison alerts the reader to another call. Invisible suggests that Tod "forgot his history" and thus died because "he thought he was a man" (457). The repetition of the phrase a few lines later forges together the lost episodes with Woodridge, Emerson, and the white wolf in the alley. Applying the phrase to Tod immediately aligns him with gay sexuality. It also raises the question of Tod's failed identity making; he couldn't be a man—nor a "lady of the races"—under uplift or communist ideology. The latter pair enforce a compulsory able-bodied masculinity that must be distanced from Black disability; otherwise, it might give credence to African Americans with a disability. As Invisible Man eulogizes his lover as an individual—and not a sublimated martyr—he removes uplift's vision of African Americans as part of a monolithic enterprise. Invisible ceases understanding Black bodies as interchangeable and recognizes individual, disabled subjects: "and as I took one last look I saw not a crowd but the set faces of individual men and women" (459). His hegemonic participation in building automatons stops; speaking as an openly disabled Black punk disrupts the reproduction of the mask of uplift and communism and his alienation from Black queer flesh. When Invisible puts into practice his queerness, he does not end with a new Black identity but rather opens the door, for the first time, to crafting a new sense of being—one that he devises in the hidden world of Black disability and Black queer flesh.

Toward Black Queer Flesh

After the narrator's identification as a person with a disability, he accelerates his process of self-abnegation. Rejecting the surplus jouissance arising from the subjectivities policed by racial uplift and communism, he no longer needs to maintain the Black subjectivities to which he clung throughout the novel. While Ellison dedicates most of the novel to showing Invisible Man his disabilities and crafting mimetic relationships with African Americans with disabilities, the process of self-abnegation occurs in a fairly condensed episode, although the Tod Clifton section reveals the emergence of Black queer flesh, but not the full process of self-abnegation. After the narrator falls into the sewer, he burns his precious documents, which symbolizes the destruction of his subjectivities. The production of light from the burned documents plays with the notion that the light produced from the disintegration of these objects will lead the narrator to knowledge instead of simply illuminating the sewer. Each item represents a subjectivity that must be abnegated. But the journey of self-abnegation is not that tidy or easy. The narrator must also turn what Melanie Klein would call "good" objects into trash. Unlike calls for spontaneous rebirths, self-abnegation involves annihilating parts of the ego.

Before falling into the sewers, Invisible Man first self-abnegates his identities associated not only with the Brotherhood but with his mentor, Jack. Invisible Man taunts his mentor by renaming him the "Great White Father" and "Marse Jack." These insults infuriate Jack to the point where his prosthetic eye pops out onto the table. Jack, too, has a disability, and this enables Invisible Man to completely rethink their relationship. Jack, he thinks, wasn't possibly upholding the norms of able-bodiedness, and thus he wasn't performatively constituting Invisible Man as able-bodied throughout the novel. Instead, this false power dissipates for Invisible Man: "his left eye had collapsed, a line of raw redness showing where the lid refused to close, and his gaze had lost its command" (474). Without constraints on his ego, Invisible Man can now self-abnegate the identities nurtured by Jack: Jack gave Invisible Man a new name and literally provided instructions on how to become a new race leader. By acknowledging that he might have misread Jack, Invisible Man no longer adheres to this philosophy; that is, he self-abnegates his connection to communism and the ways that it reorganized his psyche. In abnegating this phenomenological apparatus, Invisible Man's Black queer flesh begins to take over.

A nonnormative perception of the world arises as he purges himself of a normative sense of self. For example, he thinks, "And now all past humiliations became precious parts of my experience. . . . I began to accept my past and, as I accepted it, I felt memories welling up within me. It was as though I'd learned suddenly to look around corners" (508). This moment is important not just because the narrator is learning to self-abnegate his able-bodied identities but because he learns how to interact within the world of Black disability and Black queer flesh—to look around corners—and become more comfortable with not having a subjectivity limited by the abilities of normative able-bodied vision. This new knowledge helps him manage his relationship with Mary.

One cold day, the narrator returns to his boarding room to find that Mary has placed a piggy bank in the form of a Sambo figure underneath his bed. In Mary's unending love, she gives the narrator the bank completely filled with coins so that he could feel better—even though her own bills are running behind. The narrator smashes the bank in a fit of rage and shoves the broken pieces and coins into the Battle Royal briefcase and flees Mary's boardinghouse. While he tries to transform Mary and her gift into rubbish, the novel prevents him. An old woman calls after the narrator to reclaim the briefcase he has thrown in her trash can (328). A few minutes later, a man on the street foils the narrator's second disposal of the bag by forcing him to reclaim it; he vows to dispose of the bag once he arrives at his new Brotherhood apartment.[65]

The briefcase and its contents reappear two hundred pages later, at the end of the narrator's journeys with the Brotherhood. Though he could leave the briefcase in his frantic rush to escape the Brotherhood, the narrator grabs it as he is rushing out to the Harlem riots (527). At the riots, he deposits all of his "good" objects into the briefcase: "remembering Mary's broken bank . . . I found myself opening the briefcase and dropping all my papers—my Brotherhood identification, the anonymous letter, along with Clifton's doll—into it" (540). With all of the chaos of the unrest, the narrator almost loses the briefcase three times and retrieves his good objects at any cost—even risking his life. After being nicked by a stray bullet, the narrator falls to the ground and loses the bag. Scofield, his new friend, hands it back to the narrator, who exclaims, "I seized it with sudden panic, as though something infinitely precious had almost been lost to me" (537). In the next scene, the narrator rushes back into a burning building to retrieve his briefcase (548). And finally, as two young white male rioters attempt to confiscate his briefcase, the narrator flees from them and falls into the sewer (565). The contents of the briefcase are not merely symbolic good objects but also objects that protect his life. In a fight with Ras, before falling into the underground, Invisible Man retrieves from the briefcase "Tarp's leg chain, and I slipped it over my knuckles" (559). After piercing Ras's cheek with the spear, the narrator "hit the first [of Ras's men] with Tarp's leg chain and the other in the middle with my briefcase." He then runs to Mary's house (560). Along the way, he hits another man with Tarp's chain. The leg chain and briefcase defend the narrator from harm, and Mary remains a figure and space of protection.

Before falling into the sewer, Invisible Man begins the process of self-abnegation, and, for context, this occurs right after Tod's funeral. As Ras's lynch mob approaches him, he feels that "I had no longer to run for or from the Jacks and the Emersons and the Bledsoes and Nortons, but only from their . . . refusal to recognize the beautiful absurdity of their American identity and mine" (559). He severs the connection to these men; they can no longer control his subjectivities because he self-abnegates them. In the underground, he continues his self-abnegations by torching his formerly good objects. He burns first his high school diploma (tied to ideas of uplift); then Tod's doll (his love for Tod and the Brotherhood); the slip of paper with his new name; Jack's warning letter; his Brotherhood identification card (the Brotherhood); and finally, all of his other formative papers. Ellison confirms this reading in an interview: "Before he could have some voice in his own destiny he had to discard these old identities and illusion; his enlightenment couldn't come until then. Once he recognizes the hole of darkness into which these papers put him, he has to burn them."[66] While this burning of the past metaphor is not an original argument, I submit that it is the culmination of the queer-of-color Bildungsroman and its journey of self-abnegation. As he destroys the papers, he also liquidates those subjectivities, but Ellison fails to mention what happens to Mary, as she is not in the pile of papers.[67]

The narrator transforms fluids into a representation of Mary as a means to confront and discard the parts of his subjectivity that she sutures. Unable to confront Mary directly, her influence must be purged via aesthetics. The novel hints that Mary should be read as fluids. As Invisible Man runs to Mary's house during the riot, spilled milk recalls her: "As I ran I was trying to get to Mary's. It was not a decision of thought but something I realized suddenly while running over puddles of milk in the black street, stopping to swing the heavy briefcase and the leg chain" (560). First, Mary is aligned with the other good objects and fluids. In this instance, the mother's spilled milk seems almost like a Freudian slip—or another attempt at surplus jouissance that helps calm Invisible Man's anxieties. Besides the crude combination of the Black street, milk, and fluid as representations of the maternal body, dark fluids, on the other hand, evoke the protection of Mary. For example, the narrator thinks "to Mary, I thought, to Mary" (561) after being struck by the police's water spray and then a little later in his flight, "I would go now to Mary's. . . . I moved off over the black water, floating, sighing . . . sleeping invisibly" (567). The latter occurs right before the narrator falls asleep for the first time in the sewer. Because he did not reach Mary's home, he dreams of visiting her. After he awakes and burns all of his good objects, he again dreams of Mary, but this time she appears only as the dark fluids: "*I lay a prisoner of a group consisting of Jack and Old Emerson and Bledsoe and Norton and Ras . . . and a number of others whom I failed to recognize, but all of whom has run me, who now pressed around me as I lay beside a river of black water*" (569, italics original).

In the dream, the aforementioned group literally castrates the narrator. They then throw his testicles onto a bridge: "*they took the two bloody blobs and cast them over the bridge*" (569). Mary is included in the cast of castrators via the black water. At the end of the dream, the narrator tells Jack that "*I'm not afraid now*" (570). Severed from his subjectivities, Invisible Man awakes from the dream and ends the narrative section of the novel, before the epilogue, by declaring, "And now I realized that I couldn't return to Mary's." Mary must have appeared in the dream—either as the black water or one of the unrecognizable figures—because the narrator declares, "I had been as invisible to Mary as I had been to the Brotherhood" (571). While most of the action seems to come from those who enforce identities on Invisible Man, he proclaims that "*I'll free myself*" right before they castrate him. In doing so, he self-abnegates as they dismiss him.

In the underground, Invisible Man has disidentified with subjectivity through self-abnegation. He embraces his disabilities and gains access to Black queer flesh. He exists as Black queer flesh and performs a self-without-subjectivity in the prologue and epilogue to speak with the reader. While critics such as Robert Stepto propose that Invisible Man is "ready to birth his form" and emerge from the underground, he assumes that a revised subjectivity is the goal.[68] Robert Callahan suggests that the act of writing will emancipate Invisible Man.[69] Both accounts do not consider that Invisible Man does not want another normative or deviant subjectivity and fail to consider that he is happy and content in a world of Black disability where he isn't pressured into transforming his Black queer flesh into something recognizable, something palpable. He enjoys being invisible in regard to lacking a subjectivity: he is just Black queer flesh that cannot be comprehended by those looking at him from the standpoint of subjectivity. As the last act of queer-of-color disidentification, Ellison transforms the title of the novel from being a negative condition into a state of absolute pleasure. While Stepto, Callahan, and countless scholars suggest that Invisible Man rejoins society, they are essentially asking that he reconstruct a better subjectivity. For Ellison, though, achieving Black queer flesh and embracing Black disability are the teloi of the novel. This new state of being might disturb the reader who needs subjectivity to redispossess Invisible Man of Black queer flesh, but instead, Ellison celebrates the refusal of Black queer flesh to be repurposed or reshaped by normative forces. Invisible Man begins and ends the novel as a body speaking through and of Black queer flesh, and he hopes that normative readers, after carefully reading for disability within the narrative, will at least temporarily leave subjectivity behind and join him, that they will descend into the world of Black queer flesh not just once but forever.

4 Social Protest and the Aesthetics of Flesh in Richard Wright

Book 3, "Fate," of *Native Son* begins with an absurd scenario: after an exhausting chase by a mob of eight thousand whites bent on capturing him for supposedly raping a white woman, Bigger Thomas awakens from a long sleep in his prison cell, but not before the melodramatic arrest atop an apartment building's water tower. In his narrow cell, he is greeted by his mother's preacher, the Reverend Hammond, who is followed by Jan, the liberal boyfriend of the woman he supposedly killed, who brings his friend, the Communist Party lawyer Max, along with him. As if the space could accommodate yet another person, the state's attorney Buckley joins them, accompanied by none other than the parents of the deceased Mary, Mr. and Mrs. Dalton. Soon after, Ms. Thomas arrives with her daughter, son, and Bigger's friends: Gus, Jack, and G.H. As the litany of personages suggests, this crowded scene prompted scholars to fault the novel's spatial relations and aesthetic system.

Undoubtedly, Richard Wright's decision to pack thirteen people—not to mention the cops—into a tiny cell shatters the novel's commitment to literary naturalism. Its absurdity notwithstanding, the scene provides a glimpse into the inner mechanics of Wright's philosophy on race and Bildung. The constellation of characters represents neither a narrative oversight on the author's part nor a mere statuary of those with emotional or political relations to Bigger. Instead, the moment anchors the central point of Wright's obsession with the quest of Black self-formation. Bigger struggles to achieve the consciousness, agency, self-possession, and self-determination promised by liberal humanism's subjectivity. Wright illustrates how the characters (and what they represent) in the cell ostensibly dictate and author Bigger's quest of self-formation. They negotiate how Bigger feels agency and self-determination, for example. Wright exposes, in his critique of oppressive subjectivity, how heterosexual African American males, of the working class especially, face a cacophony of voices and vectors of power that police their sense of self and self-determination, making it nearly impossible for them to act freely. The ruse of subjectivity, for Wright, is another way to dispossess African Americans by making themselves do the work of dispossession. Subscribing to subjectivity is the major conduit for power relations to exercise control over Black men. Bigger, for instance, tries to negotiate his mother's expectations for his identity—to provide responsibly for the family as a man—with Max's expectations to be an ethical subject who has been shaped by poverty. These two disparate ways of making the self cause a riff in Bigger's psyche and provide him with a narrative of "self"-determination. A similar case can be made for the others who join him in the cell: each represents power over Bigger's subjectivity, even though Bigger is the one reproducing subjectivity. With *Native Son,* therefore, Wright explodes the fantasy of a perfect journey of self-formation for African American males—pointing to the multiplicity of Bildung available to, and imposed upon, Black men, who are hardly an exercise in self-determination.

As a landmark treatise on the dispossession, social death, and incarceration that African American families endured while struggling to combat Jim Crow racism, *Native Son* revealed the dire consequences of organizing Black lives through subjectivity. Its boundedness and interior structure, along with the myth of agency, helps reinforce power structures and, more important, their ability to permeate and dictate Black bodies through the narrative of self-formation and self-possession. For the next twenty years, Wright sought ways not only to protest normative subjectivity and anti-Black racism but also to represent how African Americans have been—and have always been—successful in making deviant selves outside the confines of the normative. He, like his intellectual interlocutors Nella Larsen and Ralph Ellison, ask how queer African Americans subvert and dismantle subjectivity. In the last work published during his lifetime, the 1958 *The Long Dream,* I take up Wright's entry point into his theory of Black queer flesh and the liquidation of subjectivity.[1] After a long engagement with Existentialism, Wright returns to protest fiction after its absence from African American literature. His queer protagonist sets out on two journeys in the Deep South: self-formation along an axis of queer sexuality in the first third of the novel, followed by the self-abnegation of this subjectivity. What is more, Wright does not stop at self-abnegation. In the sequel to the novel, Fishbelly learns to live as and in Black queer flesh.

Locating *The Long Dream* in Queer African American Literature

While Bigger fantasizes that his prison stay shapes him "like a man reborn," his quick rebirth plays into the idea that an ephemeral declaration, and not the need to thoroughly engage in a rigorous account of rebirth, can change everything about him as a person.[2] Wright refuses to embrace these magical transformations that plagued so many turn-of-the-century African American novels, such as Francis Harper's *Iola Leroy.* Self-abnegation requires an extended engagement through mimesis and cannot manifest in a culminating moment of passion or insight; these would fall under the rubric of surplus jouissance. Unlike the enduring friendship of Clare and Irene or Toni Morrison's Nel and Sula, Black male friendships do not always have the luxury of being sustainable, and so finding an enduring partner for mimesis can be a difficult prospect indeed. Clare does die, and there is a long separation in *Sula* between the friends, but African American males seem destined to exist without sustained Black male friendships in fiction—from *The Autobiography of an Ex-Colored Man*'s Ex-Colored Man and *Their Eyes Were Watching God*'s Teacake to *The Dutchman*'s Clay and *Song of Solomon*'s Milkman. This lack of male–male bonds might be attributed to the inability of African American men to remain stationary due to lynching and murder, flight and escape, incarceration, unstable and migrant employment, and discrimination in public accommodations. Such circumstances constitute much of the social and psychic worlds of African American men, so much so that enduring friendships come at the cost of living. Wright attempts to repair these missing male bonds with a double Bildungsroman novel about a father and a son, relying on a nuclear, middle-class family structure missing from canonical Black literature.

In *The Long Dream,* Wright continues to wrestle with the question of Black subject formation in the context of Jim Crow America. *The Long Dream* was to be the first part of a planned trilogy tracing the journeys of Rex "Fishbelly" Tucker in Mississippi and France. The second unpublished manuscript is housed in the Beinecke Library at Yale University. Wright, it turns out, did not even begin work on the third novel. *The Long Dream* received mixed reviews when published. Most critics expressed a deep or partial skepticism that Wright, who had lived in France for the prior fourteen years, knew the then state of race relations in America. In 1958, the civil rights movement was in full swing, with the country passing such milestones as *Brown v. Board of Education* and the nation experiencing both the murder of Emmett Till and the Montgomery Bus Boycott. The novel slightly refracts Till's murder in the lynching of Chris and attempts to undertake Black incarceration through the imprisonment of Fishbelly, but on the whole, it does not directly register the civil rights movement. In part, this reception of the novel as insufficiently in step with the times is due to critics' conception that "race" fiction should be little more than sociological transcriptions of the relative present. Many in the Black community dubbed Wright a deserter, asserting that his abandonment effectively revoked his privilege to write about race.[3] Ted Poston of the *New York Post* opined that Wright "shows no awareness of what has happened to America—and even to Mississippi—during this decade."[4] His extensive writings on race during his "exile" years prove otherwise, as Keneth Kinnamon points out—Wright voraciously read the foreign newspapers and knew of the developments in his long-abandoned homeland.[5] Taking up the question of the Black nuclear family, especially its economic privilege and respectability politics that propelled the face of the formal civil rights movement, and questions of Black masculinity as well, were major issues within the Black community. These "internal" problems were not what critics wanted to promote nationally as central to the Black experience.

While any work is, necessarily, informed by its author and usually by some measure of historical context, novels are not universally judged by the extent of their address of contemporary problems. This might seem an obvious remark, but race literature did not have roots in the academy or in the wider cultural sphere, and authors were under tremendous pressure to provide barely fictionalized accounts of current politics. Even Ralph Ellison's masterpiece, *Invisible Man,* was initially hailed more for its racial commentary than for its aesthetic ingenuity. For Wright, then, setting the novel against the grain of social politics served another purpose. In utilizing the seemingly anachronistic setting of the 1930s and 1940s, Wright engages in a productive conversation with Nella Larsen, Zora Neal Hurston, and Ralph Ellison after years of artistic and political disputes. If, as my other chapters propose, insights into the writings of the latter authors crucially depend on "symptomatic" close readings to locate their philosophies of self-abnegation, in Wright's final novel, what might elsewhere be hidden or latent queer plots rise to the "surface." His return to his own protest style of fiction honed in the late 1930s and early 1940s after forays into existential writings abroad for longer than a decade also reveals the directness in which Wright sought to protest, to make explicit the complexity of heterosexual masculinity that had paralyzed African American men from taking psychic and violent action against the self and its subjectivity.

A reader of Wright would have been expected to know about the psychoanalytic concepts he deploys so that readers growing up in the first half of the century would be familiar enough with Freud to comprehend the overdetermined imagery of his last novel. To this end, Wright presents Fishbelly walking in on his father, Tyree, having sex with a prostitute and later describes Tyree's bodily motions as a train. Then throughout the novel, the train, its forceful motion, and rides on trains become transposed, in effect, condensed, to use Freud's terminology, onto a variety of objects or people to mark sexual desire or sex itself. Typically, dream imagery might require a symptomatic reading to parse the metaphors and metonyms, but because Wright defines the meaning of the train so clearly, little decoding—and good memory—is needed to unpack Fishbelly's unconscious sexual desires. In the episode, Fishbelly watches and records in great detail his father's body in motion while barely mentioning the woman. We do not even need psychoanalysis to tell us that he finds his father's naked body stimulating. Wright even titles the book such that we know to look at the dreams for meaning. Along with clearly mapping out and displaying the meanings of his images and symbols, Wright gives rise to the notion of a Black self-abnegation and the movement toward Black queer flesh. What critic Saunders Redding of the *New York Times Book Review* has called a plot of disconnected and socially irrelevant "episode after furibund episode" is to my mind Wright's making-conscious, making-surface, of the turbulent and evolving process of Black self-abnegation and the development of a Black queer aesthetic.[6]

For Wright, I argue, the queer-of-color journey encompasses a process of self-abnegation extremely different from that imagined by other artists—a process that reflects his preoccupation with psychoanalysis, Black masculinity, and the psyche as the main battleground for political protest. This double Bildungsroman, of Fishbelly and Tyree, explores two differing, yet not necessarily competing, paths of the self. Fishbelly liquidates subjectivity, whereas Tyree dies because he attempts to subvert and recast his normative subjectivity. Critic Abdul JanMohamed has argued that Tyree follows the trajectory of the "death-bound-subject."[7] This trajectory includes Tyree risking his physical life for a more symbolic death, which would impart to his existence a greater meaning. In the novel, Tyree moves from subverting white domination by acting as a submissive partner of white criminals to exchanging his physical life for a more significant and meaningful identity as a proud African American male not restricted to the purviews of anti-Black racism. Tyree dies in an act of defiance, disrupting these criminals' corruption-extortion scheme, and continues to fight whites even after his death through the knowledge of their corruption that he imparts to Fishbelly in the form of physical evidence. Tyree's elaborate journey does indeed end in self-destruction, much like Helga's in Nella Larsen's *Quicksand,* but here I highlight Wright's efforts to craft a different type of Bildung journey for Fishbelly.[8]

Unlike other protagonists—Helga of *Quicksand,* Clare and Irene of *Passing,* Invisible Man of *Invisible Man,* and Bigger of *Native Son*—Fishbelly's self-formation and self-abnegation processes are narrated from the young age of five into his full (de)maturation. Unlike young adult characters that are presented as having undergone a racialized mirror stage, Fishbelly's negotiation of the mirror stage is actually portrayed in the novel. The process of self-abnegation works alongside self-formation as we see Fishbelly grow up. Wright comments on how race, gender, class, sexuality, and queer Blackness form a turbulent constellation of forces influencing Fishbelly's psyche. Masculinity serves as the main axis by which Wright tackles the question of self-abnegation—first through its making and then through its unmaking. I undertake Fishbelly's reactions and internalization of Black masculinity in three manifestations (heterosexual, homosexual, and subservient) and white masculinity in some depth. Doing so enables me to trace the critical potential of Black queer flesh to reject these forms of maleness, which is the life-force behind self-abnegation. As such, heteronormativity for Fishbelly becomes an expression of surplus jouissance, which aids in his mobilization of the unrepression of queer desire and the rediscovery of Black queer flesh.

The story begins in Clintonville, Mississippi, with a five-year-old Rex Tucker and proceeds with stories of his youth. The narrative takes us through how Fish acquires a nickname ("Fishbelly" or "Fish," as if "Rex" does not immediately encounter Oedipus—but in this novel, it constitutes a desire to sleep with the same-sex parent); encounters the police and their threats of sexual violence; accosts a white woman at a carnival; experiences kinship and hate with a gay boy on the playground; witnesses the lynching of his love object; and finds himself arrested, when older, for refusing to obey a corrupt and white business partner. This latter event precipitates his movement from childhood into "manhood." His short-lived manhood includes the loss of his father, Tyree, the local undertaker and landowner of most of the Black Belt, and a prostitute girlfriend. The novel concludes with his incarceration. The first third of the novel delves into the making of queer subjectivity and desires that boil right under the surface, while the second deals with questions of heterosexual and bisexual masculinity. The third section reasserts a queer identity, but this time on a journey of self-abnegation. The chapter follows this division so as to trace how queer self-abnegation shadows an attempt to integrate into a heteronormative world.

Racialized Mirror Stage: The Self-Formation of Black Queer Masculinity

True to form, the novel begins with an episode that fulfills every expectation of a classical Bildungsroman opening: the protagonist moves from amorphous child to subject. Rex earns the nickname "Fishbelly" by mistakenly calling inflated fish bladders "bellies" in a slip of the tongue for which his friends tease him. Wright appears to be depicting an innocent rite of passage for a middle-class child. This same opening scene, however, recalibrates the mirror stage by questioning the role of Black women in the self-formation of African American men. Emma, Fishbelly's mother, rarely speaks in the novel, and when she does, Wright usually endows her with the language of commander and moral judge—like mother Thomas—or language that is easily dismissed because of misogynistic positionalities. She also typically inspires dread in Fishbelly. The first sentence of the novel places Emma as a judge: "he felt seized by a whirlpool of despair as his mother tucked the bedcovers about his shoulders." Then, "she vetoes the plea" to leave the lights on and seems inordinately exhausted merely by the act of putting Fishbelly—who, albeit, is a curious and active young boy—to bed (9). Answering his penultimate question with a sigh and an exasperated "yeah," Emma bears an unpleasant atmosphere—especially so in her answer to Fishbelly's final question before she leaves his room. "Mama, do fishes bite?" "If you fool enough to put your finger in his mouth, he'll bite you" (10). Her apparent disinterest and biting reply emanate from a tired mother worn thin by caretaking, yet Wright depicts Emma as a powerful parent. In the opening scene, we do not know that Emma suffers social marginalization within the Black community because her husband openly maintains an affair with a light-skinned, younger mistress; runs two workspaces of prostitution; and exploits African Americans who live in his tenement buildings. Emma bears these burdens of bolstering intraracial oppression enacted by her husband, but Fishbelly views her as the most powerful figure in his life—the giver and taker of life.

In a classic example of the Lacanian mirror stage, Emma castrates Fish and all men. After a night of debauchery that includes catching fish, Tyree asks Emma to clean and gut the fish. She disembowels the fish and discards the entrails. Fishbelly cowers, both amazed by and terrified of his mother's powerful ability to take life. Furthermore, she discards the internals of bodies, including the phallus. When Tyree returns to the kitchen, he reaches into the pile of entrails—the remainders of castration and female agency—and inflates a fish bladder. Amazed, Rex mirrors his father: "he puffed and the fish flesh began to distend . . . I blowed up the fish's belly!" (12). Tyree undoes the castration by the mother by creating life and strength from the castrato, from the entrails, and Fishbelly identifies with his actions (this identification is Lacan's imaginary phallus: males causing the phallus to revive or enlarge). Tyree displaces Emma from the mirror. His actions demonstrate that he can protect Fishbelly by reviving—and thus mastering—the world that has been disemboweled. While Wright narrates his own struggles with Black motherhood in his autobiography *Black Boy,* he has Fishbelly turn toward the father because Tyree does not just create life but creates life from discarded flesh: "he inflated the bladders as fast as his mother disemboweled the fishes" (12–13). When asked why he mistakenly calls the bladders bellies, Fishbelly fails to conjure a response, "but in his mind there was floating a dim image of Mrs. Brown who had had a baby and her belly had been big, big like these balloons" (13).

Wright explicitly links Tyree's and Fishbelly's actions not only with reviving discarded Black queer flesh but also with creating and producing Black bodies. Rex mistakes the fish bladder for a belly and thus creates a queer moniker, "Fishbelly," which continually haunts the text as the resignification of an alternative relationship to gender, sexuality, and flesh. With each utterance of the name, the reader—and Fishbelly himself—revives Black queer flesh. As the entrails and internals of the body, Black queer flesh animates itself in the form of Fish's body. No longer is Black queer flesh required to remain as a psychic drive; it is the body itself: it just needs reviving or rebirthing. A case in point, the belly reminds Fish of pregnancy, and he assumes this role; he fertilizes the egg and carries the baby. He is both man and woman. He assumes the body of a woman who can give birth to Black queer flesh and Tyree's male ability to restore it. Fishbelly will be mother and father. The inflated bladders thereby possess a further meaning, beyond their procreative, life-giving aspect. In revivifying them, Fishbelly displaces Black queer flesh from the circuit of the drive. In doing so, he encounters Black queer flesh as a process of developing and nurturing the Black body, but learning that making subjectivity out of Black queer flesh is misguided. In the latter part of the novel, Fishbelly must self-abnegate the subjectivities he constructed out of flesh. In the process of assembling subjectivity out of Black queer flesh, Wright showcases how queer desires contribute to Blackness. Through a series of sexually charged encounters, Wright reveals the making of Black queer masculinity as a derivative of the initial mirror relation oriented around the Black phallus and Black queer flesh. This journey includes interactions with four men: Chris, Ned, Tyree, and Aggie.

Along with Tyree, the primary object of desire for Fishbelly is Chris, a boy of about nine years his senior who also doubles as the neighborhood hero. He enters Fish's imagination as a role model and as a sexual object. In the initial chapter, as Fishbelly awaits the return of Tyree from his fishing trip, he dreams of Chris. The dream begins with Fishbelly striking a gigantic fish with his baseball bat but before he can swing the fish transforms into Chris. His fear of the fish turns into joy as Chris pitches Fishbelly a ball and pronounces, "*You only five years old, but you hit like a big-league player!*" (10). Then, Chris reverts into a fish, which pitches a ball that gets stuck in Fishbelly's mouth. At this point, the fish attempts to swallow Fishbelly, who still holds the ball in his mouth. The scene reveals a complex set of sexual desires for Chris. The white ball he, as the fish, pitches into Fishbelly's mouth takes on a variety of sexual metaphors (the ejaculation that sustains queer reproduction being the most obvious; Fishbelly is penetrated by Chris). Furthermore, Fishbelly "refuses" to dislodge this sexual gift from his mouth, to discontinue his fellatio of Chris. Additionally, the complement of the "big-league player" and Fish wielding a phallus onto Chris is almost too apparent. This dream before the castration also hints that Chris is the deflated phallus revived by Tyree and that Fishbelly takes his turn at "blowing" up Chris.

Chris returns in a later episode when Fishbelly finds a discarded condom along the road and converts it into a protective sheath for this imagined sword—that is, a broken broom handle among the cinder. He shows Chris, who tells Fishbelly and his friends to throw away the sword because "that rubber's been in a woman's 'bad' thing" (30). The condom-stick might be unhygienic, as it was found on the street, and Chris's statement reveals an odd position. Chris will eventually be lynched for his supposed ongoing relationship with a white woman (Wright composes this story after the lynching of Emmett Till), but calling the vagina "bad" seems to belie another message—that heteronormativity is indeed a "bad" thing. In his late teens by this point, Chris is past the adolescent stage of "hating" girls, actively flirting with young women. Wright could have arranged this sexual awakening of the boys in a different manner, yet he marks heterosexuality as potentially dangerous, one that is riddled with uncleanliness, as the boys run to wash their hands. This degradation of heterosexuality seems to keep open the doors for both homosocial and queer relations.

Before returning to the role of Chris as an object of queer desire, I want to reveal Fishbelly's abundance of queer sexuality during his childhood and how it shapes different forms of masculinity. While Chris represents a youthful Black queer masculinity, Fishbelly also finds himself within a world of adult homosociality or pedophilia. At age six, Fishbelly walks to his father's office and encounters white men for the first time. There, they are gambling, and one man, Ned, accosts Fishbelly with the intent of extracting some luck in the form of "virgin's blood" (16). He tells Fishbelly that "niggers are born with luck. You ain't shot no dice, so you got *all* your luck. I'm going to borrow some of it" (15). When Fishbelly wins for Ned, one of the losing players threatens to kill Fishbelly, but Ned intervenes—like Tyree, he interrupts what should be destroyed, ensuring life: "Touch this nigger and I'll kill you" (16). At this point, Ned transforms into a new man: "his protector shoved the attacker away," "his benefactor put a dollar bill into his hand," and commands the others, "don't hit 'im" (17). This conversion becomes more significant when Tyree tells Fishbelly that Ned's dollar, which Fishbelly claims he found, means that "a white man dropped it and you found it, so you got some of *his* luck" (19). This exchange of luck—which I want to read as "fuck"—is extremely sexual, even bordering on the pedophilic. Ned "defends" Fishbelly from terror just as Tyree protects Fishbelly from the mother. More important, Ned protects Fishbelly, not from an African American mother, but from the more vicious and fear-inducing white men. Tyree furthers the image of Ned as a positive role model cum father. He corrects Fishbelly's fear about Ned, asking, "What you say when somebody give you something?" While he is referring here to his own gift of another dollar to Fishbelly, Tyree replaces Fishbelly's fear of Ned's gift with a command to respect and genuflect to the benevolent white father who had just violated Fish. This exchange of luck/fuck and money highlights the commodification and sexual abuse of Fishbelly (and foreshadows Tyree's business of selling women's bodies). At the same time that he frames the encounter as an exchange of capital, Wright also stages it as a sexual exchange—Ned's spilling of Fishbelly's virgin blood.

Unlike the encounter with Ned's forcible extraction of sexuality, Fishbelly actively desires Black male bodies. A year after the Ned incident, Fishbelly refines his sexual desires. In a surprise visit to his father's office, Fishbelly catches Tyree in the act of intercourse with a female prostitute. The incident is traumatic for Fishbelly, yet he experiences a thrilling taboo at seeing the "outlines of his naked father" and not the Black woman. Once his father finishes, he realizes Fish is watching in the corner, and Fish focuses not on the woman but on Tyree's "naked, black body leap[ing] from the bed" (23). Fish also registers the sex through other senses: as noise, "*bumpbump bumpbump bumpbump*" (22); as perspiration and wetness: "a slither of dim light from the edge of the window shade revealed sliding sweat on his father's concentrated face" (23); as smell: "the room's fetid air"; and as the bodily fluid odors from the first chapter: "He smelled an odd odor and was whisked back through time to that morning when his father had brought home a pail of fishes" (24). As he watches Tyree climax, Fish "managed to swallow, then his choking tension found release in tears" (23). The sexual innuendos could not be more transparent: the swallowing of cum and Fishbelly "choking the chicken" until he releases his own ejaculation. In barely veiled imagery, Fish masturbates to his father's body in action. Instead of being traumatized by this second primal scene, Fishbelly experiences sexual pleasure through the body of his father.

The solidification of "straight" Black masculinity comes together in a similar fashion as that of white masculinity. Tyree cements Fish's indoctrination by making a pact, giving Fish some cash and masculine camaraderie organized around what seems to be repression and denial: "now, just you forgit what you *think* you saw or heard, see?" and "keep your mouth shut about this 'shop,' hear?" (26). While Fishbelly walks away from the encounter feeling a false pleasure deriving from "what was most important, [that] he shared a dark secret with his father," Wright also reveals a deep incorporation, not a repression, of seeing the father's erect penis and semen, and Fish's own masturbation. In the mode of what I have described as surface-writing, Wright recycles the "*bumpbump*" and Fishbelly's description of his father's sexual motions as a train image throughout the novel to signal Black queer desire.

Upon returning home from this traumatic-pleasurable encounter, Fishbelly is seen incorporating—not repressing—the sexual acts and desires for Tyree. "That awful scene in that dim room was being replaced by a hunger to get home and play with his electric trains. From that day on, thundering trains loomed in his dreams—hurtling, sleek, black monsters whose stack pipes belched gobs of serpentine smoke." The thinly veiled sexual imagery of copulation and ejaculation continues with more metaphors, or sublimations, of sex. That same night, Fishbelly dreams of controlling a "black beautiful locomotive" for the first time (27). This is an easy replaying of his first time masturbating, during which he remembers seeing his father engaged in sex. As Fishbelly mans the controls, "the locomotive began to throb . . . and then with increasing speed . . . it plunged forward bumpbump bumpbump bumpbump," and when the train goes too fast, he gets scared and screams "Papa! Papa!" Wright does not even attempt to make the reader perform a symptomatic reading; the hurtling trains are Tyree's bodily movements or Fishbelly's masturbating hands, and the stack pipes belching gobs of smoke are the penis being stimulated toward ejaculation. The call for the father seems to mark the literal and literary climax. There is just a hint of repression at work as the dream ends with him feeling "that he had done something terribly wrong." In the context of Jim Crow, Fishbelly's mild guilt barely renders queer knowledges dispossessed or disavowed. Wright ultimately, though, rejects narrating the conscious life of queer Black lives, but this queer desire resides just beneath the surface at the level of actual Black queer flesh. Childhood queer sexuality must be socially repressed as a racialized mirror stage concludes and a period of repression takes over. This interlude of enforced heterosexuality does not last very long for Fishbelly.

When Wright pens an openly queer character, homophobia and violence quickly descend. One day, as Fishbelly and his friends play baseball, Aggie, a local gay Black boy, asks them if he can join in the game. The boys quickly turn their psychic hostilities toward Aggie as he approaches them into verbal insults. They call him pansy, fruit, fairy, homo, sissy, spook, sonofabitch, and queer nigger (38–39). Aggie stands his ground, attempting to work through their insults as a kind of initiation—if he endures the insults, they might accept him. Unfortunately, their rampant hate turns violent as they proceed to beat Aggie by kicking, slapping, punching, and hitting him with a bat until he is "blood-drenched." Like a lynch mob, the boys are hardly satisfied with the brutal attack. With a rock, they seriously injure Aggie and "a sheet of blood gushed, flooding the back of Aggie's shirt, forming a red collar about his neck" (38). This episode reveals that an out queer Black life cannot survive and will be attacked to the point of near-lynching by other Blacks. Ultimately, the boys feel ashamed of their actions because they realize how much they resembled whites lynching Blacks—for no good reason besides hate. Their final reflection is that "mebbe he can't [change and be heterosexual]. . . . Mebbe it's like being black" (39). This flash of potential acceptance of Black gays will haunt Fishbelly for the entire novel and its sequel. He cannot come to terms with being queer, even though Wright does very little in the first third of the novel to hide Fishbelly's queer sexuality.

Wright continues working through Aggie and Fishbelly's relationship in another dream, and this time Wright paints an image of Black queer flesh battling subjectivity. As Fishbelly dreams, this time while sick with pneumonia, he imagines that his friend Tony steals his shirts and taunts Fishbelly with "Black sissy boy wearing white shirts." Fishbelly not only demands that Tony return the shirts with a "heartbrokenly" whimper but also admonishes Tony, "Don't you touch 'em!" The white shirts recall Aggie's white T-shirt saturated red with his blood. Fishbelly, too, possesses these white shirts, which symbolize his queerness. By telling Tony to not touch Aggie/the shirts, Fishbelly also tries to acknowledge his own sexuality. Furthermore, Black queer flesh is constantly stolen from Fishbelly, as it cannot be the object of desire: he wants Tony to stop stealing his queerness. If the T-shirts did not convince the reader of its symbolism, Wright continues the dream by recasting the same message with gruesome details. Flies land on Fishbelly's hands and arms, and he tries to swat them away; when this fails because the flies become "sunk into his flesh," he begins to scratch them away. "To his dismay, the skin of his hands and arms began to peel, shredding off in long, shriveled strips like black rubber, leaving his flesh a gleaming, raw red" (58). This condition of exposed flesh does not last long, as the flies return: "glued to his bloody, vulnerable flesh" (59). Fishbelly successfully removes his subjectivity qua skin and exposes his raw flesh; Black queer flesh can emerge and be recognized as the force driving him. The problem, as with the other novels in this study, is that Black subjectivity (as represented by skin) covers up, metaphorically, and suffocates Black queer flesh. Even as Fishbelly succeeds in a violent self-abnegation, subjectivity—as the flies—returns almost immediately to suture Black queer flesh back into heteronormative, Black subjectivity. As self-abnegation proceeds to let Fishbelly experience his queerness as a rawness—as something miraculously uncontaminated after years of being forced into something else—Black subjectivity recaptures Black queer flesh and remolds it; the escape, the encounter with Black queer flesh, can last only a moment and is experienced as racial anxiety.

Wright voices his disdain for this suffocation of Black queer flesh. When Fishbelly wakes from this dream, he attempts to grab some food from the stove—left to simmer by his mother as she attends church events. In his delirious state, he slips, "the right side of his neck falling squarely upon sweltering metal . . . a frying crackle as his neck, like a pork chop in a red-hot, ungreased skillet, stuck itself to the sizzling iron" (60). With just hours passed since the dream of the flies and Aggie's red collar, Fishbelly burns the flies and the Black subjectivities they represent from his body so that he can reexpose his Black queer flesh. The burning of the neck refers back to Aggie's red collar of blood, a known site of Black queerness. And Fishbelly seeks to dive deeper to recover, to free Black queer flesh by burning away the subjectivity covering it up. While Wright voids the episode of the language of desire, he reveals that the queer drive somehow directs the body. This horrific deskinning reflects Fishbelly's desperate need to untether subjectivity from flesh. Wright continues this theme of exposing Black queer flesh with the lynching of Fishbelly's fantasized sexual partner: Chris.

At age twelve, Fishbelly experiences his first major introduction to Jim Crow ethics. The whites of the town lynch Chris for supposedly having had sex with a white coworker at his hotel (62). Being from the most affluent African American family in Clintonville, Fishbelly "had never experienced obvious Jim Crow," and this lynching serves as his inculcation (68). As a local mortician, Tyree recovers Chris's body, and Dr. Bruce performs the autopsy with Fishbelly present. As Dr. Bruce slowly examines the mutilated body, Fishbelly watches in both horror and fascination. Chris has a neck with at least two breaks, no nose, no right ear, protruding intestines, severed and removed genitals, missing teeth, worn lips, destroyed cheeks, and abrasions from beatings, dragging, and being hanged. The lynching and Tyree's explanations of white hate and the prohibition of sex with white women confuse Fishbelly. Typical of this first third of the novel, titled "Daydreams and Nightdreams . . . ," Wright conveys the bulk of the argument during Fishbelly's wet dream that evening.

While in the previous analysis, Fishbelly tried to expose his own Black queer flesh via the stove, in the dream, he returns to his early childhood ability to be mother. After witnessing the Black queer flesh of Chris violently exposed and probed that evening, Fishbelly rewrites the exposé of Black queer flesh as him giving birth to it. Dreaming, Fishbelly sees a "*white clock with a white face and two white hands*" that watches his every move. This imagery does not require translation. Fishbelly finds a "*fish belly wet stinking crumpled with fuzzy hair*" at his mother's dressing table. Then, he hears a train approaching, and "*the locomotive's stack pipe touched the fish belly*" (82). The fish belly expands to the size of the room and nearly suffocates Fishbelly, until it bursts. Contained within the belly is Chris, naked, and profuse amounts of blood. The blood rises so high as to drown Fishbelly, and then he awakes from the dream. Throughout the dream, the white folks qua the clock say "*DON'T DON'T*" as they watch the events. As another recycled image, Wright revises the context of the fish belly—which, remember, is really a fish bladder—as a vehicle for Fishbelly to become pregnant and give birth. The fish belly is no longer smooth, as in chapter 1 of the novel, but has "fuzzy hair" that might be Chris's hair on his head or, more likely, a revised image of Chris's genital region. Chris was physically castrated, so all Fishbelly saw was pubic hair surrounding a Black space/hole. In this way, the hairy fish belly represents Chris's castrated genitals. Then, the womb—or Chris's genitals—inflates not through air but by the touch of the train's black stack pipe, which Wright had represented as a black penis. In the previous episodes, Tyree revived the disemboweled (castrated) fish and his son. Now, Fishbelly revives Chris because Fishbelly yields the phallus that restores psychic and sexual life to Chris; his penis is the locomotive stack that creates life in Chris's castrated genitals. Wright is very clear that Fishbelly's sexual behaviors, supported by the clues for sex—"thunderingly" and the thrice repeated rhythmic "HUMPFF HUMPFF" of Fishbelly's sexual acts (thrusts)—cause a pregnancy and the resulting rebirth of Chris. At the same time, the white folks monitoring this dream keep telling Fishbelly not to act upon his desires with their "Don't Don't." Fishbelly registers his guilt for this homosexuality via his drowning in the blood of queer creation. Alternatively, Fishbelly could be seen as the pregnant body giving birth to Chris and himself. The social stigma of homosexuality cannot be expressed in lived reality but only within dreams. By lynching Chris, Wright seems to deny homosexuality as a viable expression of Black masculinity.

At stake within this dream is not just the barring of homosexuality from socially acceptable configurations of Blackness. With the negation (and here I am explicitly distinguishing from self-abnegation) of Chris's living flesh and subjectivity, Wright offers Fishbelly the chance to relate to queer Blackness. The newly born Chris is not only Fishbelly's child but also a body without subjectivity—raw Black queer flesh. Fishbelly learns that he can make Black queer flesh through sexual avenues and not just by burning away his skin. With the psychic birth of Chris, Wright signals the possibility of a new sense of self with Fishbelly as a main driver. First, the exposed Chris is all Black queer flesh that is untainted by subjectivity. Fishbelly can touch and create a queer sociality around this flesh and not have to abnegate layers and layers of Black subjectivity to forge a queer sociality. The goal of making Black masculinity comes about only after achieving Black queer flesh and not adding or shifting the layers of

Black subjectivity already present within the ego and socially inscribed body. Second, Fishbelly begins to understand that he, himself, can make Black queer flesh by stripping away—psychically rather than physically—the ego and its attachments. Mastering self-abnegation, Fishbelly comes to understand the emergence of Black queer flesh. For the rest of the novel, Fishbelly will struggle with the self-abnegation of his subjectivities. Only in the sequel to the novel will Wright be able to record how Black queer flesh can transform into a queer Blackness that does not involve subjectivity.

After a three-year "mental paralysis," Fishbelly's life and the narrative resume. It seems that for three years Fish contemplates both Chris's lynching and the possibility of self-abnegation and the recovery or creation of Black queer flesh. In this time, I propose that Fishbelly has crafted a mimetic relationship with the dead Chris that appears in an unexpected fashion. After playing on private property, Fishbelly and a friend are arrested and placed into a police car. The cops stop at an outdoor fast-food restaurant where the waitress comes to the car. While stopped, Fishbelly realizes that he is in a similar predicament as Chris: restrained by whites with an unknown fate. Fish further aligns their two situations by glaring at the white waitress—knowing that his performance of miscegenation will evoke his lynching: "Fishbelly stared at the girl's white face, her pink cheeks, her ruby-red lips, and her sky-blue eye—and he remembered Chris" (110). While Fishbelly should be looking, like the narrator and cops, at her long bare legs in tight short-shorts or her bulging breasts barely held in place by only a "brassiere," he focuses on her as an expression of the threat of death and as a linkage to Chris. She could be read as the apex of a homosocial triangle that prevents Fishbelly from ravishing Chris, but Wright prevents us from forcing her to occupy that position; Fishbelly just evokes Chris. The cops yell at Fishbelly a number of times to stop looking at the waitress, and Fishbelly disobeys: "he looked at the policemen's weather-beaten face and then felt his eyes straying magnetically toward the girl." As might be expected, the cop jumps out of the front seat of his car and threatens to lynch Fishbelly: "Nigger, I'm going to *castrate* you!" (111). With his knife at Fish's crotch, Fishbelly faints, and the cops laugh with amusement. When he awakes in the back seat of the car, now headed back to the police station, he thinks first that he is not castrated and then immediately sees again "the vision of Chris's bloody, broken body inert upon the table." Again thinking of Chris, he remembers he has a picture of a white woman in his wallet that, if found, will get him into more trouble when he is searched at the station. Unable to throw the image out the window, he decides to swallow it. This image, however, is "that photograph that he had impulsively torn out of the newspaper in the toilet on the night that Chris had been killed" (113). Once at the police station, Fishbelly is made to faint twice more, and on the third try, he refuses to do so.

The most obvious reading of the fainting accounts for Fishbelly's intersectional identity as a wealthy African American male. He is read as more "feminine" because he occupies a more rarified class position that does not require him to work. And there is the urge to coddle Fishbelly because he is narrated as young as well as innocent and naive: he is not quite a "man" and can take on supposedly "feminine" traits like fainting and emotional "hysteria" (a favorite word of Wright's). A more historically accurate reading might emphasize the humanity of passing out before a major trauma, such as jumping to one's death or, as in the case of Jim Crow life, one's lynching. The cops threaten to castrate Fishbelly—and they easily could—so he passes out from overwhelming fear and anxiety. This reading seems more plausible as Fishbelly thinks of Chris. I would like to offer another reading that disidentifies with the notion of fainting as self-preservation to argue that fainting represents a queer failure.

The act of fainting can be read from multiple vantage points, and in Fishbelly's case, it adds another dimension to this identity: "delicate nigger" (115) and "sassy nigger" (117). Both adjectives, spoken by the white cops, seem to suggest a queering of "nigger" and evoke powerlessness in gay actions. I now return to the moment of fainting to see how Fishbelly situates himself. Upon the threat of death, "an enormous curtain of black appeared and dashed itself against Fishbelly's eyes," and he becomes unconscious (111). When he awakes, the first thing he remembers is Chris and the photo in his wallet from the night of the murder. As Wright has trained us as readers, the unconscious—achieved via dreams and now fainting—helps Fishbelly protect himself by allowing him to become closer to Black queer flesh. In this instance, the unnarrated moment appears to have evoked Chris's death—he is in the positionality of lynchee after all. He rises and does not just rid himself of a potential object that will definitely get him lynched in jail. The photo of the white lady has never been examined after that night as the narrator tells us that Fishbelly does not know there is a crossword puzzle on the back; the photo is a reminder of Chris and not an object of lust for the woman. In swallowing the photo, Fishbelly imagines that "it seemed as big as a baseball" (114). If we remember, Chris throws a baseball into Fishbelly's mouth in the opening scene of the novel and repeats the image of fellatio on Chris. Thus the first two episodes of fainting represent Fishbelly's strategy to become closer to queer knowledge and queer being. In the final episode, Fishbelly changes the meaning of fainting once again.

After obtaining safety through entering a queer space of nonconsciousness, Fishbelly does not need to keep returning. When the cops want him to reproduce the fainting for their supervisor, Fishbelly rejects the idea and fashions a portion of his ego into

> a deep, small core of detached hate; he felt that black curtain swooping toward him and could sense his legs, his feet, and his arms beginning to fade. He . . . continued staring at the tip of the knife blade pointing at his groin. He was ravaged by fear, but *coldly conscious.* (120, emphasis added)

Instead of becoming overwhelmed by anxiety, Fishbelly learns to redirect anxiety to fracture his ego and create a "core" of hate that he directs and binds to the white men. This piece of himself is quite specific, too. As he begins to feel the pull on this body—through the castration threat—Fishbelly understands that the cops are trying to control his Black queer flesh by making it appear (the faint) and by controlling his subjectivity (making him delicate and sassy—a vulgar gay identity). For both scenarios Fishbelly disrupts how whites maintain their control over his flesh. First, he stops the fainting so Black flesh is not forced to be encountered against its will. Second, Fishbelly avoids his Black queer flesh being turned into a campy, white notion of a gay identity; the label of gay as a derogatory term from heteronormative white cops is not the gay subjectivity Fishbelly is going for. Finally, the core of hate that he musters is not channeled solely at the cops but back on himself. He self-abnegates a piece of his ego, and that piece becomes the bundle of hate. Fishbelly proceeds to give the white men the gift of hate and establishes a sociality with them as one of hatred. In doing so, he has self-abnegated some part of his ego—in this case, the idea of white authority as benign. This is the first act of self-abnegation in the story, and we see that the mimetic relationship with Chris, even though he has been dead for three years, sustains Fishbelly.

Upon his release from jail the next day, Fishbelly commits the ultimate act of keeping Chris with him as a mimetic partner. While Chris can remain with Fishbelly at the level of the psyche, Wright drives home his idea of psychic togetherness. As Fishbelly walks home from jail, he finds an injured dog on the side of the road. The dog was hit by a car, and his back is broken. Fishbelly understands that he must put the dog out of its misery rather than leave him wounded: "if he did not kill the dog, it would lie here and suffer for hours in this brutal sun, dying of slow torture" (133). He tries to kill the dog but cannot do it. As the dog licks his hands, he finally gains the strength to commit the act. This scene becomes an avenue for Wright to represent Fishbelly's relationship to Chris: "the dog's dying associatively linked itself with another vivid dying and another far-off death: the lynched body of Chris" (134–35). Then, in a gory maneuver, Fishbelly disembowels the dog and removes each one of its organs. In dissecting the dog/Chris, he is "trying to detect some secret that it harbored." The dissection represents not only the autopsy of Chris but also the act "enthron[ing] it [death] in himself in the same manner in which he had swallowed the white woman's picture" (135). Fishbelly believes that his experiences with Chris's and the dog's deaths prepare him to face death at the hands of white men. Wright throws a wrench in this thought pattern, however, by aligning the ingestion of the girl's photo with the exploration of the dog/Chris's body. As mentioned previously, the swallowing of the photo buttresses Fishbelly's queer sociality with Chris maintained in the psyche. Re-creating the death of Chris aids Fishbelly in trying to reconfigure his object of desire, which has been barred from consciously desiring Chris and other Black men. The secret for which Fishbelly searches is not Chris's missing genitals from the lynching but Black queer flesh within the Black body. Moreover, Fishbelly attempts to swallow it, incorporate it—not death but Black queer flesh and gay desire—just like the girl's photo represents.

A Black queer subjectivity struggles to take root in this Bildungsroman because Black queer flesh remains in the realm of dreams and the unconscious and troubles subjectivity. Fishbelly's psychic apparatus might be drawn to Black queerness, but he cannot consciously "desire" it. He moves toward it as much as he can. In this way, Fishbelly literally advances toward queer bodies, trying to focus his attention and desires toward Black men, but the text must kill the two Black men who could potentially sustain queerness: Chris and Tyree. Queer desire becomes repressed and, must be, suppressed. The object of affection must conform to heteronormativity even as Black queer flesh begins to emerge. To distance Fishbelly and the reader from encounters of queer experiences, Wright employs a sophisticated network of surplus jouissance. Heteronormativity expressed as the desire for women and as Black and white masculinity seeks to reroute queerness into a more palatable practice.

Compulsive Heteronormativity as Surplus Jouissance

The next section of the novel, titled "Days and Nights . . . ," explores Fishbelly's supposed coming-of-age experiences. In particular, Wright sets out to inquire into the different styles of masculinity that Fishbelly can adopt, but all of them require heterosexuality. The goal of this section of the novel is to somehow erase—or repress—queerness by playing into the genre's requirements that Fishbelly grow up and leave behind his youthful innocence and follies, including flirting with queer desires. Gesturing to heterosexuality as the "natural" outcome for a young boy like Fishbelly minimally distracts the reader from Fishbelly's queer life. As a response to the threat of queer bonds in the first section of the novel, Wright turns to instances of surplus jouissance to prevent the queer from emerging. While critics too easily cast Wright as homophobic, I contend that he needs the surplus pleasure—the normative pleasure in this case—of heterosexuality so that Fishbelly can practice self-abnegation. For instance, Wright ushers in heterosexual cultures in such vulgar ways that Fishbelly can easily dismiss and reject them. By exercising self-abnegation so openly against heterosexuality, Wright engages in queer-of-color critique. After the liquidation of straightness, including its erotic objects, Fishbelly can return to a queer world.

Apropos of the Bildungsroman, the appropriate sexuality and adulthood seem coconstitutive, and Wright exploits this assumption. When Fishbelly leaves jail (during his first of two incarcerations), a white cop informs him of his leaving behind of childhood: "They made a man out of you today, didn't they, boy?" (121). The castration and knife at his groin for looking at a white woman inaugurate adult Black masculinity. That same evening, Tyree, his father, reinforces this turning point as he brings Fishbelly to Maud's house of prostitution so that Fishbelly can become a "man." Upon leaving the establishment, Tyree further indoctrinates Fishbelly into straight Black masculinity with a number of banal lessons. He espouses and performs two types of subjectivity: Black submissiveness and Black manliness. Both of these normative models exclude homosexual relationships.

Fishbelly mistakes his father as only embodying a castrated and submissive Black masculinity. In the episode of Chris's lynching, Fishbelly imagines his father as being weak and powerless for not fighting the lynch mob. Later, he views his father change his posture and speech in the presence of white men, and he interprets these performances as submission and "held toward his father a nameless hatred" (79). When Tyree tries to explain his shucking and jiving as "a white man always wants to see a black man either crying or grinning. I can't cry, ain't the crying type. So I grin and git anything I want," Fishbelly cannot understand why Blacks must put on some show for whites (142). This subversive dimension to Black masculinity does not register for Fishbelly largely because he has not had to interact with whites; his parents have kept him in the Black Belt and shielded him from interactions with whites. When Fishbelly does get arrested the first time, he processes the situation as if he were a "white" citizen being arrested for trespassing. The threat of castration and arresting minors merely for playing does not register to him as Jim Crow racism; his life away from whites has not prepared him for strategies of subversion, which he wouldn't have seen in this neighborhood. Thus, when Tyree tells

Fishbelly "that's the *key*. How the white folks look at you's everything," Fishbelly's double consciousness becomes heightened and more activated than ever before (148). Told to be an Uncle Tom, Fishbelly tries to accept this new subjectivity. He tests it out by collecting rent for his father and beholds himself to the renters so that he can get the rent; in the presence of whites, he keeps quiet and tries to manage his presentation of self. All at once, Tyree enacts another masculinity inflected by his class position.

As Tyree's new sidekick and protégé, Fishbelly masters a second mask—Black masculinity in the context of other African Americans. In the previous model, Fishbelly had to imagine himself as whites imagined him, as double consciousness. Even as he collected the rent monies, Fishbelly slipped into a submissive identity because that money included a kickback to corrupt whites—who ultimately have him thrown in jail. Tyree expresses a Black masculinity uncommon to others in the community: he performs the Black businessman. When Fishbelly mistakes his masculinity within an all-Black context, Tyree scolds him: "I'm black, but do you hear me whining about it? Hell, naw! I'm a *man*! I got a business, a home, property, money in the bank" (145). He claims to own over forty thousand dollars of rental property and can be a Black "man" "'cause I 'tend to my business and leave white folks alone" (72). As the wealthiest African American in town, Tyree commands much respect within and beyond the Black community. This pleasure of wealth and power infuses Fishbelly with a rarified Black masculinity based on a large net worth.

Those without access to wealth become marginalized in Fishbelly's mind. Aggie, for one, lacks employment because he is gay and is further ostracized from masculinity (198). Fishbelly classified everyone else "into two general groups: the 'independent niggers' and the 'dependent niggers'" (199). The latter embodied the submissive Blackness because they had to interact with whites most of their lives for their livelihoods. The former were businessmen like his father, farmers, or professionals with private practices. These men also held a unique vision of the world: the privilege to try to forget the white world. While Fishbelly does splurge at times to forget his woes and white racism, Tyree tethers heterosexual sex as a pathway to forgetting anti-Black racism and double consciousness to his style of Black masculinity.

Tyree prescribes the supposed sexual domination of Black women—light and dark skinned—as the ultimate manifestation of Black masculinity and surplus jouissance. When Tyree takes Fishbelly to Maud's workers, he aims to show him that heterosexual sex can help Black men forget about their oppression. As they leave the house, Tyree asks Fishbelly three times: "Tell me: you done forgot 'em, ain't you?"; "Ain't you done completely forgot 'em?" and "Ain't you done forgot 'em" (156). The sexual distraction should have made Fishbelly forget about the police and their state power because sexual pleasure functions as surplus jouissance. Tyree tells Fishbelly that he must pay to forget white oppression. Fishbelly adopts the idea that sex produces forgetting. He describes his relationship to women as "his need of them would be limited, localized, focused toward obtaining release, solace" (60). As a "gratuitous pleasure," sex with a woman (and here Wright is explicit about framing sex with prostitutes as different from marital or romantic sex) should nullify eruptions of Black consciousness and an awareness of desires beyond what is prescribed by heterosexual Black masculinity and racism's racialized mirror stage (84). The need to keep repression intact extends beyond the need to forget about racism. Wright also slips in that women who supposedly give sexual pleasure are also equal agents in sexual exploitation. While the men use the women's bodies to forget and reinforce their masculinities, the women ensure that surplus jouissance is the product delivered. In "seducing" and paying for sex, Fishbelly needs to feel in control—to feel his sexual domination—but Wright illustrates the falsity of this feeling: "Fishbelly was deluded into feeling that he was the aggressor" (154). The prostitutes understand the need to forget to be "a man," so they orchestrate the encounters as needed to supply the surplus jouissance. Even as Fishbelly tries to engage in a conversation with his lover-prostitute Gladys, she refuses to give her opinion on topics like race and the status of colorism because she knows her role is to sell surplus jouissance and not to stir up talk about racial oppression. She helps Fishbelly forget his problems and does not help him work through them.

Fishbelly, while enacting heterosexual domination and normative Black masculinity, seems at odds with his chase of Black queer flesh in the first third of the novel. As I hoped to convey, his "first essay into manhood" occurs after his incarceration and the need for surplus jouissance to forget this supposed "manhood" (152). To remain calm in the face of the threat of death and castration, all produced because of his queer attachments to Chris, Fishbelly must latch on to a normative system: heterosexuality. By citing all the conventions of heterosexual Black masculinity, Fishbelly believes that he is becoming a "stronger" person capable of living in a world that attacks Blacks. Just as women help protect him from racial consciousness, masculinity protects him from queer abjection. While both of these institutions can potentially supply endless amounts of surplus jouissance, they also contain internal critical moments that reveal their undoing, and these flaws spark Fishbelly's self-abnegation.

While playing a heterosexual, Fishbelly fails to take his father's advice that he not get too attached to one prostitute. He tries to "date" Gladys, an extremely light-skinned woman about whom Fish often wonders why she does not pass because she looks phenotypically white. On one hand, he, as the very dark prostitute Maybelle screams at him, "think[s] it's better'n mine just 'cause it looks *white,* but it ain't white. You 'shamed of your color! You goddamn *white-struck* black fools" (172). Colorism seems to attract him to Gladys, which is partly true, but not necessarily because white skin is better. On the other hand, he picks Gladys—even though Tyree has warned him that gradations in skin color make no quantitative difference in the constitution of Black women—as she helps activate Fish's need to bond with his repressed love object. Chris was lynched because of his relationship to a white woman, and Fishbelly tries to mimetically create a similar dynamic as a tactic to remember Chris and to better understand him. Rather than not draw attention to himself and embody the Black masculinity that requires supplication, Fishbelly tries to become not only "visible" but also recognizable by whites for dating Gladys. He decides that "*you are nothing because you are black, and proof of your being nothing is that if you touch a white woman, you'll be killed*" (157). Fishbelly tries to re-create Chris's life, including the threat of death; he tries to alter Chris's life by successfully transgressing the color line and assembling himself as a gay Black man, accomplishing both without dying. By purchasing Gladys's company, he imagines transgressing the social taboo without being lynched; he "satisfies" his desires even if only as a delusion—as another manifestation of surplus jouissance. Fishbelly does not replicate Chris's adventures to "get away with" what Chris got lynched for—it does not concern improving what Chris did. Rather, Fishbelly wants to disrupt the social logic that figures Black masculinity as dangerous and powerless. This project is also in evidence when Fishbelly faints and morphs queerness into power.

By rejecting Tyree's imperative to use women to forget about racism and its constant injunction to behave in a certain way or face death, Fishbelly remains in a heightened state of fear with Gladys. "The moment he had seen her . . . she was so white that he felt that he ought to be afraid of her" (170). With her Fishbelly wavers between forgetting and racial anxiety: "never had he known so much peace as with her, yet that peace was tinged with anxiety" (174). He vacillates between peace and anxiety but prefers the latter, as it brings him closer to Black queer flesh. For example, when they ride around town together and a white man pulls alongside their car, racial tensions arise because the man thinks Gladys is a white woman. While afraid, Fishbelly relishes in the threat of death. It helps him to self-abnegate his hold on the submissive thread of Black masculinity and heterosexual masculinity, which he represses in his desire for Chris. In another example, after sex, Fishbelly begins thinking about Chris as he gazes at Gladys: "It had been for a woman who had had the color of Gladys that Chris had been killed" (178). He contemplates Chris, and not Gladys, as a way of trying to align his sexual acts, not with Gladys, but with Chris. By rewriting the sexual scene with Chris, Fishbelly tries to move toward unrepressing queer desire. By occupying a similar position as Chris—death from associating with or having sex with a white woman—queer desires creep through the back door of consciousness. Moreover, Fishbelly learns that the threat of death—being with the "white" Gladys in public or in his psyche—evokes Black queer flesh by cutting through subjectivity. Straightness, for Fishbelly, queerly recovers gay desire.

Fishbelly's heterosexual world—or, better yet, his bisexual world—cannot last too long as surplus jouissance. In a dream after he has had sex with a woman for the first time, Fishbelly is again riding a black train, a black penis. This time he occupies the engine compartment and helps to drive the train, which thinly cloaks that he assumes the role of the top (or "man") in sex. Within the pile of coal, a white woman is buried, and she frightens Fishbelly. At the same time, the white engineer, a man, demands

"MORE COAL" six times from Fishbelly to fuel the metaphorical black penis (158). Wright presents white women as sources of anxiety and precarious desire, while the man remains vigilant in trying to stoke desire. He hounds Fishbelly to keep having sex with the white woman, but Wright also cues the reader into the temporal limitations of heterosexuality: the coal will eventually run out. Fishbelly can repress his queerness for a limited amount of time before there is no "more coal" to fuel a desire for women. And true to the dream, Wright kills Gladys in a fire. Just as Fish's queer object of desire must be killed, Chris, his heterosexual object—or rather the object of surplus jouissance—must perish in a brutal fashion. The minimal psychic attachment Fishbelly had to Gladys as a person quickly reveals itself. While the fire is being put out at the bar in which Gladys and forty-one other Blacks were caught, Fishbelly asks the chief of police if his undertaking establishment could take care of all the burials. Rather than mourn the loss of Gladys, he turns to making money: heterosexuality has run out of its surplus jouissance.

The last third of the novel concludes with the murder of Tyree at the hands of the white mayor and chief of police and Fishbelly's two-year incarceration. To avoid prosecution for the fire at the bar, which Tyree co-owns, he attempts to force his coconspirators, the two aforementioned white men, either to make the jury half Black or to pin the fire on another person. They refuse, and Tyree throws them under the bus: he sends evidence of their corruption to the county prosecutor; the evidence is stolen from the prosecutor as it is being delivered to the judge and grand jury. Next, the men have Tyree killed and incarcerate Fishbelly (for supposedly attacking a white woman with the intent of rape) until he gives up the remaining evidence against them. When he is finally released from jail, he flees to Paris. The last third of the novel sorts through Fishbelly's self-abnegation of his remaining identities: those associated with his masculinities.

Self-Abnegation and Releasing Black Queer Flesh

Throughout the novel, Fishbelly has scorned his father's (and mother's) seeming refusal to directly challenge whites, and he framed this reluctance or inability to stand up as subservient Black masculinity—often associated with poorer African Americans. While abhorring this standard, Fishbelly has also internalized it and lived by its codes. As Tyree is being killed and the world reframed from Fishbelly, the process of self-abnegation begins to churn. With the chief of police questioning Tyree about the evidence against him, Fishbelly reinterprets the act of shucking and jiving: "Tyree was masking his motives to mislead the white man. . . . He was making himself the semblance of compliance" (238). Now Fishbelly understands that Tyree performs inferiority because the "chief had been trying to see if the black men before him were subservient" (239). When Tyree informs Fishbelly that Black male subservience is mostly a subversive tactic to appease whites, Fishbelly begins to disintegrate the idea that Black men's performances of Uncle Toms are authentic citations of self. He understands the fluidity of Black performances to hold multiple meanings, and unlike a perlocution that sustains the white performance of Black masculinity as truth, Black performance is not bound to such speech acts. Thus Fishbelly internalized the wrong referent and the wrong Black masculinity; he activated the lens of double consciousness that viewed African Americans as inferior to whites. He must purge this subjectivity from himself. In the next episode, Fishbelly completes the self-abnegation when Tyree, shot and almost dead, provides Fishbelly the rosetta stone needed to understand submissive Black masculinity: "You see me crying and begging—well, that's a way of fighting" (259). With this knowledge, Fishbelly can extinguish his hold on subservient Black masculinity, as it exists in reality only for whites; as a Black man, this identity functions not as a subjectivity connected to the ego but as a performance for whites. With this knowledge, Fishbelly returns to the other form of masculinity that he more admired and questions its veracity and whether it, too, should remain as a subjectivity or be jettisoned. With the self-abnegation of subservient Black masculinity, Fishbelly can continue liquidating masculinities that stand counter to Black queer flesh.

Fishbelly questions the businessman, a privileged expression of Black masculinity. He had presumed that this identity would bring him success in the world, as it was associated with wealth, property, and access to different worlds beyond other African Americans. For example, he thought himself superior to the Black people from whom he collected rent every week and better than other men because he purchased an essentially white woman. Tyree ruptures these assumptions by informing Fishbelly that "there ain't no *low* niggers and *high* niggers" (253). While the intersection of class does affect expressions of Blackness, Tyree does not want Fishbelly to enforce that white hierarchy onto Black cultural production. Fishbelly begins to self-abnegate from this masculinity by noting the contradictions in it; he has been viewing this privileged Black masculinity from the perspective of whiteness, from his double consciousness. This white gaze imposes a hermeneutic that is not compatible with the Black culture espoused by Tyree. He elaborates on this point of view as one that is far from Black, explaining his actions to the prosecutor who is trying to help him convict the "corrupt" whites. The lawyer accuses Tyree of being corrupt, and Tyree in turn shoots back, "Don't call me corrupt when I live the only way I can live. . . . My kind of wrong is right; when you have to do wrong to live, wrong is right" (273). Unlike Bigger Thomas, who tries to claim that killing Mary defines him, Tyree rejects white morality and white frames of reference that define him. The notion of corruption presented by the prosecutor suggests a free will and subjectivity not available to Tyree or other African American men. He cannot ever act morally within the context of Jim Crow; moral behavior entails not only being subservient to whites but also attaching that species of masculinity to the self as authentic Black subjectivity. Tyree cannot contort his Black flesh into such a horrid sense of self. Fishbelly, on the other hand, has done just that; he has strangled his Black queer flesh into this specific shape of Black masculinity only to learn that it, too, expresses a falseness and that it is the importation of whiteness under the guise of Black masculinity. He learns that Tyree did not bond to this masculinity but instead wielded it as drag to navigate an anti-Black world. His flattening of hierarchies between low and high "niggers" reveals that he rejects this masculinity that is based on Fish's "independent niggers" logic. Fishbelly, again, self-abnegates his identity, as he realizes it is a performance of subversion by Black men. While Tyree might own property and accumulate wealth, these, he wants to suggest, do not constitute his Black flesh into a different insubstantiation of Black subjectivity or masculinity than anyone else's. His emphasis on shared origins in Black flesh reveals to Fishbelly the urgency of returning to his own Black queer flesh, and he accomplishes this through self-abnegating his heterosexual, masculine identities—a process he completes while in jail for two years.

Fishbelly has struggled with double consciousness. He often and almost always misunderstands Black culture and can't see from behind the veil: he can see only the world outside of the veil. He approaches Black life and culture through white optics, adopting the white gaze to view the Black world and himself, which drives his construction of Black masculinity—and his repression of queerness. During childhood, for instance, Black queer flesh seems to be the main hermeneutic and form of Black epistemology. Once double consciousness kicks into full gear, Black queer flesh falls away, and Fishbelly crafts a "white" identified masculinity alongside his two Black masculinities. Smuggled in as the naivety of a child, Wright reveals that Fishbelly identifies with white culture, specifically its ability to produce fear in African Americans. The most poignant moment of "bad" reflection occurs after Fish is released from jail the first time and he must rationalize why whites have power over him and how he can fix that problem: "That white world, then, threatened as much as it beckoned. . . . He was fatally in love with that white world, in love in a way that could never be cured" (158). Double consciousness, for Wright, could not be "cured" or purged from the Black psyche: as Du Bois theorized, the white world was always part and parcel of the Black psyche. Per Wright's mission, Fishbelly must tackle this white psychic intrusion and not just focus on the self-abnegation of Black masculinity. White masculinity as embodied by Black men must also be considered. The entire notion of liberal humanism's subjectivity—white, Black, or double consciousness—must be abnegated.

When Fishbelly feels ashamed of Black responses to racism, he makes a snide remark, valorizing whiteness over Blackness. During the lynching of Chris, both of his parents tell him to keep quiet and to keep the lights off so as not to alert the white lynch mob passing near their home. Fishbelly whispers, but he unconsciously lifts his hand to flip the light switch on—this as a reaction to his parents' overt demonstration of fear. While his "daring idea to switch on the light" fails, the fear that his father seems to possess drains "all the reverent awe he [Fishbelly] had once felt for his father" (69). Whites do not seem to be afraid, and their positionality of creating fear rather than feeling fear appeals to Fishbelly. At one point, he openly suggests that he embodies white masculinity: "he was really much whiter mentally than she [Gladys] was or ever could be, though she was whiter of skin than he" (207). Aroused by the confidence, the utter strength, inherent in white masculinity, Fishbelly embraces the white portion of his double consciousness. He is "whiter mentally" than the white-skinned Gladys. We should remember that his first encounter with a white man, Ned the gambler, also reappears: Ned is not afraid of his white peers. He defends Fishbelly from the other men's threats of death, an image of white masculinity that Wright recycles as not merely protective but as fearless amid violence and danger. Fishbelly indulges in this limited version of white masculinity that seems to operate without fear. Even as the white cops and corrupt politicians threaten Tyree and himself, Fishbelly still holds on to the ideals of white masculinity: the white men threaten Black men, and whiteness, from his perspective deep on the other side of double consciousness, remains king and remains fearless.

With his father dead, and having self-abnegated the Black masculinities available to him, Fishbelly must manage the whites who seek to put him into prison until he hands over the remaining evidence that could convict them. Without much wisdom under his belt, and just months after Tyree's death, the sixteen-year-old Fishbelly is framed for the attempted rape of a white woman. He sits in jail for two years. During this time, he does not do much besides complete his self-abnegations from Black masculinity. When he leaves jail, the only thing that remains in him is his attachment to Chris and his queerness—although both remain highly repressed—and his white masculinity. The latter, after all, had the power to kill his father and incarcerate him for two years without an actual trial or conviction. The day after his release, his mother and stepfather (she married Tyree's right-hand man while Fishbelly was in jail) try to speak with Fish. Understandably, he feels "helpless to do anything about it [being controlled by whites], he grew angry and ashamed." In trying to calm him, Jim, his stepfather, provides an eye-opening lesson that transforms his entire worldview: "the white folks think you're after them and they're scared" (344). Jim alerts Fishbelly that whites can be filled with fear, and this shatters his connection to white masculinity because it is not supposed to be afraid. This is not the first time Fish has heard this line; Tyree instructs Fish when he is fifteen that "white folks is scared to death of us!" That fear, though, will only come about "if they give us *half* a equal chance" (143). Tyree qualifies white fear as only occurring when equal rights—or half rights—enter the public sphere. For all of the critiques leveled at Wright for not understanding America's battle over civil rights, he seems to capture the fear running through white America, and more important, he provides a model for Black people who admire white culture to extricate themselves from the false power and attraction that whiteness might hold. With this qualifier about rights, Fishbelly can dismiss Tyree's claim and thus keep whiteness as a space that lacks fear, especially fear of African Americans. In Jim's formulation, on the other hand, whites are already scared because Fishbelly secures the upper hand. The roles invert, and whiteness becomes a space of fear. This new knowledge ruptures the surplus jouissance supplied by an identification with white masculinity. At this juncture, Fishbelly begins to self-abnegate his bonds to whiteness and its masculinity.

When the whites frame Fishbelly for the supposed intent to rape a white woman and he is sent to prison for two years, his world begins to collapse. He endures incarceration as a "rite of passage" that facilitates his becoming a Black man and, in the process, injects new meanings into punishment and solitude. The gesture is largely absent to "punish" and destroy Fishbelly. He witnessed the debacles that led to the murder of his father, his girlfriend burning to death in a club co-owned by his father, and the lynching of his queer love object. And long ago, he had distanced himself from his mother. Instead of allowing whites to distort and remake him into a criminal—this should evoke Irene's refusal to let Clare be remade by whites and thus the need for her death—Fishbelly disidentifies with the space of the prison and its impulse to strip him of his humanity into the act of self-abnegation that will lead him to Black queer flesh. In this way, he disidentifies with the carceral state and his own heterosexual subjectivities.

In his prison cell, Fishbelly is visited by the man who framed him and who desperately seeks the evidence that will convict him of corruption. Fishbelly refuses to give up the evidence and instead halts the progress of the novel and of his formation. First, he suggests to the man, "Awright, kill me," in response to his pursuit of evidence. Fishbelly has achieved what critic Abdul JanMohamed calls a "symbolic death," whereby Fishbelly no longer responds to the threat of death; he accepts this threat and his imminent death for disobeying whites.[9] He accepts the exchange of his incarcerated, bare life for the pleasure of refusing white control of his body. From this psychic standpoint, he discontinues his life. As the narrator continues, a second "stopping" of the narrative—or of subjectivity—comes into focus. At this juncture, remember that Fishbelly has self-abnegated both of these Black masculinities, most of his white masculinity, and the class privilege he occupies. The major remaining "faux" subjectivity is his socially defined bisexuality, but it is trapped within the cycle of the psychic drive and not of the ego (save that repressed bond with Chris). Fishbelly returns to the realm of the queer—to the unconscious: "he felt himself sinking into a cold numbness into which human voices could not penetrate. He did not wish to speak ever again, to look with his eyes again, to listen again." Then he "partially blacked out" rather than fainting (356). Fishbelly "sinks into" Black queer flesh. As a consequence, the frail ego comes close to completing its liquidation. The subjectivities that constrained and tortured his Black queer flesh have been self-abnegated, and Black queer flesh can emerge.

While Wright revamps the fainting scene from earlier in the novel into a controlled descent into Black queer flesh while Fish waits in prison, the text struggles with making queerness a central axis. When Fishbelly awakes from his descent, he cannot "remember" Black queer flesh and can only register its absence: "he began to realize dimly that there was something missing in him" (356). The dim realization that cannot penetrate the conscious mind involves the fabric of Black queer flesh that remains barred from social and psychic expression by the ego. The ego exists in a precarious state and has been eviscerated of its subjectivities. Fishbelly needs to completely eradicate it for Black queer flesh to come out. At the same time, Black queer flesh must remain unrepresentable. Wright needs this to be the case; otherwise, Fishbelly could embrace queer subjectivity and thus bolster the ego. The scenario recalls Irene's refusal of John Bellew, a man who sought to reinscribe a formless Clare Kendry with the identities of an African American, a divorcée, and a poor, fallen woman. Larsen does not want a queer subjectivity to defend Clare, as it would undo a journey of self-abnegation.

At the same moment that Fishbelly descends into Black queer flesh to reveal a precarious ego, Wright stops any signs of a journey of self-formation. By expelling self-formation from the novel, Wright exposes that the novel cannot be a Bildungsroman. In jail, for example, Fishbelly embraces stagnation and the refusal to save his ego: "there was no adventurous journey he wanted to make, no goal toward which he sought to strive" (356–57). Furthermore, he had "no mores to sustain him" (357). Wright rejects any suggestion of his novel being a Bildungsroman by showing that not only has self-formation ceased but also the text has been moving Fishbelly on a journey of self-abnegation since the first page of the text, when his name "Rex" is abnegated and replaced with a queer moniker: Fishbelly. As a Black male, he was always already destined to be incarcerated and forced to live a life with the constant threat of death. The text did not make this his self-formation journey and instead showed the unfolding of an already mapped-out future—Fishbelly was just catching up. Wright works against this unfolding of self by endowing Fishbelly with the agency to self-abnegate.

During the two years that Fishbelly is incarcerated, nothing really happens in the novel—and it should not, because Fishbelly as we knew him has completely disintegrated. All of his psychic attachments have dissipated, and the ego with which he entered prison no longer exists. Wright narrates this egoless state in a letter Fishbelly writes to the prosecutor—and while he is on a plane to Paris. Immediately after being released from jail, Fishbelly collects the evidence to convict the whites and begins his long journey, about three weeks, to Paris. He writes that, entering jail, he was "scared, more scared than you will ever think," yet adamant about not handing over the evidence. He signs the letter "Rex (Fish) Tucker" instead of "Fishbelly." In his two years of sitting and thinking, he cannot be Fishbelly—the person we saw since the third page of the text. He and that ego are gone. The idea of letters is important, as they provide much of the narration for his time in jail; he reads letters from others, but he does not send them out. When asked to write a letter, Fishbelly tells his stepfather, "Write it for me, Jim . . . I ain't got hold of myself" (358). In jail, Fishbelly cannot grasp "myself" because he has become formless and without subjectivities. "He" cannot write a letter because that person is gone. What remains is that "something missing in him," which is Black queer flesh.

Only after leaving jail and having reconstituted himself as Black queer flesh can Fishbelly—or the formerly legible Rex (Fish)—compose a letter. As Black queer flesh, Fishbelly performatively constitutes an ephemeral self-without-subjectivity: an archived Rex that mingles with other histories and experiences in Black queer flesh that come together as a speaking entity. On the journey to Paris, Fishbelly begins inhabiting Black queer flesh and learning how to express it. Wright communicates this transcendence of subjectivity while Fishbelly flies across the Atlantic Ocean: "that in him which had always made him self-conscious was now the bud of a new possible life that was pressing ardently but timidly against the shell of the old to shatter it and be free." Fishbelly must adjust to Black queer flesh as queer histories and as plural being. For example, they feel the residual pains of double consciousness when the white hostess asks them a question. They speak without the "intonations of 'nigger' obsequiousness" and with "muscles [that] had tautened." The body remembers fear, but a "bud of a new possible life" springs forth, and they are now "relatively free from fear and pressure." With the liquidation of the ego and subjectivity, they do not need to feel the constraints, the "pressure," of the superego enforcing normalcy. In the penultimate paragraph of the novel, Wright introduces us to the new Fishbelly when he explains that "he was not voluntarily longing to pledge allegiance to a world whose brutal might could never compel him to love it with threats of death" (383). Fishbelly is not organized around an ego that is susceptible to double consciousness; there is no subject or ego to internalize double consciousness. Embodying and living as Black queer flesh extricates them from double consciousness and the psychic configurations that bar queerness.

The ending is anything but utopian. Wright acknowledges that Fishbelly will continue to exist in a hostile, anti-Black world. The queer-of-color Bildungsroman cannot solve the problem of racism, but it does suggest a way to terminate double consciousness and the cult of subjectivity. Fishbelly's Black queer flesh can now be tested out in "Gay Paree" (359). In the sequel to *The Long Dream,* Fishbelly creates queer bonds while also exploring desire for male, female, and cyborg bodies. Even though double consciousness has been eliminated, Fishbelly must still contend with external racism and navigate the protocols of a homophobic society. Life after the creation of uninhibited Black queer flesh is not easy, and there will be many failures as Fishbelly experiments with living without subjectivity.[10]

5 Toward a Black Queer Utopia

> How else were they to express the longing to be free? How else were they to make plain their refusal to be governed?
>
> —Saidiya Hartman, *Wayward Lives, Beautiful Experiments*

Nella Larsen refuses to allow Black queer flesh to be reappropriated or transformed into subjectivity. In *Passing,* she would rather kill Clare Kendry, given this character's neophyte existence of Black queer flesh at the end of the novel, than allow her to succumb to the control of society—including her husband, John Bellew, and upper-middle-class African Americans. Ralph Ellison, too, illustrates a similar journey of self-abnegation. Invisible Man performs Black queer flesh in the prologue and epilogue of the novel. Still, with this character at least, Ellison remains elusive and does not particularly flesh out the contours of Invisible Man's life as Black queer flesh. In *Wayward Lives, Beautiful Experiments,* Saidiya Hartman takes the work of her novelist peers a step further. She represents Black queer flesh as a mode of being without dominating it through definitions, exactness, or precision. Moreover, she devises a new narrative technique, which she terms "close narration," as a style to give voice to Black queer flesh without forcing it to abide by subjectivity within representations in language and visual culture. Hartman communicates ephemeral selves-without-subjectivities. These performances of the self reveal not only the precarious nature of Black queer flesh but also a queer-of-color critique against a reading practice that desires stability, a unified self, or typical sources of evidence. She crafts a hybrid text that blends fiction, nonfiction, literary criticism, history, and ethnography to discuss the lives of queer women in early twentieth-century Philadelphia and New York City. For Hartman, Black queer flesh can be an archive, and in drawing from this archive, she is able to perform the lives and histories that it contains.

Prior to discussing Hartman's thrilling and beautiful experiments in Black queer flesh, I address the one instance in which her predecessor Ellison devised a character who successfully liquates his subjectivity and manages to self-abnegate and embody Black queer flesh. Like Hartman, Ellison does not seek either to define or to provide a standard representation of Black queer flesh, with the exception of his representation of Jim Trueblood in *Invisible Man*. Even in the midst of a horror story, Ellison emplots Black queer flesh within a scene that is not only difficult to read closely but also nearly impossible to reread. Ellison's morally bankrupt character, like the the wild and wayward characters Hartman introduces, has rejected subjectivity and is living as Black queer flesh. Ellison's Jim Trueblood and Hartman's *Wayward Lives, Beautiful Experiments* reveal what is at stake with queer self-abnegation.

"To Move without Moving": Jim Trueblood

Houston Baker famously interpreted the Jim Trueblood episode from Ralph Ellison's *Invisible Man* in what is now a classic reading of the scandalous yet aesthetically vibrant world of Jim Trueblood. He argues that Trueblood renders Black expression, folklore, and blues into commodities, proposing that the blues represent a complex language of Black experience. My sense of this process of commodification and of Trueblood's radical deployment of the blues is that they are only possible by a more sophisticated, revised Trueblood who has liquidated his subjectivities: one who performs a self-without-subjectivity. To Baker, no form of rebirth occurred; Baker notes that "Trueblood realizes that he is not so changed by catastrophe that he must condemn, mortify, or redefine his essential self" because he has "incorporated his personal disaster into a code of blues meanings."[1] I think Baker would agree that Trueblood must undergo a rebirth when we revisit the character's penultimate line, which Baker memorably cites: "I make up my mind that I ain't nobody but myself and ain't nothin' I can do but let whatever is gonna happen, happen."[2] As I will show, Trueblood activates his Black queer flesh when he draws upon the blues tradition, which contains contradictions of love, fear, anger, joy, and betrayal, including the entire spectrum of affects associated with the blues. Unlike Invisible Man, who spends the entire novel self-abnegating, Trueblood accomplishes this task within a brief period and by way of immoral actions.

As Invisible Man wanders in the prologue and epilogue as Black queer flesh, Ellison teases the reader that Invisible Man is attempting to put into practice the veteran's cryptic advice to "be your own father" (156). The narrator could be writing himself anew by retelling his story. Critic John Callahan has suggested that the narrator becomes a writer to gain perspective on himself, engaged in a process of reorientation rather than a project of rebirth.[3] Constant readjustment of the body is exactly what Jim Trueblood does in the story. As the story goes, Jim Trueblood, a poor farmer, unconsciously raped his daughter while sleeping next to her on a cold winter night (recall that southern cold is not New England cold but rather an element of the trickster's tale). As he wakes raping his daughter, who is crying and beating him, he rationalizes that he must continue abusing her until he climaxes even after he, along with everyone else in the house, is now awake. Incensed, his wife, Kate, also beats him, managing to bring down an axe upon him that slices his face open. She kicks him out of the house, but Trueblood eventually returns to raise his two new children—his wife and daughter became pregnant simultaneously. News of the events quickly spreads upon his return to the household. While fascinated whites give him money to tell the story over and over, African Americans associated with the college offer him money to leave. Invisible Man deplores Trueblood, as the reader should, given Trueblood's horrible behavior. Yet Ellison designates Trueblood as both a trickster and a morally bankrupt person. In doing so, he covertly slips a critical project into the Trueblood episode, and no one is the wiser.

Ellison complicates the idea of disability by incorporating Jim Trueblood into the mix. Cloaked within the traumas of incest—and according to the medical doctrine at the time, incest was a manifestation of a severe mental illness and moral failing—Ellison details how Trueblood, via conduits in jazz and the blues, manages first to self-abnegate his identities, if only to rejoin the community as if he had reconstructed his ego. From one perspective, the entire Trueblood episode produces racial anxiety: Trueblood's neighbors in the country and in town do not think of him as either a "human" being or a subject. Instead, whites keep him alive as a disabled "monster," defining Black subjectivity as a species of disability; Black people, by contrast, want to drive him out of town for this very reason, given his reprehensible actions. In these ways, both groups keep him in a state of queer (as in nonnormative) flesh. For African Americans, Trueblood signifies their racial anxiety. He is a phobogenic body. Local whites are, rather, amused with his story instead of appalled; they send out reporters, enjoy the retelling of the story, and provide Trueblood with work to ensure he remains in the Black community. Knowing his family partially undoes the work of uplift for the entire race, whites support Trueblood's claim to being a "model" subject; the family is therefore represented in anti-Black white culture as the quintessence of Black subjectivity (as disabled, as inhuman, as immoral). Ellison complicates these racial dynamics by making Trueblood a trickster who exploits said situations.

The trick is that Trueblood constantly performs a false subject and that that false subject is not the same but different in each performance. Ellison reveals that Trueblood's performances are ephemeral and not stable, fixed, or unified but created for each listener. As a self of Black queer flesh, Trueblood performatively constitutes a self-without-subjectivity upon each encounter with the townsfolk and visitors. The entity that they meet appears to be a subject with an ego—and Trueblood loves to toy with the idea that his ego is corrupt or bad and that he possesses an ego in the first place. In crafting a new self-without-subjectivity for each encounter, Trueblood does not repeat subjectivities. By not repeating or constantly citing and reciting a specific subjectivity or subject position, Trueblood does not make a stable, consistent, or unified gender, race, or sexuality that might arise from constant repetition or from hegemonic knowledge. Instead, living as Black queer flesh, Trueblood reconstitutes a plural self without an ego. By self-abnegating these identities, he opportunely engages Black queer flesh, recrafting what appears to be a more suitable, more moral, more kind, and more normative ego and subjectivity. Ellison sought to reject subjectivity and was not about to revive it. The idea of rebirth is a trickster ruse that prevents readers or listeners from registering (and then dominating or appropriating) Black queer flesh. In addition to this subversive act, Trueblood recounts his self-abnegation, which suggests a road map for Black emancipation, in a scene that will illustrate the mechanics of living as Black queer flesh and performing a self-without-subjectivity.

During the so-called dream-sin, as Trueblood likes to call the event when he raped his daughter, he insists that the dream itself—and not his desires—is to blame for the rape. On the day we encounter Trueblood, he is telling the story for Norton, a trustee for the college and a potential rapist of his own daughter. In the overdetermined dream, Trueblood assigns numerous images of him penetrating his daughter and ejaculating as if he recycled those particular images in his multiple retellings, and the same act occurs many times, as if to excite his audience. He crafts this particular version of the narrative for his pedophilic listener; otherwise, the story does not logically follow, and he would not need to "move without moving" once awake, either. Even his recounting of his wife's responses seems fictionalized; his style, including its musicality and suspense, overcomes the question of whether he accurately remembers the dream and aftermath. His story emphasizes multiplicity over truthful reproduction. Trueblood's tale provides graphic details and wonderful prose while also being a horrible series of events; they imperfectly replicate the original scene.

Trueblood, the Br'er Rabbit salesman, crafts an original copy of the master story for each listener; as such, he tweaks the imagery and its frequency to satisfy the customer.[4] The listener wants to consume the horrific story, not assure its accuracy. Thus his reproductions can serve as a form of art if he, as artist, embeds a critical message of how to combat racial anxiety within the reproduction. I would like to argue that Trueblood's stories only appear as reproductions when instead each story is an original and contains a unique message to eradicate surplus jouissance. As such, I believe his story reveals his self-abnegation (with some violent assistance) and emergence as Black queer flesh in four movements.

First, the stories do not exactly reproduce the master original. They are sold as copies (Norton gives him one hundred dollars at the end of the tale), but in fact Trueblood weaves anew the images, frequency, and order of events, including his asides, to meet the consumer. He passes off an original as a copy. This quality of substitution, then, can be read into Trueblood's own being: he appears as a deviant subject for whites, but he is really creating art and his own Black queer flesh into a self-without-subjectivity. He is not layering or developing a unified identity but constantly remaking what appears to be a self in front of whites and Blacks. In this way, he embodies C. Riley Snorton's theory of trans as the capacity to remake personhood.[5] Trueblood remakes his stories—and thus himself as actor of those stories—for each guest, even though he appears to be a stable, unified, and bounded subject. They misread Black queer flesh for deviant subjectivity. Second, Ellison can openly reveal the queer-of-color methodologies of self-abnegation within Trueblood's tale, given that the text forecloses the possibility of a close reading of the heinous moral crimes, implying a critical moment of freedom within a narrative of incest. The raw, open wound on Trueblood's face, for example, is quickly dismissed as a remnant of his incest instead of a symbolic gateway to Black queer flesh. Few readers reread this scene, and many skip sections to avoid the graphic details, so this episode is a strategic way of communicating a complex theory of self-abnegation that will be overlooked by most readers—including Invisible Man himself.

Third, Trueblood achieves formlessness and ushers in Black queer flesh. After being isolated by the community, the women surround and protect Matty Lou, his now pregnant daughter, and Kate, his pregnant wife. Ostracized from the community, Trueblood loses his hold on being a father, moral heterosexual, and church performer. These are essentially his only identities, as he does not care much for manual labor, and he readily transgressed heteronormativity (he is also a minor character, so there is not much history to him). As his daughter's rapist, Trueblood self-abnegates (with some help from the townspeople and his own family) from being a heteronormative or deviant father. The entire matrix of fatherhood has been stripped away by his actions. A moral heterosexual is also gone as an identity for obvious reasons, and he becomes a person with a mental illness (and this categorization of his mental illness as a disability taints the characterization of the other disabilities in the novel).

While fatherhood and heteronormativity require self-abnegation by himself, he does willfully act as a rapist and thus disinvest from these identities (even though that might not have been his goal). Unlike Invisible Man, Trueblood is forcibly stripped of many of his identities by the community. His final self-abnegation requires more contemplation.

As the best singer in church and town, Trueblood loves to perform with others and to express feelings and stories beyond the use of standard language. Self-abnegating from this subjectivity requires much more work for Trueblood, as he does not have a force helping him to strip it away. One night, after being thrown out of the house, he goes to confession as a way of trying to rejoin the community and to repair his bond with the church. He decides against this: "I leaves trying' to pray, but I caint. I thinks and thinks, until I thinks my brain go'n bust." He understands that there is no forgiveness or rejoining the community; there is no way to heal the rupture, so he continues to enlarge it. He sings the blues and descends into Invisible Man's lower frequency and self-abnegates his ties to the church and community. He cannot rely on his old subjectivities—especially of a choir singer—so he rejects them. His transformation occurs as he channels the blues: "I'm singin' them blues I makes up my mind that I ain't nobody but myself and ain't nothin' I can do but let whatever is gonna happen, happen." Remember that Trueblood is telling this tale for Norton, so the intricacies of self-abnegation are not needed for this audience. Nonetheless, I believe Trueblood signals it with his telling statement. Even though these are pejorative phrases, I suggest that Trueblood completes his self-abnegation realizing that he lacks subjectivity when he says "I ain't nobody." He has no identities and apprehends that he no longer has an agency that is tied to an ego: "ain't nothin' I can do." With his mind "go'n bust," Trueblood liquidates his ego. He then reconstitutes the self as Black queer flesh when he admits, "I made up my mind" (66). A moment prior, his mind had exploded and disappeared, whereas now he seems to have a new one. As Black queer flesh, Trueblood—if that is how he still identities—can build new relationships with Matty Lou, Kate, and various communities. In this short scene, there is no apparent queer lover or mimesis that aids in self-abnegation, even as Ellison offers some insights into the transcendence of subjectivity. By singing and descending into the blues, Trueblood can improvise from the ensemble of Black queer flesh that lingers within phonic substance. To adapt Fred Moten's concept of the Black sonic, Trueblood can find a mirror within one (or many) of the phonetic substances, and with them, he can perform and then abnegate a self-without-subjectivities as needed from Black queer flesh.[6] His stories shift with each new performance of self because flesh comes together in a random fashion to weave a new, temporary self.

Ellison did not narrate a deep mimetic relationship for Trueblood, instead providing a mimesis that operated on a different time and physical scale. The episode was too short to develop a long relationship, so Ellison exploited an overlooked Black tradition that does not obey chronological time and questions of duration. As a blues singer, Trueblood called forth from Black queer flesh itself a myriad of histories and experiences that could mingle in an improvisation to create the sonic material behind and of the blues. Over an unspecified period of time, Trueblood sings the blues by himself, and from what Ellison provides us, Trueblood self-abnegates his church bond by singing and wallowing in the blues.[7] Within music's phonic landscape, Trueblood conjures a constellation of mimetic relationships with other Black phonic material. He says, "One day, early in the mornin,' I looks up and sees the stars and I starts singin'"—without intentionality and possibility with some embellishment of the morning sky—and comes across an ensemble of Blackness that improvises in a way that appeals to him (66). From this concert of Black queer flesh acting as mirror, he reconstitutes the self as Black queer flesh and returns home as a new plural and ephemeral person. Thus the character we meet in the novel is not a subject but Black queer flesh performing just one self-without-subjectivity. When talking about Trueblood, I now employ third person plural pronouns to designate the multiplicity of selves performed by Black queer flesh as well as the nonfixed status of Black queer flesh.[8]

Trueblood retains the past, but it does not haunt them—the incest haunts their former identities with guilt, but this new self relates to the event as a historical trauma that must be addressed with care. They establish new relationships to their community and family and build relations with whites. This new self, organized by Black queer flesh and not subjectivity, though an example of my main argument, is often neglected and ignored because of the moral absurdities involved—that Trueblood would return to their family and prevent the abortions of their grandchild and child and become a "good" provider. In their reconfigured relations, though, Trueblood seems content with their family not speaking to them and being able to work and speak with the white community; they are not afraid of anti-Black racism and do not let others author their life. Rather, Trueblood now performs a self-without-subjectivity as an art. Each time they tell a story, they make themselves and the story anew and sell it to captive listeners as if they had just made a simple adjustment to themselves to come back into society, as Baker has argued. The works of art—subjectless subjectivities and the stories—all contain the critical moment needed to transcend subjectivity. They write in each story the methods of self-abnegation and of remaking of the self through knowledges from Black queer flesh. If only the listener could actually hear the Black phonic dimension of the story and not react with fear, scandal, shame, anxiety, or masochistic pleasure, he, too, might be able to descend into the blues of Trueblood's stories. This requires relating to the new Trueblood, the artist, and not the old ego and set of subjectivities.

This reminds me of Trueblood's ironic rationale that they had to "move without moving." When they supposedly awake from their sleep-rape, they convince themselves, as the tale goes, that they must ejaculate; otherwise, their rape would be a sin—if they transform the act into procreation, then their actions would not necessarily be rape, they argue. With Kate beating them and their daughter screaming, Trueblood has to "move without moving" to ejaculate, and they wrongly believe this will help them avoid the charge of rape. Recycling this metaphor, I regard Trueblood's subjectivity as changing before our eyes without notice. Other people view them as the same person, but Trueblood has undergone a radical transformation. In this context, they self-abnegate and reorganize the self as Black queer flesh—they "moved without moving," again performing the trickster by pulling a fast one before our eyes. This subtle, almost imperceptible transformation enables Trueblood to restart their life: they transform from subjectivity to flesh without visible movement. If Invisible Man could relate to the new Trueblood—as morally impossible as that might be—he, too, could live and work in the social world as a self not terrorized by subjectivity, double consciousness, and uplift. Invisible Man could craft himself as Black queer flesh, just like Trueblood.

If Invisible Man or readers happen to miss Trueblood's self-abnegation and rebirth, then their raw wound, like Tod Clifton's wounded face, Supercargo's bloody wound, and Ras's punctured face, offers another avenue to experience Black queer flesh. After unsuccessfully chasing Trueblood from the house, Kate brings down an axe upon their face but produces a deep wound that refuses to heal. "The man had a scar on his right cheek, as though he had been hit in the face with a sledge. The wound was raw and moist and from time to time he lifted his handkerchief to fan away the gnats." This literal cutting away of their body and subjectivity creates a physical entrance to Trueblood's Black queer flesh. Their wound represents the condition of Oedipus, who comes to blind himself. When Trueblood replies in the affirmative to Norton's question if they were okay after the incest, Norton eagerly responds, "You do? You feel no inner turmoil, no need to cast out the offending eye?" (51). Norton views the need to blind "the offending eye" like Oedipus for committing incest. Norton wants access to whatever enabled Trueblood to "cast out the offending eye" without becoming Oedipus; he wants the secrets of rebirth but forgets that the Trueblood with whom he is speaking is hardly the same person from the stories. The wound signals an escape from death and permanent physical injury to Norton, but Ellison's invitation to that wound gives access to Black queer flesh. Trueblood, the trickster artist, manages a rebirth into and as Black queer flesh—their art facilitates the same journey of self-abnegation for others. The open wound, too, serves as a more literal access point to Black queer flesh. Invisible Man misses both of these opportunities.

Living as Black Queer Flesh: Saidiya Hartman's *Wayward Lives, Beautiful Experiments*

Ralph Ellison not only portrays Jim Trueblood as fully immersed within a fabulation of Black queer flesh, but in the opening pages of *Invisible Man,* he also intimates that his eponymous character and narrator achieves this important feat, especially in the prologue and epilogue, where his protagonist's experience of a self as Black queer flesh is most pronounced. This self—this state of being—is endowed with the discerning ability "to *see* around corners" and, more significant, "to hear around them" (13). A trait of going beyond the impossible—from the position of subjectivity—percolates in the act of making visible the performance of Black queer flesh. As a unified subject, these modes of perception seem absurd. Constructing a character that has transcended subjectivity requires crafting not the impossible but something beyond it: one that has insight, with the capacity to see and hear around corners.

Literary critic Saidiya Hartman writes about encountering the impossible in Black studies. In "Venus in Two Acts," she describes the difficulties of trying to capture the everyday experiences of those excluded from the traditional archive.[9] This historical narrative chronicles the horrors, pains, and offenses wreaked by slave owners and anti-Black whites in the aftermath of Emancipation on legions of African Americans. While many have written of these experiences and of their violence, authors are faced with the challenge of "revisit[ing] the scene of subjection" so as to remake, and perhaps even to put Blackness into, Black flesh (4). Missing from these narratives are first-person accounts that chronicle the multifaceted ways African Americans not only lived but also experienced their lives. And even as historians have spent decades recovering first-person narratives of African Americans, this limited archive, as far as Hartman is concerned, is impossibly narrow; she yearns for the accounts of the many who were denied the opportunity to record their histories. One response to this dilemma, for Hartman, hinges on trying "to imagine what might have happened or might have been said or might have been done" (11). Engaging in a sort of historical fiction for her is ostensibly "not to *give voice* to the slave, but rather to imagine what cannot be verified, a realm of experience which is situated between two zones of death—social and corporeal death" (12). For Hartman, this narrative practice of narrating the impossible—"what cannot be verified"—calls for an art of "critical fabulation" or "recombinant narrative" (11, 12) as she aims to create a mode of writing that can represent the impossible: the conditions and experiences of African Americans in the zone of death, in the zone of Black flesh.

Not until a decade later does Hartman solve the problem of being limited to narrating Black flesh. Her final line in "Venus in Two Acts" suggests that she experimented with the rejection of subjectivity, embracing not Black flesh but Black queer flesh. She concludes the essay with an insight about the limits of critical fabulation, observing that insofar as "we" is written as a collective, rather than I, "we too emerge from the encounter with a sense of incompleteness and with the recognition that some part of the self is missing as a consequence of this engagement" (14). After descending into the text—similar to when Ellison's narrator descends into music—Hartman returns feeling herself as a collective and "incomplete." This incompleteness signals that self-abnegation has begun; it signals her disavowing subjectivity. This article is written after the publication of her splendid text *Lose Your Mother.* In this book, Hartman finds herself confined to "the stuff of subject and plots and ends" (10). In other words, Hartman feels bound to remaining a subject of Black flesh, whereas in "Venus in Two Acts," she begins the journey of rejecting subjectivity. In *Wayward Lives, Beautiful Experiments,* by contrast, Hartman transcends subjectivity, going beyond Black flesh, and beyond the impossible and incomplete: here she narrates from the position of Black queer flesh, even with occasional returns to performing life as an academic, as she puts into narrative the lives of those selves existing as Black queer flesh.[10]

Wayward Lives recounts the stories of Black women's experiences in New York City and Philadelphia at the onset of the twentieth century from what seems a hybrid of first-person accounts, academic critic, and omniscient narrator. Drawing purposefully from archival sources, including police and social worker records, as well as diaries, hospital records, and local government documents, Hartman provides glimpses into the lives of working-class women—queer and otherwise—as they set out to explore and live their lives through nonnormative, wayward behaviors and practices. Unlike historiographies, which attempt to re-create the lives of their subjects, Hartman discovers that no archive contains the histories and experiences of her women, from their own perspective; "History" chooses to preserve not their views but rather their records—at least from the vantage point of state power—and casts these women as dissolute vagrants and criminals. In response to the paucity of data, Hartman, according to Sam Huber, "authorizes herself to fill them [nonexistent archives] with her own speculations about her protagonists' most private fears and preciously guarded desires."[11] In speaking of Hartman's methodology, Joanna Scutts echoes this observation: "Because there's so little concrete evidence about who these women are, Hartman's book takes deliberate liberties with the usual constraints of history."[12] What is more, some critics find that Hartman adds "speculative or fictionalized interjections" in "creating a composite of ordinary Black womanhood from the fragments of life" that are missing from the archives.[13] *Wayward Lives*, in fact, commingles the genres of autoethnography, historiography, visual studies, and creative fiction and nonfiction. As such, Hartman conjures histories, experiences, and perceptions because we lack traditional archives that can give us first-person accounts.

Hartman does more than straddle the genres of creative writing and history in advancing worlds of Black queer flesh. Indeed, I propose that we recast claims, such as those made by critic Parul Sehgal that her project is one of "speculation and sometimes fictional imagining," as instead Black queer flesh attempting simultaneously to speak.[14] For me, the text operates through multiple registers insofar as it represents an amalgam of queer histories and of Black queer flesh within the "lost" or nonexistent, nonnormative archives Hartman pursues. In this fashion, she both finds and founds an archive of Black queer flesh by showcasing stories from her journey into it for her narratives.

Illustrating the impossible in *Wayward Lives,* Hartman includes, within this impossibility, the horrid, heavily policed lives of Black women and men. Through the stories of characters who are struggling against the enforcement of dominant gender and sexuality, she articulates that "the failure to comply with or achieve gender norms would [ostensibly] define black life," "and this 'ungendering' inevitably marked black women (and men) as less than human" (186). Being called "*half a woman*" inevitably compelled Black women to conform, "to be normal," as it were (184). Consequently, such despoiling of humanity into Black flesh, and the concomitant enforcement of normative systems, constitutes the experience of the impossible, the experience of Black flesh. Even so, Hartman's text does not traffic solely in Black flesh. Rather, a large part of the text conveys the significance of going beyond Black flesh. The text shows life as Black queer flesh and the joy and beauty that emerge from this way of life, from this mode of being without subjectivity or Black flesh haunting the self with horror.

Actor, musician, and womanizer Gladys Bentley captures the most visible and practicable example of Black queer flesh—given that he essentially "reconstructed [life] along radically different lines" (197). All things considered, he strips away cultural norms, especially his own subjectivities, as a woman and as a singular self to become a person who dons a new costume every night—on stage and out and about on the street.[15] He dated different women as often as he changed the performance of himself-without-a-subjectivity. In taking control of the process of flesh making, Bentley made himself Black queer flesh, and this powerful refashioning continually inaugurates a new self in process that enables him to more readily practice a main tenet of the wayward or of Black queer flesh: he has the capacity to "improvise the forms of life, experiment with freedom, and refuse the menial existence scripted for [him]" (4). As a celebrity, he makes his life and his selves as he experiments with new modes of understanding gender and sexuality that radically depart from subjectivity. His well-known story, however, is not particularly the principal focus in Hartman's exploration of Black queer flesh; rather, Bentley's cultural and economic capital merely bolster historians to document his beautiful life.

More intensely focusing on the precarious lives of those embracing Black queer flesh, Hartman tells the story of how Bentley's wealth isolates him from state-sanctioned interventions, namely, from social services and the police; the others in *Wayward Lives* find themselves in different class positions, embodying Black queer flesh in various, wayward ways—prompting readers to decode the project as an exercise in telling stories about Black queer flesh. Not surprisingly, in the opening section, "Methods," Hartman refers to the text as "the fugitive text of the wayward, and it is marked by the errantry that it describes" (xiv). She then proceeds to inform the reader that "in this spirit, I have pressed at the limits of the case file and the document, speculated about what might have been, imagined the things whispered in dark bedrooms, and amplified . . . the vision and dreams of the wayward" (xiv–xv). Evoking the demonstrative pronoun "this" (with spirit) makes one wonder about its referent. Hartman seems to suggest aberrant behavior might just be the animating spirit. And, nearly two hundred pages later, she defines these terms and offers no less than fifty options. Is she playing the trickster, one wonders? Within this family of definitions lurks the idea of Black queer flesh, given that she references the act of performance itself when she acknowledges that "*what might be* . . . is an improvisation with the terms of social existence" (228). Then, she interestingly plays with how one might take ownership of flesh making, particularly when she invokes Baby Suggs's resonant message in *Beloved*: "to love what is not loved" (227). In her wisdom, Baby Suggs does nothing short of miraculous when she shepherds her congregation to turn Black flesh into Black queer flesh, instructing them how to "love it [flesh]. Love it hard . . . love your hands! Love them. . . . You got to love it. This is flesh . . . flesh that needs to be loved."[16] Loving Black flesh, for Baby Suggs, constitutes the removal of her congregation's subjectivities until they achieve Black queer flesh. Hartman, for her part, defines waywardness as self-abnegation and the rejection of subjectivity as "the avid longing for a world not ruled by master, man or the police" (227). In her compendium of definitions, she essentially describes the qualities of Black queer flesh. In toto, *Wayward Lives* not only narrates a story of people who have rejected subjectivity but also powerfully embraces Black queer flesh.

Hartman's great innovation in terms of aesthetics and her contribution to culture in general are no less than the communication of stories, especially of those experiencing and living daily as Black queer flesh. While her invention of critical fabulation puts into language the experience of Black flesh, Hartman develops "close narration" as a technique to talk about Black queer flesh. She describes this aesthetic as "a style which places the voice of narrator and character in inseparable relation, so that vision, language, and rhythms of the wayward shape and arrange the text. The italicized phrases and lines are utterances from the chorus. This story is told from inside the circle" (xiii–xiv). Close narration includes, at a minimum, three key elements. The first is the narrator, who could be an academic or a temporary academic subject-without-subjectivity improvised from Black queer flesh. Hartman as narrator cannot exist as a singular subject: she in fact informs us that her style is "inseparable" from

Black queer flesh, given that she herself has achieved this state of being. The second element of close narration is a character who has rejected subjectivity and remade the self along the lines of Black queer flesh. The text denotes a large cast of characters who reside in this state. In each moment of "inseparability," Hartman and the character produce a new interaction, thereby evoking a different ensemble of Black queer flesh that will improvise and usher into existence a different speaking voice and narrative trajectory. In this way, the writing itself exemplifies two additional definitions of the wayward: a "sojourn without a fixed destination" (227) and a "directionless search" (228). By combining multiple experiences of Black queer flesh—one living as Hartman, one historical as the character—the text moves in unpredictable directions. If Hartman is an ever-changing, improvised product of Black queer flesh that is never singular—never a subject—and the characters emerge on their own terms from Black queer flesh, the comingling in the final analysis cannot be anything but wayward. Consequently, this union crafts an errant narrative. If two queer and unknowable selves complicate the text, the final contributors further increase the opacity of the text.

Speaking from the depths of Black queer flesh, the chorus introjects their utterances into the text in short phrases. Hartman italicizes their words to help readers distinguish her intertwining with a specific character over and against the "chorus," which represents one sliver of Black queer flesh that finds it necessary to call out—in a call-and-response fashion—to the events happening in the main story line. In her "Cast of Characters" catalog, a list that appears in any playbill, Hartman defines the chorus as "all the unnamed young women of the city trying to find a way to live and in search of beauty" (xvii). One axis for the search for beauty involves overturning the construction of gender and sexuality. Hartman extensively writes about how these categories arise as practices that reshape Black women and men into controllable subjects in *Scenes of Subjection.*[17] Once reduced to a state of flesh, these bodies become remade so that power can easily penetrate and control them. The chorus, however, refuses this process of self-making and desubjectification into flesh. In the closing chapter of the text, Hartman elaborates on the chorus—perhaps once again playing the trickster—as if to ask for a rereading of the text once readers grasp the significance of the chorus. The chorus, too, refuses the concept of the "sovereign" and subjectivity (349). In complete alignment with Black queer flesh, the chorus lacks shape, besides an amorphous assemblage: it is "an assembly sustaining dreams of the otherwise" (348). Returning to the notion that the text is writing within an unknown "circle," the chorus constitutes that circle, and as such, the text is written by Hartman calling upon and immersing herself in Black queer flesh. The chorus assembles Black queer flesh to "gather in the circle and fall into the line where all particularity and distinction fade away. One girl can stand in for any of them, can serve as the placeholder for the story, recount the history from the beginning" (345). The evanescence evokes both the rejection of subjectivity and the embrace of Black queer flesh, and additionally, the metaphor of existing as a multiplicity by becoming part of the vast assemblage of Black queer flesh. The chorus refuses subjectivity and instead seeks collectivity as a mode of self-making; they reject the fetish of modern sovereignty and subjectivity. Furthermore, as a plural self, the chorus can share histories and experiences: "marvel at their capacity to inhabit every woman's grief as their own" (345). This quality of "marveling" helps readers grasp the elation of being Black queer flesh; it also helps readers process that Hartman has moved from Black flesh to explore the positive dimensions of directing flesh making to join the assembly, the circle of Black queer flesh. The triumvirate of academic narrator, character, and chorus composes the contributors to close narration, but all of them emerge from the same source: Black queer flesh. Thus close narration is an aesthetic practice that captures the "voice" of Black queer flesh. In other words, as Black queer flesh needs to communicate with subjects, such as readers, an ensemble of it comes together—like the chorus—and improvises speaking subject-without-subjectivity that can pass on knowledge, as when Hartman and her characters morph into a plural self.

Wayward Lives presents countless case studies that serve as illustrative examples of people who have pursued self-abnegation and undone subjectivity, of individuals who, in a very practical sense, have reconstructed plural selves while asserting Black queer flesh as an ontology. Early in the text, Hartman alerts readers to an alternative mode of reading, one that parallels Ralph Ellison's call to see and hear around corners and in which Invisible Man "not only entered the music but descended, like Dante, into its depths."[18] Like Ellison, Hartman insinuates that but a few will register the language of Black queer flesh in her story, posing this insight not as a question but as a riddle of sorts: "what you can hear if you listen" (7). Readers familiar with Ellison's great work will immediately apprehend this intertextual conversation. Hartman performs the receptivity and attentiveness to Black queer flesh required by her text. When describing a street corner, Hartman's thick descriptions include colorful statements like "'hey girl, send it on'" that emanate from pimps. She also records the internal thoughts of bulldaggers who "undressed the pretty ones with a glance" (87). This is a prime example of close narration: Hartman recovers the histories and experiences of "bulldaggers" that reside in Black queer flesh endemic to her narrative.

Close narration occurs throughout the text, but the story of Esther Brown, a "chippie and rebel, who insists on being treated the same as white girls," constitutes a preeminent example of this "style" (xx, xiii). The chapter begins with Hartman's introduction of Esther and her "refusal to be governed." In the subsequent line, the chorus interrupts Hartman's point to add their own insights to the topic. In the two lines that follow, the chorus at least waits until Hartman concludes her thoughts before chiming in:

> Esther Brown did not write a political tract on the refusal to be governed, or draft a plan for mutual aid or outline a memoir of her sexual adventures. A manifesto of the wayward—*Own Nothing, Refuse the Given, Live on What You Need and No More, Get Ready to Be Free*—was not found among the items in her case file. She didn't pen any song lines: *My mama says I'm reckless, My daddy says I'm wild, I ain't good looking, but I'm somebody's angel child.* She didn't commit to paper her ruminations on freedom: *With human nature caged in a narrow space, whipped daily into submission, how can we speak of potentialities?* (229)

While the first introjection presents a series of shouted manifesto titles that the chorus cites, the second literally celebrates, through song, Bessie Smith's "Reckless Blues." The final addition is painstakingly summoned by the chorus directly from Esther. Close narration leads Hartman to engage in a call and response with Black queer flesh. As she writes, the chorus, which emanates from Hartman herself, contributes in multifaceted ways. For the chorus to simultaneously improvise and perform a speaking voice, it must first call upon Black queer flesh to assemble and form an ensemble. Yet, the parameters that encompass *what* and *who* assembles are not up to Hartman herself, or to the chorus, for that matter. Given this unknowability and inability to command or master the constituents of Black queer flesh, Hartman cannot direct who speaks or when. As such, the chorus is able to interject with various historical voices and lived experiences all at once. At first, it is the different voices that the chorus speaks that then morph into a Bessie Smith song, finally giving way to Esther's thoughts, which conclude the above scenario. Esther's chapter, in which the aforementioned scenario appears, "The Anarchy of Colored Girls Assembled in a Riotous Manner," is characteristically replete with extensive narration by the chorus. This, in part, is because Esther herself engaged in "wandering and drifting" as the way that "she engaged the world and how she understood it" (234). The close narration, in fact, aligns perfectly with Esther's "errant path" to living life, where she pursued many unexpected cuts and detours because she, too, allowed the chorus to mingle with her sense of self. The remainder of the chapter, in sum, repeats this initial relationship between narrators, and in doing so, Hartman's close narration shifts as the participants change. Ultimately, Esther's wayward drift resurfaces as the text itself refuses vehemently to be governed. By listening to the "rhythm and stride" of close narration, readers can discern Hartman adroitly conjuring Black queer flesh (234). As such, *Wayward Lives* effectively presents these stories of existence beyond subjectivity.

The subsequent analyses consider three case studies that powerfully illustrate what can be heard and heeded from Hartman's enduring experiments. Eva Perkins, nineteen and a factory worker, marries Aaron Perkins (aka Kid Chocolate), a boxer and elevator operator, and the two enjoy life together dreaming and playing in the streets of Harlem and the surrounding neighborhoods. The two learn to reject subjectivity early in their lives by eschewing the concept of property—particularly, of ownership. "They were radically disenchanted with the idea of property," Hartman-Aaron-Eva informs us.[19] The chorus, for its part, observes that the notion of property recalls the condition of "*being an object of property*"

(270). The three or four, they claim, "had endured the life of the commodity," and "if the past taught them anything, it was that the attempt to own life destroyed it" (271, 270). Forced to inhabit the condition of property or "the life of the commodity," African Americans endure both a psychic and social prison—one that must be broken entirely. Christina Sharpe expounds upon this notion of "the hold" as an act of being held in captivity given that enslaved peoples painfully anticipate the torture of being sold, the literal hold of the slave ship being one manifestation of this condition, and the planation economy being the other predicament that will hold them perpetually against their will.[20] Contemporary aspects of this phenomenon include well-known examples of the carceral system, such as police brutality, the choke hold, the prison cell, the interpellating gaze of the cops, and the presumption of criminality. In like fashion, what literally holds Black queers as nonnormative is none other than a life-denying "grammar of the human that regarded them both as monsters and deviants" (274). Within this picture, subjectivity does nothing short of pinning them to these identities—with the possibility of bearable versions of the human if, and when, they subscribe to the mandates of racial uplift. Subjectivity in this scenario demands that they police themselves by continually berating themselves with questions, not unlike the chorus's when they ask, "*Am I human flesh? Am I not a man and a brother? Ain't I a woman?*" (275). Tethering oneself to subjectivity produces a humiliation to prove and assert one's humanity perpetually. In rejecting the horrors associated with ownership and Black flesh, Aaron, Eva, and Hartman disidentify with the hold of subjectivity because they exercise the power and "the willingness to lose oneself and become something greater—a chorus, swarm, ensemble" (285). They self-abnegate and thereby join the chorus of Black queer flesh.

Living "in the life" often led African Americans to uncover Black queer flesh. Edna Thomas, a "stage and screen actor," lived their life as Black queer flesh; their beautiful life was an experiment in playing with the ensemble, in calling forth bits and pieces of Black queer flesh to come together. Edna married Lloyd Thomas, a Harlem nightclub manager who was also attracted to queer men. Eventually, when Edna meets Olivia Wyndham, an English noble lady, at a party thrown by A'lelia Walker, the three end up living life together. Similar to Eva and Aaron, Edna and Lloyd learned early in their lives the significance of not being "fixed by the coordinates of identity" (209). Subjectivity was seen as a burden to be disregarded. As a stage actress, Edna doubly performed and played with Black queer flesh as an expression of plurality at work and in everyday life. The ensemble, for Edna, was the "domain of collective bodies," where "all other roles had to be relinquished" (211). Edna felt and embodied plurality and yet manages to turn away from individuality; not unlike Aaron, Eva, and Hartman, they "become something greater—a chorus, swarm, ensemble" (285). In this modus operandi, Edna "slip[s] into someone else's existence" and is "no longer bound to her personal history." Thus Edna relinquishes a performed self-without-subjectivity and, as a result, "disappeared into other lives; she became other selves. This was exquisite. It was the most sustained joy she had ever experienced" (211). As such, Edna moves through the stage and the world as the ensemble dimension of Black queer flesh—and in lieu of existing in the amalgam of Black queer flesh, Edna thrives in playing with its ensemble dimensions, with its multiplicity of experiences they occasion. Unlike Aaron and Eva, who find the "chorus, swarm, and ensemble," Enda, rather, creates art out of slipping into other lives while experiencing what comes of this amalgamation; they create drama by performing the ensemble as a self-without-subjectivity. The chorus concludes Edna's story by describing them as "*an artist without an art form*" (214). Edna's performed selves-without-subjectivity always changed and could never really be pinned down into a specific form of art. The normative world does not have a way of capturing how those organized by Black queer flesh are crafting new selves on a daily basis. It is the illegibility of Black queer flesh that cannot be given a permanent form: it adapts, waywardly, and it changes errantly, improvising queerly. In these crucial ways, Edna's art is "to be lost to the world": not fully knowable, not fully recognizable, and not fully recordable by normative history. Edna's art, however, helps constitute Black queer flesh as nothing short of this beautiful experiment of theirs. Edna's making art of their performances of Black queer flesh invokes the approaches taken by Jim Trueblood to create art in their every performance. The final case study provides another glimpse of a character, Mabel Hampton, employed as a professional entertainer, who refuses fixed, normative, or deviant identities, on and off the stage, by pushing subjectivity aside. A wayward soul in Hartman's magnum opus, they will also play with Black queer fleshy existence by living life waywardly. Not only will they reject gender assignments but they will also disavow the notion of queer bodies.

A working-class lesbian and intellectual, Mabel's equally beautiful experiment involves questioning the construction of the self, race, gender, and sexuality. Hartman-Mabel annoyingly ask themselves, "What was it that a colored woman was supposed to be?" This interrogation of hegemonic categories seeps into other domains as Mabel ponders "who she was and who she wanted to be. Did she have to be a woman? Did she have to be a man? Did she have to be anything at all"? (338) These questions plague a younger Mabel, who clings to subjectivity in public spaces like the cabaret, where the police spy upon lesbian desires. But Mabel does not want to be a subject and finds their way out. Mabel transforms dancing and singing on the stage into an opportunity to be free of subjectivity and live as Black queer flesh. They find that moving their body in certain ways can defy the mandates of liberal humanism. In equal measure, they tremendously dislike moving their body for acts of servitude: for cleaning, wiping, mopping, and saying yes to white employers. Instead, Mabel experiences tremendous joy in being one of the "anonymous members of the ensemble" of the streets, an actual chorus line, as they stroll through life—refusing to be governed (301). For Mabel, a walk down the streets of Harlem—while encountering debauchery—was "another elaboration of the general strike" against normativity, against being a singular subject, and against being a domestic worker (299). Similar to Edna, being a performer enables Mabel to slip into "the costume of another existence, inhabiting a body different from the one violated in a coal bin" (302). Like wayward movements in the streets and private parties, dancing facilitates Mabel not to have to relive the pains of rape and Black flesh and instead to enjoy the pleasures of not nurturing a subjectivity. By following the encouragement of the chorus, which shouts at Mabel, "*I am unavailable for servitude. I refuse it,*" Mabel can cultivate a plural self (299). On the stage, in the streets, and in private queer worlds, they become a "shared body" with a "common rhythm" (303). In private parties—far from the eyes of the police and social reforms—Mabel re-creates their stage self: one in which they "refused the world that refused" them (305). These queer spaces allow Mabel and their friends to perform in movements that resemble Black queer flesh, mobilizing to perform a self-without-subjectivity: the music and passions "call to assembly" the bodies in the room, and for Mabel, they manage to embrace a "body unmarked by stigma and undisciplined by servitude" (306). This involves the party-goers becoming "unmade men and women" and enjoying "the utter dissolution of the bounded, discrete self was a gift" (324). Poor queer bodies assembling together improvise new plural selves united in the wayward pleasures of Black queer flesh.

From the outset, Hartman promises in her text that her technique of close narration requires the narrator to merge with the character. We find, however, that this merging constitutes the expression of plural selves that comingle as Black queer flesh. While Hartman and her characters exemplify Black queer flesh: improvising and performing a self-without-subjectivity, the chorus embodies the remainder of the experiences and histories of Black queer flesh. In a brilliant act of call and response, the chorus and Hartman inform the reader at the end of the narrative that they will continue to be the archive of lost voices: "*Somewhere down the line the numbers increase, the tribe increases.* The chorus increases. *So how do you keep on?* She can't help it. . . . *The struggle is eternal. Somebody else carries on*" (348). As more selves reject subjectivity, and pursue self-abnegation, they will inevitably join the chorus, Hartman, Mabel, Edna, Eva, Aaron, and Esther, in the wild and wayward and promising amalgamation of Black queer flesh.

Life as Black Queer Flesh

Nella Larsen paved the way for the queer-of-color journey and brought life to a new queer literary genre and a new mode of Black selfhood. Next came Wright's and Ellison's transformation of the genre, where they finally rescue Black queer flesh, expounding upon how Black queers would find their way into a society that revolves around questions of identity, subjectivity, and desire driven by an individual ego. They rehoused Black queer flesh—their freeing it from its captivity within double consciousness and white and Black uplift's control—helping us understand the scope and necessity of how Black queers engage in the work of queer bonds, sociality, and kinship, with the hope that they can act as role models for others who need to self-abnegate and learn to express their Black queer flesh too. With the eradication of double consciousness, there is no nagging question of inhumanity, subhuman, the animal, or the like. This ideology might exist in the world, but Black queer flesh does not have this preprogrammed into its core to make its sense of self always be in question. By rejecting the normative idea of subjectivity through the art of Black queer abnegation, these queer characters can serve as exemplars of characters not dominated by society; they serve as the Clare Kendrys for the Irenes of the world who need help conceptualizing alternative ways of living a life of undominated and desubjected Black queerness. At the center of this innovative literary and radical political project is not simply the avocation of new modes of queer existence but an emphasis on healing old wounds, freeing Black queer flesh, and celebrating loving relationships.

As I have proposed, Black queer flesh enabled African American authors to imagine alternative paths to the making of the self. Rejecting the idea that Black authors could somehow wrestle away the reins that were placed around Black subjectivity and write their own narratives of self-formation, the authors in this study refused that project. They asked what knowledges might have been trampled over by the cult of Bildung and subjectivity. Furthermore, how might Black queer flesh—as opposed to the nominally unmarked straight Black flesh—disrupt and irritate hegemonic desires and the underworld of repression to expose alternative worlds and socialities that lie unconscious? My analysis shows that Black queer flesh—itself dispossessed from dispossession—demands an alternative narrative and way of life: a life of self-abnegation, a life of the chorus, a life of selves-without-subjectivity. Black queer flesh, denied representation in the normative world, finds expression through racial anxiety and, ultimately, in Hartman's close narration. When racial politics and racial fear escalate, the subject fractures and often ruptures to expose the universe of the drive and the existence of Black queer flesh. In this situation, the subject can either embrace this flesh—at the cost of continuing to experience anxiety and tortuous affects—or seal the wound with surplus jouissance. This extra pleasure not only metaphorically sutures the wound but also distracts such that anxiety and Black queer flesh that has either popped out or dragged the character into itself become neutralized and return to the drive. The most prominent example of surplus jouissance in this study manifests as racial uplift and, in particular, its fascination with the idea of self-formation, or being a normative human. By disseminating this idea, advocates of racial uplift plant the seeds of surplus jouissance into each African American reader, who can draw upon this resource as needed to deflect racial anxiety, to deflect Black queer flesh. As the saying goes, ignorance is bliss. By forcibly ignoring Black queer flesh and adopting the idea of self as wholly independently constructed, African American authors and community leaders effectively condone the work of double consciousness.

Queers of color disidentify with this mode of distraction and dispossession. Instead of calling forth surplus jouissance as a salve to racial anxiety, they latch on to anxiety until it helps them decathect from the subjectivity initiating the anxiety. This process of self-abnegation—of refusing to control anxiety—enables the queer character to play with Black queer flesh, which also participates in the process of decathection. This purging of subjectivities from the ego repeats until there are no more—or often just one—identities forming the ego. With a queer lover at their side, the character can self-abnegate the final subjectivity (usually something having to do with that lover) and undergo a radical reshaping of the self. In doing so, they reconstitute the self in the context of Black queer love—and not anti-Black racism, which fueled the installation of double consciousness. A new self can emerge informed by Black queer flesh.

The question arises: what happens to Black queer flesh after it aids the subject in destroying herself? As I have argued, the ideology of subjectivity as a permanent, solid, or quantifiable entity ceases. There are no false faces or "white masks," to riff on Fanon. The notion of a socially constructed identity, too, falls away even when it is understood to be flexible or constructed. Queer Blacks need not "resist" how they are made because they do not have an ego or psychic world that is automatically programmed for the internalization of anti-Black racism.[21] The self becomes, as Hartman models in *Wayward Lives,* an improvisation between all the constituents of Black queer flesh and a performance of that flesh in the form of a self-without-subjectivity, the chorus, and the amalgam of Black queer flesh as an archive. These performances will depend on what aspects of Black queer flesh might be available for participation in an ensemble at the moment when social interactions require a speaking body; the performance is highly contingent on Black queer flesh and the improvisation driving the pieces that happen to show up in the ensemble. Thus Black queer flesh is a performance—much in the manner of Trueblood's storytelling: a new storyboard unfolds that appears to represent the original (imagined to be some quantifiable subjectivity or "core" self) when in fact the story is a new creation dependent on previous versions of that story and who might be the listener.

By creating new performances of self for each interaction with the world, Black queerness expresses itself after a long life in the closet. Unlike straight Black flesh, Black queer flesh is not bound to dominant Black histories and experiences that fill history textbooks, the oral tradition, or sanitized family histories. These records, particularly documents from slavery and the slave narrative, either suggest—or erase—queer desire and Black queer sociality. If we consult the "historical" record proper, queer Blackness would be a recent invention of the late twentieth century in Black culture; Black queers continually struggle to gain a positive representation and political position within the Black community. Queer desire endures as abjection in heteronormative Black communities. Thus Black queer flesh must perform itself and make itself felt in the social world as much as possible to ensure that it is not excluded once again, and this exploration of the archives of Black queer flesh is endemic to Hartman's beautiful experiment. The queer, too, as a nonnormative presentation of self, is vital to sustaining Black queer flesh as exposed, accessible, wayward, and just plain "odd" and "different." The extravagance of Black queerness allows for, invited sometimes for those extroverts, a pleasure in being socially different—and almost always in a deviant way. With the performance of a self-without-subjectivity refreshed and reconfigured with each improvisational quilting of Black queer flesh, the self becomes increasingly comfortable, transcending subjectivity and with a sense of belonging in Black queer flesh.

Acknowledgments

I owe a great many thanks to many people and institutions. I acknowledge the generous support of St. Lawrence University and Dean Karl Schonberg for a faculty sabbatical and a Bradbury Faculty Award, which facilitated the completion of this book project. I am also grateful for my colleagues at St. Lawrence University who have been supportive, especially in the English department. At Middlebury College, I had time to rethink and rework the project while also teaching undergraduates through the benefit of an Andrew W. Mellon Foundation C3 Diversity Postdoctoral Fellowship. Deans Shirley Collado and Andi Lloyd provided support and funds for indispensable research in the Richard Wright Papers at the Beinecke Library, Yale University. My writing group at Middlebury, Toni Cook, Jessyka Finley, Ellery Foutch, and Anson Koch-Rein, held me accountable as the book took shape, offering encouragement and advice. The Disability Studies Collective there, particularly Susan Burch and Eli Clare, workshopped chapter 3. My co-organizers, Jessyka Finley and Susan Baldridge, ensured a successful Diversity at Liberal Arts Colleges conference hosted at Middlebury. Cheswayo Mphanza and Tamir Williams provided much-needed research assistance. The Mellon Foundation provided a needed Digital Liberal Arts grant that enabled me to travel to the Ralph Ellison Papers and Photographs at the Library of Congress. Much gratitude goes to the expert librarians at the Beinecke and Library of Congress for their generous assistance.

A big thanks to Seulghee Lee for reading the manuscript in various stages and collaborating on new work. Zakiyyah Jackson has offered support and friendship since the early days of graduate school. I am also grateful to a larger collective of editors, mentors, and colleagues who helped me clarify my ideas: Tavia Nyong'o, Josh Chambers-Letson, Eric Zinner, Aida Levy-Hussen, Juliet Flower MacCannell, Stephen Best, Thadious Davis, Herman Beavers, Richard Yarborough, Sookyoung Lee, Mary Jane Smith, Timothy Billings, Michael Bronski, Robert Cohen, Brett Millier, Marion Wells, Arlene Keizer, Cheylon Woods, and Susan Schweik.

Thanks to all those at Berkeley who made graduate school a magical time of intellectual inquiry and personal discovery. Noa Farchi, K-Sue Park, Simon Porzak, Batya Ungar-Sargon, and Damon Young fiercely unpacked Lacan, Freud, and Deleuze with me at our Townsend Center Working Group on Psychoanalysis. I cherish my discussions with the late Janet Adelman and am grateful to Peter Glazer for a life-changing experience when I served as dramaturg for a production of *Measure for Measure.* My committee not only supported the dissertation project but also fed me an endless list of books and articles. Gautam Premanth opened my eyes to decolonial critique and African literatures. Paola Bacchetta encouraged me to read Lacan and Irigaray in the original to better grasp these thinkers' humor and wit. Bryan Wagner started me down the rabbit hole of archives, and I've been diving ever since. I appreciate his thoughtful and eye-opening insights. Carol Stack stuck with me after retirement, both through generous conversation and in writing, and that meant the world to me. Kent Puckett entertained my obsession with literary theory and fueled my hunger for more. Maire Jaanus introduced me to Lacanian psychoanalysis and kindly allowed me to squat in her office hours until my endless queries were exhausted. My advisor, mentor, and friend Abdul JanMohamed ensured that graduate school and its afterlives were intellectually stimulating and personally enriching. I cannot thank him enough for his infinite patience and wisdom. He always makes time for me to ask, wonder, and converse about conundrums.

The monograph greatly improved because of a Mellon-funded manuscript workshop. A heartfelt thanks to Nadia Ellis, Roderick Ferguson, Abdul JanMohamed, and Darieck Scott for their insights and scholarship. Nadia helped me rethink assumptions and frameworks, while Darieck helped me more precisely frame the nexus of race, affect, and psychoanalysis. Roderick pushed me to advance queer-of-color critique, and for this challenge I remain in his debt.

Thank you to my wonderful editors at the University of Minnesota Press, Dani Kasprzak, Jason Weidemann, and Leah Pennywark. Jason and Leah provided tremendous support and wonderful advice. Gary Holcomb and Amber Musser cannot be thanked enough for their feedback in their incisive and generative reader reports. I also thank Anne Carter and Holly Monteith for their invaluable help with the manuscript. My appreciation to Mike Stoffel and the entire team at the Press as well.

Larry and Louise, you have given me a peaceful place to write, and the many jokes and meals we have shared for years have sustained me, so thanks to you both. I thank Adrienne for her careful reading of the manuscript. Danny, Julia, Sandy, and Michael, you have been dear friends whose love and fellowship these many decades have meant the world to me, humoring me through ups and downs. I can't wait for you, Charlotte and Eliot, to read this book and for us to take many more vacations. Mechel, thank you for opening your heart and family to me. The book benefited greatly from the invaluable assistance of Miguel Segovia, whose willingness to generously read and provide thoughtful suggestions has been invaluable, influencing my perspectives and prose in the process. And, finally, a big thank-you to you, Ryan, for countless meals and critiques.

Notes

Introduction

1. Michel Foucault, *Power/Knowledge: Selected Interviews and Other Writings, 1972–1977* (New York: Random House, 1980), 95.

2. Roderick A. Ferguson, *One-Dimensional Queer* (Cambridge: Polity, 2019), 3.

3. Walter Johnson, "To Remake the World: Slavery, Racial Capitalism, and Justice," *Boston Review*, February 20, 2018.

4. Charles Taylor, *Sources of the Self: The Making of the Modern Identity* (Cambridge, Mass.: Harvard University Press, 1992).

5. Along with scholars Paget Henry and Lewis R. Gordon, who have powerfully challenged Black studies to both understand and dismantle anti-Black racism from the perspective of a "regime of truth" not predicated on anti-Black racism, Sylvia Wynter has intervened to make a case for a sociogenic perspective; see Greg Thomas and Sylvia Wynter, "Proud Flesh Inter/Views: Sylvia Wynter," *ProudFlesh: A New Afrikan Journal of Culture, Politics, and Consciousness*, no. 4 (2006). In her work, da Silva, too, has emphasized the role of science "as the proper domain for the production of truth of man." See Denise Ferreira da Silva, *Toward a Global Idea of Race* (Minneapolis: University of Minnesota Press, 2007), xviii.

6. Saidiya Hartman, *Scenes of Subjection: Terror, Slavery, and Self-Making in Nineteenth-Century America* (New York: Oxford University Press, 1997), 116.

7. Alexander Weheliye has asked "what different modalities of the human come to light if we do not take the liberal humanist figure of Man as the master-subject." Alexander G. Weheliye, *Habeas Viscus: Racializing*

Assemblages, Biopolitics, and Black Feminist Theories of the Human (Durham, N.C.: Duke University Press, 2014), 8. This is a question Jared Sexton poses differently when he explains that "slavery is not a loss that the self experiences—of language, lineage, land, or labor—but rather the loss of any self that could experience such loss." Sexton, "The Vel of Slavery: Tracking the Figure of the Unsovereign," *Critical Sociology* 42, no. 4–5 (2016): 9. Theirs is a preoccupation of leading scholars in Black studies, particularly of Afro-pessimists who generally question the contemporary Black self as a subjecthood that is insufficient to register this loss of selfhood. Given this questioning of how a liberal human Black subject cannot by definition experience this loss of slave history, in *Black Queer Flesh,* I posit that a self of, and performing of, Black queer flesh could be thought of along the lines of Sexton's lost self, yet imagined in a queer elsewhere to evoke the formulation of queerness propounded by Nadia Ellis in *Territories of the Soul: Queered Belonging in the Black Diaspora* (Durham, N.C.: Duke University Press, 2015).

8. Hortense Spillers, "Mama's Baby, Papa's Maybe: An American Grammar Book," *Diacritics* 17, no. 2 (1987): 65.

9. Tavia Nyong'o, *Afro-Fabulations: The Queer Drama of Black Life* (New York: New York University Press, 2018), 20.

10. Spillers, "Mama's Baby, Papa's Maybe," 67.

11. Scholars often describe Black flesh as a site of horror. For Stephens, Black flesh maintains itself as "everything abject, vulnerable, fleshy, de-idealized." Michelle Ann Stephens, *Skin Acts: Race, Psychoanalysis, and the Black Male Performer* (Durham, N.C.: Duke University Press, 2014), 196. Beneath skin resides "the raw, holey fleshiness of the subject within" (199). "Flesh connotes objectification, woundedness, and a lack of agency," and Black flesh "produc[es] guilt and shame" in the early work of Amber Musser's *Sensational Flesh: Race, Power, and Masochism* (New York: New York University Press, 2014), 20, 170. Fred Moten argues that flesh means the "condition of not having a body of one's own" and the state of being "unprotected" in Saidiya Hartman and Fred Moten, "Fugitivity and Waywardness," Episode 6, "Make a Way Out of No Way," http://arika.org.uk/archive/items/episode-6-make-way-out-no-way/fugitivity-and-waywardness. Moten's usage taps into the liberal human notion of self-ownership as the first metric of subjectivity. Christina Sharpe, when she eloquently states that contemporary Black lives possess an "inheritance of a life of precarity," addresses the reproduction of precarity as the reproduction of flesh as pain, suffering, woundedness, and death. See Sharpe, "Black Studies: In the Wake," *Black Scholar* 44, no. 2

(2014): 63. The distortion and dispossession of Black lives, she proposes, enact themselves over time along with the production of flesh.

12. Michelle Ann Stephens, a careful reader, interprets Spillers to mean that "the flesh represents the body that sits on the very edge, on the underside, of the Symbolic order, pre-symbolic and pre-linguistic, just before words and meaning" in *Skin Acts,* 3.

13. Amber Musser, *Sensual Excess: Queer Femininity and Brown Jouissance* (New York: New York University Press, 2019), 6.

14. In reflecting upon her childhood, Hortense Spillers thinks of herself as a seven-year-old "fleshed, natural girl," sitting in the front row of church, in "'All the Things You Could Be by Now If Sigmund Freud's Wife Was Your Mother': Psychoanalysis and Race," *Critical Inquiry* 22 (Summer 1996): 710. In this brief interlude, she imagines an adult self reclaiming Black flesh as a positive experience.

15. Frantz Fanon, *The Wretched of the Earth* (New York: Grove Press, 2005), 19.

16. Darieck Scott, *Extravagant Abjection: Blackness, Power, and Sexuality in the African American Literary Imagination* (New York: New York University Press, 2010), 65.

17. Judith Butler, "Critically Queer," *GLQ: A Journal of Lesbian and Gay Studies* 1, no. 1 (1993): 19.

18. Jennifer Christine Nash, *Black Feminism Reimagined: After Intersectionality* (Durham, N.C.: Duke University Press, 2019), 3.

19. Nyong'o, *Afro-Fabulations,* 18; Musser, *Sensual Excess,* 17.

20. Joshua Chambers-Letson, *After the Party: A Manifesto for Queer of Color Life* (New York: New York University Press, 2018), xii.

21. C. Riley Snorton, *Black on Both Sides: A Racial History of Trans Identity* (Minneapolis: University of Minnesota Press, 2017), 59.

22. Fred Moten, *In the Break: The Aesthetics of the Black Radical Tradition* (Minneapolis: University of Minnesota Press, 2003), 22.

23. Tavia Nyong'o, "Wildness: A Fabulation," *Scholar and Feminist Online* 12, no. 1–2 (2013–14).

24. Tavia Nyong'o, "Little Monsters: Race, Sovereignty, and Queer Inhumanism in Beasts of the Southern Wild," *GLQ: A Journal of Lesbian and Gay Studies* 21, no. 2–3 (2015): 262.

25. Snorton, *Black on Both Sides,* 2.

26. E. Patrick Johnson, *Appropriating Blackness* (Durham, N.C.: Duke University Press, 2003), 2.

27. Saidiya Hartman, *Wayward Lives, Beautiful Experiments: Intimate Histories of Social Upheaval* (New York: W. W. Norton, 2019).

28. Jafari Allen, "Black/Queer Rhizomatics," in *No Tea, No Shade: New Writings in Black Queer Studies,* ed. E. Patrick Johnson, 27–47 (Durham, N.C.: Duke University Press, 2016).

29. José Esteban Muñoz, "Ephemera as Evidence: Introductory Notes to Queer Acts," *Women and Performance: A Journal of Feminist Theory* 8, no. 2 (1996): 6.

30. Jafari Allen, "Black/Queer/Diaspora at the Current Conjuncture," *GLQ: A Journal of Lesbian and Gay Studies* 18, no. 2–3 (2012): 215.

31. Jennifer DeVere Brody, "Passing Strange: E. Patrick Johnson's Strange Fruit," in *Blacktino Queer Performance,* ed. E. Patrick Johnson and Ramón Rivera-Servera, 213–28 (Durham, N.C.: Duke University Press, 2016).

32. Johnson, *Appropriating Blackness,* 2.

33. Hartman, *Wayward Lives,* xiii.

1. Passing into Racial Anxiety

1. Fanon, *Wretched of the Earth,* 19.

2. Scott, *Extravagant Abjection,* 65.

3. Reinhart Koselleck, *The Practice of Conceptual History: Timing, History, Spacing Concepts* (Palo Alto, Calif.: Stanford University Press, 2002), 185.

4. Franco Moretti, *Maps, Graphs, Trees: Abstract Models for a Literary History* (New York: Verso, 2005), 19. The data are for Britain, and the date is approximate, as read from a graph.

5. Viviana Zelizer, *Pricing the Priceless Child: The Changing Social Value of Children* (Princeton, N.J.: Princeton University Press, 1994).

6. Booker T. Washington, *Up from Slavery* (New York: Dover, 1995).

7. Jessie Redmon Fauset, *Plum Bun: A Novel without a Moral* (Boston: Beacon Press, 1990), 17.

8. Rita Felski, *Beyond Feminist Aesthetics: Feminist Literature and Social Change* (Cambridge, Mass.: Harvard University Press, 1989), 122–53.

9. Deborah McDowell, "Regulating Midwives," in Fauset, *Plum Bun,* xvi.

10. McDowell, xxi, xxi.

11. James Weldon Johnson, *The Autobiography of an Ex-Colored Man* (New York: Dover, 1995), 67.

12. Abdul JanMohamed, *The Death-Bound-Subject: The Archaeology of Richard Wright* (Durham, N.C.: Duke University Press, 2007).

13. Nella Larsen, *Quicksand,* in *The Complete Fiction of Nella Larsen* (New York: Anchor, 2001), 132, 104.

14. Max Horkheimer and Theodor Adorno, *Dialectic of Enlightenment,* ed. Gunzelin Schmid Noerr, trans. Edmund Jephcott (Palo Alto, Calif.: Stanford University Press, 2007), 111.

2. Nella Larsen and the Emergence of Black Queer Flesh

1. Moten, *In the Break,* 5.

2. Franco Moretti, *The Way of the World: The Bildungsroman in European Culture* (London: Verso, 1987).

3. Amritjit Singh, *The Novels of the Harlem Renaissance: Twelve Black Writers, 1923–1933* (State College: Penn State University Press, 2001), 36.

4. Genevieve Fabre and Michel Feith, eds., *Temples for Tomorrow* (Bloomington: Indiana University Press, 2001), 11.

5. Petrine Archer-Straw, *Negrophilia: Avant-Garde Paris and Black Culture in the 1920s* (New York: Thames and Hudson, 2000), 13.

6. Marianna Torgovnick, *Gone Primitive: Savage Intellects, Modern Lives* (Chicago: University of Chicago Press, 1990), 8.

7. Carole Sweeney, *From Fetish to Subject: Race, Modernism, and Primitivism 1919–1935* (Westport, Conn.: Praeger, 2004), 3.

8. For an extended analysis of Josephine Baker and French negrophilia, see Anne Cheng's *Second Skin: Josephine Baker and the Modern Surface* (Oxford: Oxford University Press, 2011). For an extended analysis of literary usages of the primitive, see Ben Etherington's *Literary Primitivism* (Palo Alto, Calif.: Stanford University Press, 2017).

9. Sieglinde Lemke, *Primitivist Modernism: Black Culture and the Origins of Transatlantic Modernism* (Oxford: Oxford University Press, 1998), 8–9.

10. Nathan Huggins, *Harlem Renaissance* (Oxford: Oxford University Press, 2007), 188.

11. Singh, *Novels of the Harlem Renaissance,* 34.

12. Shane Vogel, *The Scene of Harlem Cabaret: Race, Sexuality, Performance* (Chicago: University of Chicago Press, 2009), 6.

13. Kennedy Center, "Jazz History," http://www.kennedy-center.org/programs/jazz/ambassadors/Lesson9.html.

14. Deborah E. McDowell, *The Changing Same: Black Women's Literature, Criticism, and Theory* (Bloomington: Indiana University Press, 1995), 75.

15. Torgovnick, *Gone Primitive,* 18–19.

16. Sweeeny, *From Fetish to Subject,* 16, 17.

17. Martin Jay, *Adorno* (Cambridge, Mass.: Harvard University Press, 1984), 62.

18. Horkheimer and Adorno, *Dialectic of Enlightenment,* 21.

19. Adorno and critical theorists use the term *identity* to mean "identical." Because studies in racial formation use the term *identity* in a very different manner, I substitute critical theory's term with "the identical," "the same," etc.

20. Gunter Gebauer and Christoph Wulf, *Mimesis: Culture, Art, Society* (Berkeley: University of California Press, 1995), 25.

21. Martin Jay, *Marxism and Totality: The Adventures of a Concept from Lukács to Habermas* (Berkeley: University of California Press, 1984), 269. The process of dereification for Lukács also depends on a value-creating power of labor that forms the basis for a new collective unalienated social practice (270).

22. Theodor Adorno and Walter Benjamin, "Letter 117 from Adorno to Benjamin, dated 29 February 1940," in *The Complete Correspondence, 1928–1940* (Cambridge, Mass.: Harvard University Press, 2001), 321.

23. Theodor Adorno, *Negative Dialectics* (New York: Continuum, 1981), 53.

24. Judith Butler, *Bodies That Matter: On the Discursive Limits of "Sex"* (New York: Routledge, 1993).

25. bell hooks, *Killing Rage: Ending Racism* (New York: Henry Holt, 1995).

26. Jay, *Adorno,* 156.

27. José Esteban Muñoz, *Cruising Utopia: The Then and There of Queer Futurity* (New York: New York University Press, 2009), 1.

28. Theodor Adorno, "Letter to Benjamin 18 March 1936," in *Aesthetics and Politics: Debates between Block, Lukács, Brecht, Benjamin, Adorno* (London: Verso, 1980), 104.

29. Nella Larsen, *Passing,* in *The Complete Fiction of Nella Larsen: "Passing," "Quicksand," and "The Stories"* (New York: Anchor, 2001), 180.

30. Cheryl Wall, "Aspects of Identity in Nella Larsen's Novels," in *Passing,* ed. Carla Kaplan (New York: W. W. Norton, 2007), 361.

31. Helena Michie, "Sororophobia," in Kaplan, *Passing,* 411.

32. Moten, *In the Break.*

33. Adorno, *Negative Dialectics,* 53.

34. Adorno, *Dialectic of Enlightenment,* 112–13.

35. Michie, "Sororophobia," 416.

36. Ann DuCille, "*Passing* Fancies," in Kaplan, *Passing,* 438.

3. Queer Underworlds in Ralph Ellison

1. Josh Lukin, "Disability and Blackness," in *The Disability Studies Reader,* ed. Lennard Davis (London: Routledge, 2013), 311.

2. Dea H. Boster, *African American Slavery and Disability: Bodies, Property and Power in the Antebellum South, 1800–1860* (New York: Routledge, 2012).

3. Jennifer James, *A Freedom Bought with Blood: African American War Literature from the Civil War to World War II* (Chapel Hill: University of North Carolina Press, 2007), 13–15.

4. Dennis Tyler, "Disability of Color: Figuring the Black Body in American Law, Literature, and Culture" (PhD diss., UCLA, 2010), 40.

5. Ralph Ellison, "Out of the Hospital and Under the Bar," in *Soon, One Morning: New Writing by American Negroes, 1940–1962,* ed. Herbert Hill, 244–90 (New York: Random House, 1963).

6. Michal Raz-Russo et al., *Invisible Man: Gordon Parks and Ralph Ellison in Harlem* (Pleasantville, N.Y.: Gordon Parks Foundation, 2016).

7. Ralph Ellison, "Harlem Is Nowhere," *Harper's Magazine,* August 1964.

8. American Psychiatric Association, *Diagnostic and Statistical Manual of Mental Disorders* (Washington, D.C.: American Psychiatric Association, 1952).

9. Goodwill Industries of America, "The Goodwill Way: 1946 Annual Report," 1946, http://www.disabilitymuseum.org/dhm/lib/catcard.html?id=1973.

10. Paul Longmore and Lauri Umansky, "Disability History: From the Margins to the Mainstream," in *The New Disability History* (New York: New York University Press, 2001), 4, 12.

11. Rosemarie Garland Thomson, *Extraordinary Bodies: Figuring Physical Disability in American Culture and Literature* (New York: Columbia University Press, 1997), 15.

12. Christopher M. Bell, "Introducing White Disability Studies: A Modest Proposal," in Davis, *Disability Studies Reader,* 275–82.

13. Alison Kafer, *Feminist, Queer, Crip* (Bloomington: Indiana University Press, 2013); Robert McRuer, *Crip Theory: Cultural Signs of Queerness and Disability* (New York: New York University Press, 2006).

14. Ralph Ellison, "Wheelchair," folder A, box I:146, Ralph Ellison Papers, Manuscripts Division, Library of Congress, 514.

15. Ellison, folder A, 515, 515, 348.

16. Ellison, folder A, 513, 348.

17. Ellison, folder A, 353.

18. Ellison, folder B, box I:146.

19. Ellison, folder B, D replaced by page H.

20. Ellison, folder A, 354.

21. Ellison, folder B, 280, 18.

22. Ellison, folder A, 524.

23. Ralph Ellison, "Invisible Man," *Horizon: A Review of Literature and Art,* October 1947.

24. http://ehistory.osu.edu/osu/mmh/machinery/1to8.cfm. This includes permanent partial disabilities and temporary total disabilities but does not comprise permanent total disabilities or deaths, which were 75,400.

25. *The Municipal Code of Chicago: Comprising the Laws of Illinois Relating to the City of Chicago and the Ordinances of the City Council* (Chicago, 1881), 325.

26. Susan Schweik, "Begging the Question: Disability, Mendicancy, Speech and the Law," *Narrative* 15, no. 1 (2007): 59.

27. Susan Schweik, *Ugly Laws: Disability in Public* (New York: New York University Press, 2009), 186.

28. Michelle Jarman, "Coming Up from Underground: Uneasy Dialogues at the Intersections of Race, Mental Illness, and Disability Studies," in *Blackness and Disability: Critical Examinations and Cultural Interventions,* ed. Christopher Bell (East Lansing: Michigan State University Press, 2011), 17.

29. Ellison, "Harlem Is Nowhere," 320.

30. Letter to Richard Wright, cited in Arnold Rampersad, *Ralph Ellison* (New York: Knopf, 2007), 219.

31. Ellison, "Harlem Is Nowhere," 323, 324–25, 322.

32. Rampersad, *Ralph Ellison,* 219.

33. George Chauncey, *Gay New York: Gender, Urban Culture, and the Making of the Gay Male World* (New York: Basic Books, 1995), 83, 88.

34. A limited amount of scholarship covers sexuality in the novel. For example, Claudia Tate's "Notes on Invisible Women in Ralph Ellison's *Invisible Man*" examines the role of women as sexual objects and conduits for knowledge; Tate is in John Callahan's *Ralph Ellison's Invisible Man: A Casebook* (New York: Oxford University Press, 2004), 253–66. Michael Hardin's "Ralph Ellison's Invisible Man: Invisibility, Race, and Homoeroticism" examines the narrator's homosexual desires. Hardin is in *Southern Literary Journal* 37, no. 1 (2004): 96–120.

35. Ralph Ellison, *Invisible Man* (New York: Vintage, 1952), 22.

36. Daniel Y. Kim, *Writing Manhood in Black and Yellow: Ralph Ellison, Frank Chin, and the Literary Politics of Identity* (Palo Alto, Calif.: Stanford University Press, 2005).

37. José Esteban Muñoz, *Disidentifications: Queers of Color and the Performance of Politics* (Minneapolis: University of Minnesota Press, 1999), 31.

38. Judith Halberstam, *The Queer Art of Failure* (Durham, N.C.: Duke University Press, 2011), 11.

39. Moten, *In the Break,* 17–19.

40. Moten, 69.

41. Ellison, "Out of the Hospital and Under the Bar," 287.

42. Ralph Ellison, "At Mary's," box I:142, Ralph Ellison Papers, Manuscript Division, Library of Congress.

43. Ralph Ellison, "Pictorial Problem," box I:100; "Harlem Is Nowhere," folder 3, Ralph Ellison Papers, Manuscripts Division, Library of Congress.

44. David J. Alworth, *Site Reading: Fiction, Art, Social Form* (Princeton, N.J.: Princeton University Press, 2015), 122.

45. Ralph Ellison, "Vet," box I:146, Ralph Ellison Papers, Manuscript Division, Library of Congress.

46. Ralph Ellison, "Emerson," box I:144, Ralph Ellison Papers, Manuscript Division, Library of Congress.

47. Ralph Ellison, "Uncle Charles," box I:146, Ralph Ellison Papers, Manuscript Division, Library of Congress.

48. Lawrence Jackson, *Ralph Ellison: Emergence of Genius* (New York: John Wiley, 2002), 135.

49. Barbara Foley, *Wrestling with the Left: The Making of Ralph Ellison's Invisible Man* (Durham, N.C.: Duke University Press, 2010), 166. I was

unable to find this exact reference in the Ellison papers during my research trips.

50. Schweik, *Ugly Laws,* 144.

51. Siobhan Somerville, *Queering the Color Line: Race and the Invention of Homosexuality in American Culture* (Durham, N.C.: Duke University Press, 2000), 37.

52. Ralph Ellison, "Woodridge," box I:146, Ralph Ellison Papers, Manuscript Division, Library of Congress.

53. Kim, *Writing Manhood in Black and Yellow,* 321; Douglas Steward, "The Illusions of Phallic Agency: Invisible Man, Totem and Taboo, and the Santa Claus Surprise," *Callaloo* 26, no. 2 (2003): 522–35.

54. Roderick Ferguson, *Aberrations in Black: Toward a Queer of Color Critique* (Minneapolis: University of Minnesota Press, 2003), 65.

55. Ellison, "Woodridge."

56. Ellison.

57. Ralph Ellison, "Working Notes for Invisible Man," in *The Collected Essays of Ralph Ellison* (New York: Modern Library, 2003), 345.

58. Ralph Ellison, "Notes, 1942–1950," box I:151, Ralph Ellison Papers, Manuscript Division, Library of Congress, cited in Foley, *Wrestling with the Left,* 206.

59. Emphasis added. Ellison, untitled note ["At what point . . ."], "Emerson," box I:49, Ralph Ellison Papers, cited in Jackson's *Ralph Ellison: Emergence of a Genius,* 387.

60. *Calamus* refers to the gay-themed section of the same name in Walt Whitman's *Leaves of Grass* and has become a code word among gays. The full title of Sigmund Freud's work further illuminates Ellison's playing with the connection of gay and Black lives: *Totem and Taboo: Resemblances between the Mental Lives of Savages and Neurotics.* Furthermore, the text could be read as Emerson asking Invisible to join him in killing the primal father who rejects the "unspeakable" gay son.

61. In his notes, Ellison characterizes one of the veterans as flamboyantly gay. He describes a vet who "reveals a definite homosexual personality and 'acts out' his acceptance of Park's theory that Negro people are the 'lady of the races.'" Ralph Ellison, "Campus," folder F1, box I:144, Ralph Ellison Papers, Manuscript Division, Library of Congress.

62. Ellison, "Out of the Hospital and Under the Bar," 254.

63. Ellison.

64. Ellison, "At Mary's."

65. Ellison, *Invisible Man,* 332. Another briefcase used for work appears on p. 408.

66. Ralph Ellison, "The Art of Fiction: An Interview," in *Collected Essays,* 219.

67. The narrator also drops the Rinehart sunglasses during his fight with Ras, and the leg chain from Tarp is not accounted for, although I assume he discarded it in his stay underground.

68. Robert Stepto, *From Behind the Veil: A Study of Afro-American Narrative* (Urbana: University of Illinois Press, 1979), 381.

69. John Callahan, *Ellison's Invisible Man* (Washington, D.C.: Library of Congress, 2001).

4. Social Protest and the Aesthetics of Flesh in Richard Wright

1. Richard Wright, *The Long Dream* (Boston: Northeastern University Press, 2000).

2. Richard Wright, *Native Son* (New York: Harper, 2005), 111.

3. Hazel Rowley, "The Exile Years? How the '50s Culture Wars Destroyed Richard Wright," https://hazelrowley.com/articles/article-6/.

4. Ted Poston, "Wright: He's Out of Touch," *New York Post,* October 26, 1958.

5. Keneth Kinnamon, foreword to Wright, *The Long Dream,* viii.

6. Saunders Redding, "The Way It Was," *New York Times Book Review,* October 26, 1958, 4, 38.

7. JanMohamed, *Death-Bound-Subject.*

8. I want to distinguish self-abnegation from actual death: the former involves decathecting from identities that ultimately dismantle subjectivity and the psyche, whereas the latter can or cannot be included in this process. The main emphasis of a queer-of-color critique involves the displacement of social structures and their meaning and infusing that same form with queer politics and aesthetics. Helga, for instance, retains all of her psychic identities when she dies; they happen to overwhelm her, but she dies with them fully intact and bound to her ego.

9. JanMohamed, 253.

10. Fishbelly's adventures as Black queer flesh appear in the unpublished sequel "Island of Hallucination."

5. Toward a Black Queer Utopia

1. Baker Houston, "To Move without Moving: An Analysis of Creativity and Commerce in Ralph Ellison's Trueblood Episode," *PMLA* 98 (1983): 337.

2. Ellison, *Invisible Man,* 66.

3. Callahan, *Ellison's Invisible Man.*

4. Houston Baker, in *Blues, Ideology, and Afro-American Literature* (Chicago: University of Chicago Press, 1987), points out that Trueblood's story relies on multiple frame narratives to draw in the reader (176). Baker also argues that we must not forget that the story is a commodity (192).

5. Snorton, *Black on Both Sides,* 74.

6. Moten, *In the Break.*

7. George Kent, "Ralph Ellison and Afro-American Folk and Cultural Tradition," in *Speaking for You,* ed. Kimberley Benston, 95–104 (Washington, D.C.: Howard University Press, 1988). Kent agrees that the blues aids Trueblood in reentering the social world. He claims that Trueblood sings the blues to "get himself together" after the rape (98).

8. The chapter should refer to Trueblood with the pronoun "they" to reference the character as Black queer flesh from the first mention. To avoid confusion, I switch pronouns at this juncture for the purposes of clarity.

9. Saidiya Hartman, "Venus in Two Acts," *Small Axe* 12, no. 2 (2008): 1–14.

10. Hartman, *Wayward Lives.*

11. Sam Huber, "Saidiya Hartman's Astounding History of the Forgotten Sexual Modernists in 20th-Century Black Life," May 1, 2019, https://www.thenation.com/article/archive/saidiya-hartmans-astounding-history-of-the-forgotten-sexual-modernists-in-20th-century-black-life/.

12. Joanna Scutts, "The Art of Unruliness," *New Republic,* April 26, 2019, https://newrepublic.com/article/153693/art-unruliness.

13. Keeanga-Yamahtta Taylor, "Saidiya Hartman's 'Beautiful Experiments,'" *Los Angeles Review of Books,* May 5, 2019, https://lareviewofbooks.org/article/saidiya-hartmans-beautiful-experiments/.

14. Parul Sehgal, "An Exhilarating Work of History about Daring Adventures in Love," *New York Times,* February 19, 2019, sec. Books, https://www.nytimes.com/2019/02/19/books/wayward-lives-beautiful-experiments-saidiya-hartman.html.

15. Hartman refers to Gladys Bentley with the pronoun "he" to reflect

Bentley's self-identification. I employ the pronoun "they" when referencing characters who subscribe to Black queer flesh, unless Hartman specifically utilizes a different designation.

16. Toni Morrison, *Beloved* (New York: Vintage, 2004), 103–4.

17. Hartman, *Scenes of Subjection.*

18. Ellison, *Invisible Man,* 9.

19. Since close narration fuses identities, I employ the designation of narrator-character(s) to indicate the combined plural subject-without-subjectivity speaking, which makes it difficult to decipher who is talking. This usage also helps reinforce the performative aspect of Black queer flesh and its plural structure.

20. Christina Sharpe, *In the Wake: On Blackness and Being* (Durham, N.C.: Duke University Press Books, 2016).

21. While racism is no longer an internal structure of the psyche, the culture industry is another story. The workings of capitalism and commodification can operate on subjects without their involvement. Nella Larsen begins to analyze how African Americans can undo reification in *Quicksand.*

Index

Aberrations in Black (Ferguson), 141
abjection, 82, 184, 222; Black disability and, 17, 125; corporeal spasms through prism of, 7, 22; creation of alternative culture via, 127; positionality of, 90, 125; primitive and, 70–71. *See also* self-abnegation
ableist discourse of subjectivity, 1, 82, 110–11, 114, 120–22; anti-Black racism as, 115–16; medical model and, 106–7, 111, 117; rejection of, 106, 153; unconscious reading practices, 127; uplift as, 115–16, 121–22, 132–33, 151–52
abnegation. *See* desubjectification; self-abnegation
Adorno, Theodor, 43, 66–69, 71, 73, 232n19; artwork, idea of, 69, 83–84
aesthetics, 13–14; anti-Black, 43, 55; avant-garde, 127, 163; Bildungsroman and, 8, 14, 59, 65; Black, 37, 40–43, 57; Black queer, 14, 17, 164, 213; failed, 42, 65–66; of literary modernism, 59; Naturalist, 105, 145; queer-of-color, 105
African American novel: Bildungsroman as quintessential genre, 8, 28; queer literature, 161–65; tragic mulatto novel, 27–28, 44; writers expected to write about contemporary Black issues, 162–63. *See also* Bildungsroman; uplift, racial
African Americans: dehumanization of, 1–2, 81; disability as trope for, 106–7, 110–11, 121–24, 134–35, 139, 199–200; subjectivities prefabricated for, 40, 42–45, 56–57, 68, 105, 133
African American Slavery and Disability (Boster), 106
African Americans with disabilities: as awaiting able bodies and access to subjectivity, 107; disruption of uplift ideologies, 131–33,

137–38; in Ellison archives, 107–8; knowledge production by, 114–15, 120, 126–27, 136; silencing of, 126–27; subjectivity rejected by, 106, 116, 126–28, 142, 153
African art, 62
Afro-pessimism, 4, 228n7
agency, 1–5, 10, 37–38, 40, 53, 128, 160; liberal humanist view, 2, 25; limited, 64, 105, 228n11; refusal to claim, 32–33; self-abnegation of, 193, 203
Allen, Jafari, 14
Alworth, David, 137
American Psychiatric Association, 119, 140
anti-Black racism, 4, 116, 205, 227n5; African Americans constructed as disabled, 116; forgetting of, 182–83; freedom from, 77–78; psychological effects of, 118–19
archive: Black queer flesh as, 198; disability and, 105–16; first-person accounts lacking, 207–9. *See also* Hartman, Saidiya; *Wayward Lives, Beautiful Experiments*
Aristotle, 67–68
Asiatic primitive, 66
Autobiography of an Ex-Colored Man (Johnson), 15–16, 27–28, 143; male privilege in, 33–34; reception of, 38

Baby Suggs (character, *Beloved*), 211
Baker, Houston, 198, 205, 238n4
Baker, Josephine, 62, 63, 66
Bakhtin, Mikhail, 87, 95
Barthé, Richmond, 63, 139–40
beauty, narrative of, 61
beggars, as "handicapped," 117–18
Bell, Derrick, 108–9
Beloved (Morrison), 27, 211
Bentley, Gladys, 210, 238n15
Bildung, 125, 129; genealogy of concept, 25; heteronormative, 95; as imposed, 159–60, 220; normative white model of, 45–46, 54, 56–57, 68; "primitive" model of, 44–46; rejection of, 92–93; as self-formation, 25–26
Bildungsroman, 15; adapted to protest literature, 105; African American, 8–9, 43; anti-Black aesthetic, 43, 55; Black queer flesh repressed by, 59; Black women limited by genre, 56–57, 60, 65–66, 77, 92–93; disidentification from, 13–14; domestic sphere destroys self-formation, 43; double, 69–70, 103; education as central to, 44–46; endings, 31–32; episodic structure, 43–44, 55; eradicating, 55–57; friend as helper, convention of, 92–93; ideology of subjectivity promoted by, 8–9, 15–16, 23; limitations of, 24, 42–43; marriage as end of for female protagonist, 32, 41; narrative closure, 103–4; nineteenth-century, 43; policing via, 9; post-1848, 26; as propaganda, 25; queer-of-color critique, 7, 10, 13–14, 142, 181, 194, 197,

237n8; as quintessential African American genre, 8, 28; rejection of subjectivity in, 41–42; surplus jouissance aligned with, 8–9, 23–28; as white literary form, 42–43, 55–56, 59–60, 73; *Wilhelm Meister's Apprenticeship*, 124. *See also* uplift, racial
biracial characters, in tragic mulatto novel, 27–28, 44
Black Boy (Wright), 18, 167
Black flesh, 3–6, 178, 188–89, 207–20, 228n11; disidentification with, 79, 81–83; policing of, 209; Spillers' theorization of, 4–6, 79, 81. *See also* Black queer flesh
Blackness, 7; commodification of, 27, 36–37, 40, 50–54, 80–81; hegemonic, 126; multiplicity inherent in, 9–10; as performative and embodied, 15; as radiance, 44–46, 48–50, 55–57, 60–61, 65, 72; as "savage," 44, 53–55, 62, 64
Black queer flesh, 3; as archive, 198; as basis for emancipated sense of self, 97–98; chorus in alignment with, 211–13; defined according to context, 7; disorganic nature of, 11, 13; ensemble dimensions of, 9–10, 19, 79, 96, 204, 212–13, 215–18, 222; erasure of, 82, 180, 222; fainting, and closeness to, 177–78, 185, 192; heteronormativity and, 180–82; as hypervisible, 82; Larsen's exposure of, 44–45; life as, 219–22; as life-force, 7, 13, 22–23, 165; lived experiences of historic queer identities, 6–7; as ontology for being, 7–8, 23; as part of Black women's history, 73; performance of, 11–12, 14–15, 207, 217; pronouns use to indicate, 101–3, 204–6, 238n15, 238n8; psychic drive and, 7, 23, 80, 167–68, 192; repression of, 59–60, 75–76, 81–83, 89–90, 185–86; rhizomatic metaphor, 14; rise of, 80–83; self-abnegation and releasing of, 186–95; sonic materiality, 79, 96, 101, 204; as stolen, 172–73; after subjectivity, 9–10, 13, 16–18, 197–222; subjectivity, rejection of, 2–3, 6–7, 13, 50; subjectivity assembled out of, 168; undominated, 61–65, 69, 73–74, 78–80, 89–93, 101–4, 220; "voice" of, 213. *See also* chorus
Black subjectivity. *See* subjectivity, Black
Bledsoe (character, *Invisible Man*), 46, 140, 143
Boas, Franz, 62
Boster, Dea, 106
bourgeoisie, Black, 44, 138–39
Brockway, Lucius (character, *Invisible Man*), 130
Brody, Jennifer, 15
Brown, Esther, 214–15
Brownies' Book, The (magazine), 27
Brown v. Board of Education, 162
Burke, Kenneth, 124
Burnside (character, *Invisible Man*), 137–39, 143
businessmen, Black, 182, 187–89
Butler, Judith, 10, 61, 70, 71

Calamus, 144, 236n60
Callahan, John, 199
Callahan, Robert, 156
carceral system, 216
Chamber, Josh, 10
Chauncey, George, 119, 140, 141
chorus (Hartman), 18–19, 211–22; as Black queer flesh, 211–13; call and response, 19, 214–15, 219; "Cast of Characters" catalog, 212; plurality of Black queer flesh as, 19, 211, 213, 217, 219; rereading of text via, 212–13
Chris (character, *The Long Dream*), 168–69
civil rights movement, 45, 162; white fears of, 191
Clifton, Tod (character, *Invisible Man*), 130, 148–52
close narration, 18–19, 197, 220, 239n19; academic narrator, character, and chorus, 211–13, 239n19; improvisation and, 210–15, 217, 219, 221–22
Cloutier, Jean-Christophe, 108
colorism, 184
commodification: of Blackness, 27, 36–37, 40, 50–54, 80–81; in *Invisible Man,* 130, 138, 198; in *Passing,* 72, 74, 80–83; property, rejection of, 215–16; in *Quicksand,* 36–37, 40, 42, 50–57, 60, 72–74, 80; of sexuality, 50–51, 72
commodity fetishism, 50–54, 56, 72
communism, 124, 127, 134–35, 152–53
Cotton Club, 64
Crane, Helga (character, *Quicksand*), 40–57, 60, 69, 72, 164; as commodity, 42, 52–57, 60, 80
Crisis, The (NAACP), 27
critical fabulation, 207–8, 211
culture industry, 69, 71, 73, 89, 239n21
cultures: *Bildung* across, 25; disability, 124, 125, 132–33; heterosexual, 180–81; non-value, 127; "primitive," 62; queer, 7, 12, 17, 125

death, zones of, 207
death-bound-subjectivity, 41, 164, 192
decathection, 102, 221, 237n8
Deleuze, Gilles, 10
Demoiselles d'Avignon, Les (Picasso), 62
Dennis, Tyler, 106–7
desubjectification, 7–8, 12, 16, 212, 220
deviant subjectivity, 7, 126–28, 140, 156, 202
dialectic of enlightenment, 66–67
Dialectic of Enlightenment (Adorno and Horkheimer), 66–67
difference: as disability, 116; forgetting of, 67; mimesis preserves, 67, 71, 84, 95; nonidentical, 69, 84
disability, 6–7; as abject, 17, 125; African American, celebration of, 107, 138; African Americans policed into, 115–16; anti-Black ma-

nipulation of medical discourses, 118, 133, 199–200; archive and, 105–16; as basis of community, 135; beggars, as "handicapped," 117–18; Black cultural definitions, 114; Black punk, 17; Black queer disability history and culture, 142; blindness metaphor, 121–22, 134–36; as chance to reject subjectivity, 106, 127–28, 142, 153; communities, African American, 126–27; cripping the Battle Royal chapter, *Invisible Man,* 120–24; deficit model of, 111, 132; designed to oppress African Americans, 115–16, 121, 126, 132–33; gay and fairy identities as, 108, 118; "handicap" as category, 7, 108, 113, 117; hegemony of visual register, 135; histories of, 116–20; homosexuality as, 108, 117, 119, 140, 143–44; incest as mental illness, 199–200, 202; infirmity, 130–33; "insanity"/mental illness/cognitive disability, 108, 132, 137–39; medical model, 106–7, 111, 117; as non-value culture, 127; queerness, intersection with, 109; as source of strength, 134–35; subjectivity denied, 126–30, 135, 137; subversion of oppression via, 135, 142; trickster figure and, 128–31; triple intersectionality, 150; as trope for African Americans, 106–7, 110–11, 121–24, 134–35, 139, 199–200; two systems of, 113; *Ugly Laws,* 117–18, 130, 133, 139, 140; Union Army's use of, 106; visible, 118, 126

disability studies, 17, 106; as "white disability studies," 108–9

discipline, 8, 21, 43–44, 67

disidentification, 122; with Black flesh, 79, 81–83; with carceral state, 191; with disability as normative ideology, 125, 134, 141; with heteronormativity, 125, 143; with ideology of subjectivity, 13–14, 85, 130, 156, 216; queer, 44; queer-of-color, 125; with social structures of primitivism, 70–71; from surplus jouissance, 71–72; with uplift's philosophy and methods, 124–30; from whiteness, 87–88, 123

Disidentification (Muñoz), 125

dispossession, 220; of knowledge, 3, 59, 61, 115, 129, 171; productive, 142; psychological, 137

domination, 2, 6, 16–19; Black subjectivity as, 17, 74, 77–80; forgetting, and nature, 66–67; fragmenting of subjectivity, 77–80; freedom from, 73, 77–78, 84–88; self-abnegation and, 72–73; surplus jouissance eradicates feeling of, 30; trajectory away from, 73–77; undominated Black queer flesh, 61–65, 69, 73–74, 78–80, 89–93, 101–4, 220; undominated primitive, 68–69, 71, 73, 78, 94

double consciousness, 14, 30, 60, 79,

97, 220, 221; in *The Long Dream,* 182, 187–90, 194–95
drive, the, 22–23, 83, 91, 168, 220–21
Du Bois, W. E. B., 24, 27; "Talented Tenth," 45
DuCille, Ann, 92

écriture feminine, 73–74
education, suppression of Black culture by, 44–46
Ellington, Duke, 64
Ellison, Ralph, 17, 46, 104, 105–57, 219; avant-garde aesthetics of, 127, 163; "Harlem Is Nowhere," 107–8, 137, 140; Lafargue Psychiatric Clinic and, 118–19, 136–37; queer-of-color critique, 142, 202; Wright's conversation with, 163. See also *Invisible Man*
Emerson (character, *Invisible Man*), 143–44, 147
Emerson, Ralph Waldo, 142
Emma (character, *The Long Dream*), 166
enslaved people, 2–5, 106, 216
Ex-Colored Man (character, *The Autobiography of an Ex-Colored Man*), 32–38
exotic, 61–62

Fabre, Genevieve, 61
fabulation, 11, 206–8, 211
fairies, as third sex, 107, 119, 140–41
Fanon, Frantz, 7, 22–23, 221
Fauset, Jessie Redmon, 16, 27–32, 37, 39, 41
Feith, Michael, 61
Felski, Rita, 29
feminism, Black, 10
Feminist, Queer, Crip (Kafer), 111
Ferguson, Roderick, 2, 15, 141–42
Fishbelly (Rex Tucker; character, *The Long Dream*), 161–95; bisexuality of, 165, 185, 192, 195; fainting episode, 176–77, 185, 192; letters, role of, 193–94; in prison, 162, 190, 191–92
flesh, 5–6; as life-force, 22–23; unmarked, 5, 72, 219–20. *See also* Black flesh; Black queer flesh
Foley, Barbara, 140
forgetting: of anti-Black racism, 182–83; in *The Autobiography of an Ex-Colored Man,* 32; domination of nature and, 66–67; gendered, 33–34; immediate transitions in novel, 35–37; as "passing" device, 38; of racial anxiety, 8, 21, 34–36, 38, 40, 185; reification and, 69; as surplus jouissance, 34–39, 183
Foucault, Michel, 2
France, Black expatriates in, 63
freedom, 94–95, 202, 210, 214; from domination, 73, 77–78, 84–88; integral, 73; liberal humanist, 25; (pre)historical, 94, 103; radical, 11, 84–85, 99; from subjectivity, 101; from white assimilation, 28, 54
Freud, Sigmund, 22, 81, 163, 236n60
Fry, Roger, 62

Garland-Thomson, Rosemary, 108
Garvey, Marcus, 24
Gay New York (Chauncey), 140
gay people and culture: fairies, as third sex, 107, 119, 140–41; "mentally handicapped" designation, 117, 119, 140; modes of being early twentieth century, 139–40, 149; "punks," 119–20, 139–48; "wolves," 119–20, 143, 147–48
gaze, white, 188–89
gender, 167, 209; forgetting as gendered, 33–34; intersectionality of, with race and disability, 32, 74, 76, 109–12; performance of, 70; shifting categories of, 6
Gilroy, Paul, 11
Goethe, Johann Wolfgang von, 124
Gone Primitive (Torgovnick), 62
Goodwill Industries, 108, 113, 116–17
Great Migration, 24, 118

Halberstam, Jack, 126
Hampton, Mabel, 217–19
happiness, norms of, 47
Hardin, Michael, 141
Harlem, mental illness in, 108, 118, 136–37
"Harlem Is Nowhere" (Ellison), 107–8, 137, 140
Harlem Renaissance, 38, 39; primitivism and, 63–64; social reality of, 71
Harper, Francis, 161
Hartman, Saidiya, 3, 5, 12, 104, 238n15; "chorus," concept of, 18, 211–22; close narration, 18–19, 197, 211–15, 219, 220, 239n19; critical fabulation, 207–8, 211; *Lose Your Mother,* 208; *Scenes of Subjection,* 212; as trickster, 211, 212–13; "Venus in Two Acts," 207–8. See also *Wayward Lives, Beautiful Experiments*
heteronormativity, 6, 95, 173, 178, 202–3; ableist rhetoric and, 120, 124–27, 129; as "bad," 169; in Black communities, 222; Black primitive in framework of, 65; compulsive, as surplus jouissance, 180–86; disidentification with, 125, 143; mimesis and, 100–101; recovery of gay desire through, 185; self-abnegation of, 91, 150, 165; subjectivity, 60, 173; surplus jouissance and, 50, 165, 180–86
historical fiction, 207
historiographies, 208
history, as means to terminate reification, 68
hold, the, 216
Home to Harlem (McKay), 63–64
homosexual, as term, 119, 140–41
hooks, bell, 70–71
Horkheimer, Max, 66–67
Huber, Sam, 208–9
Huggins, Nathan, 63, 64
Hughes, Langston, 139
humanism. *See* liberal humanism
Hurston, Zora Neale, 1, 2, 163

identity: Black and white stereotypes, 44; as "identical," 67, 232n19; intersectional, 3, 9, 33,

74, 107, 125, 177; multiplicities of, 109; performance of, 6–7; socially constructed, 221
"Illusions of Phallic Agency, The" (Steward), 141
Imaginary, the, 5, 22–23
improvisation, 10–12, 17–18, 79, 96, 204; close narration and, 210–15, 217, 219, 221–22
individual: identity making at level of, 14; individuation of, 3; plural selves, 213, 217; standardized behavior imposed on, 67–68; uplift, role in, 24–25, 135
instrumental rationality, 67
intersectionality: critique prior to, 75; of disability, gender, and race, 32, 74–76, 109–12; of disabled and racial identities, 106–7, 110–11, 114, 124–26; of sexuality and race, 75
In the Break (Moten), 79
"in the life," 144–45, 147, 216
"Invisibility, Race, and Homoeroticism" (Hardin), 141
Invisible Man (character, *Invisible Man*): Black queer flesh achieved by, 156–57, 197, 206–7; limited sexuality of, 125; mimetic relationships, 128–32, 143, 148–52, 203–4; misreading of, 17; as punk, 139–48; self-abnegation of, 17, 128–29; in "Wheelchair" chapter, 109–15
Invisible Man (Ellison), 46, 105–57; "Battle Royal" episode, 105, 115–16, 120–24, 145; "Blackness of Blackness" episode, 128–29, 131; Black queer flesh, move toward, 152–57; Black queer flesh in, 107, 128–30, 132–35, 138, 206–7; blues tradition, role in, 198–99; Brotherhood episodes, 133, 134–35; commodification in, 130, 138, 198; as "Disabled Man," 135; document burning scene, 152, 154–55; draft chapters, 107, 109–15, 134; dream/castration scene, 155–56; factory episode, 130–33; lobotomy scene, 122, 132, 148; normative readings of, 125; post-1940s reading of, 149; punk sexuality and, 139–48; queer love and mimesis in, 148–52; racial anxiety in, 120, 124, 141, 150; reviews focused on racial commentary, 163; self-abnegation in, 128–30, 141, 144, 150, 152–57, 199–206; self-without-subjectivity in, 17, 128, 156, 197, 198, 200–201, 204–5; surplus jouissance in, 129, 132, 145–46, 201–2; Trueblood scenes in, 46, 198–206; veterans, 137–39; "Wheelchair" (purged chapter), 109–15
Iola Leroy (Harper), 161
Irigaray, Luce, 73

Jack (character, *Invisible Man*), 152–53
Jackson, Lawrence, 140, 144
Jacobs, Harriet, 9
James, Jennifer, 106
JanMohamed, Abdul, 41, 164, 192
Jarman, Michelle, 118

Jim Crow system, 105, 131; lynching, 174–75; morality not possible within, 188; subject formation in context of, 162
Johnson, E. Patrick, 12, 15
Johnson, James Weldon, 15–16, 27–28, 32–39, 143
Johnson, Walter, 2
jouissance, surplus: Bildungsroman aligned with, 8–9, 24–28; as defense mechanism, 16; as disciplinary, 8, 21; disidentification from, 71–72; as distraction, 21–22, 40, 50, 183, 221; fairy tales about marriage, 30; as false pleasure, 8, 21; financial success as, 46; forgetting as, 34–39; as form of repression, 21–22; heteronormativity as, 50, 180–86; in *Invisible Man,* 129, 132, 145–46, 201–2; Lacan devises, 21; marriage naturalized as legitimate source of, 32; neutralizing, 78; normative pleasure and, 14, 180–81; as oppressive, 40, 46; in *Passing,* 76–78, 80–81, 89–91, 93, 97; in passing novels, 28–39; in *Plum Bun,* 28–32; racial anxiety avoided by use of, 8, 15, 21–24, 44, 46–49, 201; rejection of in *Quicksand,* 39–59, 73; security as, 89–92, 94, 97

Kafer, Alison, 109, 111
Kendry, Clare (character, *Passing*), 60–61, 67–104; commodification of, 72, 74, 80–83; death of, 98–100, 191, 197
Kent, George, 238n7
Kim, Daniel, 125, 141
Kinnamon, Kenneth, 162
Klein, Melanie, 152
knowledge: Black queer flesh as source of, 9; dispossessed, 3, 59, 61, 115, 129, 171; production by African Americans with disabilities, 114–15, 120, 126–27, 136
Koselleck, Reinhart, 25, 26

Lacan, Jacques, 8, 21–23, 96, 166–67. *See also* psychoanalysis
Lafargue Psychiatric Clinic (Harlem), 118, 136–37
language: of Black queer flesh, 96–97; complete utterance, 86–87, 95–96; hegemonic, 17
Larsen, Nella, 16–17, 116, 161, 219; critique of Bildungsroman, 40; new genre inaugurated by, 16; rejection of subjectivity within Bildungsroman, 41–43; Wright's conversation with, 163. See also *Passing*; *Quicksand*
Lawrence, D. H., 62
lesbian primitive, 66
lesbian readings, 61, 65
Levi-Strauss, Claude, 62
liberal humanism, 1–3, 14–16, 108, 218, 227n7, 228n11; Bildungsroman as promotion of subjectivity, 8–9, 15–16, 23; self-abnegation destroys, 6, 189; self as subjectivity, 1–2, 19, 25, 27–28, 160; uplift discourse and, 74
literary artists, primitivism and, 62–63

lived experiences, 6–7
Locke, Alain, 63
Long Dream, The (Wright), 18, 161–95; Aggie episode, 172, 173, 182; Bildungsroman rejected, 192–93; bisexuality in, 165, 185, 192, 195; Black queer flesh in, 167–68; castration imagery in, 166–67, 168, 175, 176–78, 181, 184; childhood sexuality, repression of, 171–72; compulsive heteronormativity as surplus jouissance, 180–86; critiques of, 162, 164; "Days and Nights . . ." section, 180–86; as double Bildungsroman, 162, 164; double consciousness in, 182, 187–90, 194–95; dreams, importance of, 163–64; fainting episode, 176–77, 185, 192; "Fishbelly" nickname in, 166–67, 193; Gladys scenes, 184–86; locating in queer African American literature, 161–65; lynching of Chris in, 174–80; mimesis in, 176–79, 184; mirror stage, racialized, 166–80; Ned scene, 169–70; nuclear, middle-class family structure in, 162; prison episode, 162, 190, 191–92; psychoanalytic concepts in, 163–64; racial anxiety in, 173, 185; self-abnegation in, 175–76, 178–79, 186–95; self-formation expelled from, 192–93; sequel to, 162, 176; Tyree scene, 170–71; Tyree's murder scene, 186
Longmore, Paul, 108
love story, 60–61
Lukács, Georg, 68, 232n21
Lukin, Josh, 106
lynching, 37, 41, 92, 93, 154, 161; in *The Long Dream,* 174–80

"Mama's Baby, Papa's Maybe" (Spillers), 4
"Man": domination of nature, 66–67; Eurocentric ideal of, 3, 227n7
"many, the," 11
marriage: as end of Bildungsroman for female protagonist, 32, 41; fairy tale, 30; as means of access to power, 29; to "upstanding men," 30–32
Marx, Karl, 21, 54
Marxism, 134
Mary (character, *Invisible Man*), 128, 134, 136, 141, 146–47, 153, 154–55
masculinity: achieving Black queer flesh, 175–76; Black male friendships, 161–62; compulsive heteronormativity as surplus jouissance, 180–86; in context of other African Americans, 182; gay subjectivity, white notion of resisted, 178–79; heterosexual, complexity of, 163; homosexuality denied, 175, 180; as the "lady of the races," 142, 151; self-abnegation of, 165, 185–92; submissive, 164, 181–82, 186–87; subversion, performance of, 188; three types of, 165, 181, 189, 192; white, Black appropria-

tion of, 189–91; white, as fearless, 189–91
materiality, sonic, 79, 96, 101, 204
McDowell, Deborah, 29, 30, 61, 64–65, 71, 75, 76, 92
McKay, Claude, 63–64
meta-subject, 68
Michie, Helena, 75, 89
middle class, Black, 48–49; assimilation into white culture, 54; businessmen, 182, 187–89; disciplining powers of, 67; nuclear family, 162; in *Passing,* 68–70, 73, 89; quest for "happiness," 47; rejection of, 55; sexuality as repressed, 65; standardization, 68–70, 89; uplift propaganda about, 24
mimesis: alter libido, 92; difficulty of, in Wright, 161; identification vs., 84; in *Invisible Man,* 128–32, 143, 148–52, 203–4; in Larsen, 16, 68–71, 73–74, 78, 83–95, 97, 99–101; in *The Long Dream,* 176–79, 184; mimicry vs., 68, 91; mirror stage, 101; necessity of among African American women, 72–73; primary, 100; referent, 68–70; replication of original, 67–68; secondary, 101; self-abnegation and, 16, 74, 83–93; semblance as promise of nonsemblance, 69–70, 71, 83
mirror stage, 101, 165; racialized, 166–80
modernism, 59–61, 105; primitivist, 63, 72; queer-of-color aesthetic, 105
Moretti, Franco, 26
Morrison, Toni, 21, 27, 161. See also *Beloved*
Moten, Fred, 11, 15, 59, 79, 81, 96, 129–30, 228n11; "nonvalue," 127
motherhood, reproduction of oppression via, 41–43
multiplicity, 9–10, 160, 201, 204, 213, 217
Muñoz, José, 11, 14–15, 66, 73, 125
Murray, Angela (character, *Plum Bun*), 28–32
Musser, Amber, 6, 10, 81

Nash, Jennifer, 10
Native Son (Wright), 17, 18, 159–60, 188
Naturalist aesthetic, 34, 105
Nazis, 62
Negative Dialectics (Adorno), 69
negrophilia, 63
new African Americans, 24
New Negro, The (Locke), 63
Nigger Heaven (Van Vechten), 63
normative methodologies, 108–9
normativity, rejection of, 14, 16, 47–48, 103, 218
nuclear family, Black, 162–63
Nyong'o, Tavia, 10, 15

object, captive body as, 4–5
Oedipus, 165, 206
old age, Black, 134
oppression, 160; disability discourse and, 121, 132–33; forgetting through surplus jouissance, 183; intraracial, 166, 172; reproduced via motherhood, 41, 43, 88;

subversion of, 128, 142; surplus jouissance as, 40
ownership, 52, 211, 215–16; self, 1–2, 228. *See also* self-possession

Park, Robert, 142
Parks, Gordon, 107, 136–37
passing: in *The Autobiography of an Ex-Colored Man,* 32–39; forgetting and, 38–39; limbo state of racialization, 72; passive position toward, 32–34, 37; in *Plum Bun,* 28–32; public discussion of, 38; switching between races, 76–77; tragic mulatto novel, 27–28
Passing (Larsen), 40, 60–61, 67–104; Black queer flesh articulated in, 61, 67, 72–74, 77; Clare's death in, 98–100, 191, 197; commodification in, 72, 74, 80–83; as double Bildungsroman, 69–70, 103; heteronormative and homonormative readings, 81; love story in, 60–61; mother–daughter relationship in, 87, 88; move toward no domination in, 73–77; narrative closure, 16, 103–4; opening scene, 80; rise of Black queer flesh in, 80–83; self-abnegation, achieving in, 93–104; self-abnegation and mimesis in, 83–93; self-abnegation in, 72–75, 77–80, 83–104; subjectivity rejected in, 16–17, 23–24; surplus jouissance in, 76–78, 80–81, 89–91, 93, 97; undomination in, 61–65, 69, 73–80, 89–93, 96, 101–4
performance: of Black queer flesh, 11–12, 14–15, 207, 217; of false subject, 200; of gender, 70; of identity, 6–7; of self-without-subjectivity, 11–12, 210–11, 221–22; skin as site of, 4–5; of subjectivity, 4–5, 40, 56; of subversion, 187–88
performance studies, Black and Black queer, 14–15
Perkins, Aaron (Kid Chocolate), 215
Perkins, Eva, 215
Petry, Ann, 105
picaresque narrative, 43, 56
Picasso, Pablo, 62
Plum Bun (Fauset), 16, 27, 37; marriage as end of Bildungsroman, 41; surplus jouissance in, 28–32
plurality of self, 10–11, 18–19, 194, 213, 217, 219
policing: African Americans forced to embody disability, 115–16; archival record of, 209; Bildungsroman and, 9; of self-formation, 159–60; into specific, historically contingent categories, 6; of subject through power, 3, 218
pornotrope, 4, 6
Poston, Ted, 162
power/knowledge system, 1, 6, 14
powerlessness, 4, 177
primitive, the, 36, 54–55, 72–74, 84, 96, 103; abject form of, 70–71; applied to Jews, 62; Asiatic, 66; culture industry's effect on, 71; disidentification

with, 71–72; "jungle style" of jazz, 64; lesbian or Black queer, 67; as origins/original, 66–69, 71, 84; as overly sexualized, 70–71, 72; as queer origins, 65–73; as radiance, 44–46, 48–50, 55–57, 60–61, 65, 72; reification of, 72; sixteenth-century definition, 66; stereotypes of, 44–45; undominated, 68–69, 71, 73, 78, 94
pronouns, used to indicate Black queer flesh, 101–3, 204–6, 238n15, 238n8
property, rejection of, 215–16
protest tradition, 18, 105, 161, 163
psychoanalysis, 14, 21, 163–64. *See also* Lacan, Jacques
"punks," 119–20, 139–48, 149
punk sexuality, 139–48

queer cultures, 7, 12, 17, 125
queer failure, 125–27, 177
queer histories, 6–7, 10, 100, 194, 209
queerness: categories of, 6; disability, intersection with, 109; fairy as third sex, 107, 119; as the non-normative, 82; one-dimensional, 2–3; as point of departure, 10; as same-sex love, 81–82
queer-of-color critique, 7, 10, 13–14, 125, 197, 237n8; Ellison's, 142, 202; Wright's, 164, 181, 194–95
queer sociality, 7, 10–12, 50, 81, 100, 132, 175, 179, 222
Quicksand (Larsen), 16, 27, 39–55, 161; Bildungsroman critiqued in, 40; circulation metaphor, 51–52, 57, 80; commodification in, 36–37, 40, 42, 50–57, 60, 72–74, 80; critiques of, 42, 46, 59; double consciousness reproduced in, 60; ending of as aesthetic failure, 42; introduction of, 80; objectification in, 50–55; place in, 48–50; primitive/"savage" trope in, 44, 53–55, 60, 62, 64; queer disidentification in, 44; "radiance" in, 44–46, 48–50, 55–57, 60–61, 65, 72; self-racializaton in, 48; sexuality in, 50–52, 65; social realism in, 56; surplus jouissance, rejection of, 39–59, 73; surplus jouissance, to avoid racial anxiety, 44, 46–50

racial anxiety: desire for racial freedom, 85–87; desubjectification propelled by, 7–8; embrace of, 27, 39; forgetting of, 8, 21, 34–36, 38, 40, 185; in *Invisible Man,* 120, 124, 141, 150, 200–201; in *The Long Dream,* 173, 185; mimetic relationships and, 74; as "muscular spasms" of the colonized, 7, 22; psyche and, 22; self-abnegation and, 12, 221; sexual desire and, 76; as shame, 37; surplus jouissance used to avoid, 8, 15, 21–24, 44, 46–49, 201
racialization, 74, 99, 141; limbo state of, 72; self-racialization, 48; skin as, 5

radiance, Blackness as, 44–46, 48–50, 55–57, 60–61, 65, 72
radical humanism, 66–67
Rainey, "Ma," 64–65
Ralph Ellison Archive (Library of Congress), 17, 107
Rampersad, Arnold, 119
reading, alternative modes of, 213–14
Real, the, 5, 22–23, 81; eruptions of, 96
Reality, 22
"Reckless Blues" (Smith), 214
recovery: of Bildung, 43, 68; of feelings and narratives of slavery, 3; of prehistoric/primitive, 65, 68–69; of subjectivity, 5, 55
Redding, Saunders, 164
Redfield, Irene (character, *Passing*), 60, 67, 69–104, 128; Clare's death and, 98–100, 191, 197
reification: dereification, 232n21; history as means to terminate, 68–69; of primitive, 72; of self-formation, 50, 52, 55, 57, 65, 239n21
Reis, Winold, 63
repression, 189–90, 220; of Black queer flesh, 59, 60, 75–76, 81–83, 89–90, 185–86; of desires, 65, 67–68, 89; surplus jouissance as form of, 21–22, 182–83; unrepression of queer desire, 165
respectability politics, 116, 162
revolution (Europe, 1848), 25

"savage" trope, 44, 53–55, 62, 64
Scenes of Subjection (Hartman), 212
Schweik, Susan, 117–18
Scofield (character, *Invisible Man*), 154
Scott, Darieck, 7, 22–23
Scutts, Joanna, 209
Second World War, 116–17
security, as surplus jouissance, 89–92, 94
Sehgal, Parul, 209
self: collective, 9–10; plurality of, 10–11, 18–19, 194, 213, 217, 219; skin as site for performance of, 4–5; slavery and loss of, 228n7; sovereignty over, 2, 3, 16, 213; as subjectivity, 1–2; submissive masculinity not authentic, 187; transcendence of subjectivity, 12, 16, 205; trans practices of, 11–12; unified, ideology of, 8, 10, 12, 18–19, 23, 25, 197
self-abnegation, 6–9, 11, 116; achieving, 93–104; death distinguished from, 93–94, 237n8; domination and, 72–73; in Ellison, 17, 18, 128–30, 141, 144, 150, 152–57, 197, 199–206; formlessness, state of, 72, 94, 98–100, 202; against heterosexuality, 181; journey of in Wright, 18, 165, 193; in Larsen, 16, 18, 72–75, 78–80, 83–104, 193, 197; of masculinity, 165, 185–92; mimesis and, 16, 74, 83–93; mutual, 73–74; as process, 97; queer, 16, 165; queer-of-color, 95; releasing Black queer flesh, 186–95; self-realization through, 97; surplus

jouissance required for, 180–86; waywardness as, 211
self-acceptance, 142–43
self-determination, 1–2, 26, 160; Bildung predicated on, 25; ideologies of, 44–45, 59, 67, 127–28; new forms of, 105; as success, 29
self-formation, 1–3, 8–11, 98–100, 160, 212–13; Bildung as, 25–26; deviant, 15; dictated by oppressive subjectivity, 159–60; failure of, 29–32; as ideology of subjectivity, 23–24; impossibility of, for African Americans, 34–35, 41–43, 59–60; incompatibility of, for African American women, 56–57, 60, 65–66; limited for Black people, 34–35; through marriage, 30–32; normative models of, 15–16, 103; policing of, 159–60; through profession, 30; reification of, 50, 52, 55, 57, 65, 239n21; rejection of, 164–65, 192–93; unified subjectivity and, 25; uplift stories and, 26–27; white journey of, 33–35; women's determined by marriage, 29; Wright's obsession with, 159–60
self-ownership, 1–2, 228
self-possession, 1–3, 8, 15, 23–28, 55, 59, 77, 135, 160; as cultural practice, 24; as ideology of subjectivity, 23; queering of, 77, 127–28
self-racializaton, 48–49
self-reflection, 1, 25, 44, 46, 83, 136; "bad," 189
self-reliance, 142
self-without-subjectivity, 2, 9, 17, 19, 98, 239n19; Bentley as, 210; in *Invisible Man,* 17, 128, 156, 198, 200–201, 204, 205; in *The Long Dream,* 156, 194–95; in *Passing,* 98–99, 102, 104; performance of, 11–12, 210–11, 221–22; in *Wayward Lives, Beautiful Experiments,* 197, 210–13, 217, 219–20, 222
sexuality: bisexuality of, 165, 185, 192, 195; childhood, repression of, 171–72; exchange value, 50–51, 72; homosexuality as disability, 108, 117, 119, 140, 143–44; punk, 139–48; race linked with, 75; shifting categories of, 6
shame, 37
sharecropping (indentured servitude), 24
Sharpe, Christina, 216, 228n11
Singh, Amritjit, 61
skin: bodies bounded by, 2; flesh as separate from, 4–5, 22; as site for discursive formations, 4–5
slavery, 2–5, 106, 216, 228n7; recovery of, 3
slave ship, 216
Smith, Bessie, 64–65, 66, 214
Smith, Valerie, 124–25
Snorton, C. Riley, 10–11, 14, 202
social construction, 89, 105
social inequalities, 105
sociality, queer, 7, 10–12, 50, 81, 100, 132, 175, 179, 222
Somerville, Siobhan, 140

sonic materiality, 79, 96, 101, 204–5
sovereignty, over self, 2, 3, 16, 213
species imperialism, 66–67
Spillers, Hortense, 4–6, 81, 229n12, 229n14
standardization, 67–70, 73–74, 89
Stephens, Michelle Ann, 15, 81, 228n11, 229n12
Stepto, Robert, 156
Steward, Douglas, 141
Strange Fruit (Johnson), 15
subject, 1–2; false, 200; individual, 25; meta-subject, 68; rights-bearing, 3
subjectivity: desubjectification, 7–8, 12, 16, 212, 220; deviant, 7, 15, 126–28, 140, 156, 202; disidentification with, 13–14, 85, 130, 156, 216; female, 32; freedom from, 101; multiple ideologies of, 10, 23; self as, 1–2; transcendence of, 12, 16, 205; white, self-determination allowed by, 28–29. *See also* ableist discourse of subjectivity; self-without-subjectivity; subjectivity, Black
subjectivity, Black: ablation of, 6, 23, 129; attempt to escape, 47–48; autonomy and, 3, 25–27, 43, 46; Bildungsroman promotes, 8–9, 15–16, 23, 59; Black queer flesh after demise of, 9–10; Black queer flesh at odds with, 7; categories required, 13; challenges to, 3, 7; commodity fetishism and abandonment of, 50–54; as cultural mandate, 15; death-bound, 41, 164, 192; disability and, 126–30, 135; as domination, 17, 74, 77–80; fetishization of, 23, 26; flesh not grounds for, 81; as heteronormativity, 173; impossibility of, 56–57; of middle-class African American woman, 43; normative, 27, 47–48, 126, 160, 164; as oppressive structure, 7, 13–14, 160; policing enabled by, 3; post-slavery appeal of, 25; prefabricated for African Americans, 40, 42–45, 56–57, 68, 105, 133; racial anxiety tears apart, 22–23; recovery of, 5, 55; rejection of, 2–3, 6–7, 13, 16–17, 23–24, 41–43, 83, 127–28, 142, 208–9, 211, 213, 220; rejection of, via objectification, 50–55; reworking/reconstruction of, 25; skin's false account of, 22
subversion, performance of, 188
Sula (Morrison), 21, 161
Supercargo (character, *Invisible Man*), 145–46
Symbolic, the, 5, 22–23, 80, 96, 229n12

"Talented Tenth," 45
Their Eyes Were Watching God (Hurston), 1, 2
Thomas, Bigger (character, *Native Son*), 159–60, 188
Thomas, Edna, 216–17, 218
Thomas, Lloyd, 216–17
Till, Emmett, 162, 169
Tocqueville, Alexis de, 24
Torgovnick, Marianna, 62, 63

tragic mulatto novel, 27–28, 44
trans practices, 11–12, 14, 202
trickster figure, 128–31; Hartman as, 211, 212–13; Trueblood as, 199–202, 205–6
Trueblood, Jim (character, *Invisible Man*), 18, 46, 198–206, 217; pronouns used for, 238n8; as trickster figure, 199–202, 205–6
Tuskegee Institute, 140, 141
Tyree (character, *The Long Dream*), 163–71, 174–75, 180–91

Ugly Laws, 117–18, 130, 133, 139, 140
Ugly Laws (Schweik), 140
undominated Black queer flesh, 61–65, 69, 73–74, 78–80, 89–93, 101–4, 220
Union Army, 106
Up from Slavery (Washington), 26–27
uplift, racial, 8, 24–28, 31, 216, 221; as ableist discourse, 115–16, 121–22, 132–33, 151–52; as appropriation of whiteness, 44; critiqued in *Invisible Man,* 115–16, 120, 122, 124–27, 135–36, 152; disabled African Americans disrupt, 131–33, 137–38; disabled African Americans excluded from, 126; disidentifying with philosophy and methods of, 124–30; essential Black journey of development vs., 45; in *Passing,* 93, 101; pleasures of, 24–25; in *Quicksand,* 40, 44–45; self-abnegation works against, 129; as self-formation, 26–27; surplus jouissance of, 124, 221
utopia, 79, 127; false, 73; mimetic moment as, 71; queer, 12, 66, 73–74, 82, 103

Van Vechten, Carl, 63, 143
"Venus in Two Acts" (Hartman), 207–8
Vevers, Margaret (character, *Invisible Man* excised chapter), 109–15, 124
Vision and Design (Fry), 62
Vogel, Shane, 64

Walker, A'lelia, 216–17
Wall, Cheryl, 75, 92
Walls of Jericho, The (Fisher), 63
Ward, Jesmyn, 9
Washington, Booker T., 24, 26–27; Atlanta Compromise speech, 122
Wayward Lives, Beautiful Experiments (Hartman), 12, 18, 206–19; "The Anarchy of Colored Girls Assembled in a Riotous Manner," 215; "Cast of Characters" catalog, 212; chorus in, 19, 211–22; "Methods" section, 210; reading, alternative modes of, 213–14; self-without-subjectivity in, 197, 210–13, 217, 219–20, 222
Wertham, Fredric, 137
whiteness: Black appropriation of, 44; disidentification from, 87–88, 123; morality of, 188; performance of, 70; production of

flesh as tactic of domination, 6; as "refined," 44; tropes of, 70
Wilhelm Meister's Apprenticeship (Goethe), 124
"wolves," 119–20, 143, 147–48
women, African American: marriage as end of Bildungsroman for, 32, 41; nurturing and emotionally caring stereotype, 33; power limitations on, 40; self-formation destroyed by domestic sphere, 43; subjectivities limited by stereotypes, 4. See also *Passing*; *Quicksand*
Woodridge (character, *Invisible Man*), 141–43
Wretched of the Earth (Fanon), 22
Wright, John, 125
Wright, Richard, 17–18, 104, 137, 159–95, 219; *Black Boy,* 18, 167; cast as homophobic, 180; Ellison's letter on Lafargue Clinic to, 118; *Native Son,* 17, 18, 159–60, 188; protest fiction, 105, 161, 163; psychoanalytic concepts in, 163–64. See also *Long Dream, The*
Wyndham, Olivia, 216–17

Zelizer, Viviana, 26

Alvin J. Henry is assistant professor of English at St. Lawrence University in New York and the editor of *Psychoanalysis in Context*.